GUERRILLA GOVERNMENT

Political Changes in the Southern Sudan during the 1990s

DATE DUE

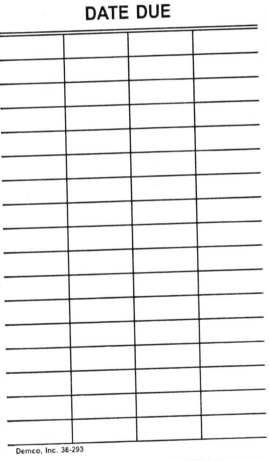

Demco, Inc. 38-293

NORDISKA AFRIKAINSTITUTET 2005

Indexing terms

Sudan
Southern Sudan
Sudan People's Liberation
Movement
Sudan People's Liberation
Army
Government
Civil war
Conventions
Political development
Political reform

Cover photo: Øystein Rolandsen
Cdr. Rin Teny, County Secretary for Yirol in his office.

Language checking. Elaine Almén

Index: Margaret Binns

© the author and Nordiska Afrikainstitutet 2005

ISBN 91-7106-537-7

Printed in Sweden by Almqvist & Wiksell Tryckeri AB, 2005

Contents

TABLES

The boundaries and names shown and the designations used on this map do not imply official endorsement or acceptance by the United Nations.

EGYPT

SAUDI ARABIA

Lake Nasser

Administrative boundary

Halaib

RED SEA

Wadi Halfa
Selima Oasis
Semna West
Lake Nubia
Kumma

Salala

Muhammad Qol

N u b i a n   D e s e r t

NORTHERN STATE

Laqiya Arba'in
Nukheila
Kerma
Dongola
Karima

Abu Hamed

RED SEA

Port Sudan
Suakin

El'Atrun

Old Dongola

Merowe
RIVER
Atbara

Haiya

Tokar

Karora

Jebel Abyad Plateau
Jebel Nagashush
Jebel Abu Dulu
Wadi el Milk

Ed Damer
NILE
Meroë

Gadamai

Wadi Howar

Shendi

ERITREA

Abu 'Uruq

KHARTOUM
Omdurman
Khartoum

KASSALA
Halfa al Gadida

Kassala

Asmara

NORTHERN DARFUR
Miski

NORTHERN KORDOFAN
Umm Badr
Sodiri
Dar Hamid

GEZIRA
Wad Medani
Gedaref

GEDAREF

Yekere

Al Fasher

El Obeid

Kosti

Gonder

WESTERN DARFUR
Geneina

En Nahud
Abu Zabad

WHITE NILE

SINNAR
Sinnar

T'ana Hāyk
Abay (Blue Nile)

Nyala

WESTERN KORDOFAN
Ed Da'ein
Al Fula

SOUTHERN KORDOFAN
Nuba Mts.

Renk

BLUE NILE
Ed Damazin
Famaka

Tullus
Buram
Muglad
Kadugli
Kologi
Talodi

Paloich

ETHIOPIA

Abay

SOUTHERN DARFUR
Radom
Kafia Kingi

Abyei

UNITY
Bentiu

UPPER NILE
Malakal

Kigille

Ādīs Ābeba (Addis Ababa)

CENTRAL AFRICAN REPUBLIC

Bahr el'Arab

NORTHERN BAHR AL GHAZAL
Aweil
Raga

Fathai

WESTERN BAHR AL GHAZAL

WARAB

Akobo

JONGLI

BAHR AL GHAZAL
Wau

Rumbek

BUHEYRAT

Bor

Ukwaa
Towot

Administrative boundary

SUDAN

⊕ National capital
⊙ State (wilayah) capital
○ Town
✈ Major airport
— International boundary
—·— State (wilayah) boundary
— Main road
— Track
— Railroad

Li
Yubu
WESTERN EQUATORIA
Yambio
Maridi
Amadi

EASTERN EQUATORIA
Juba
Torit
Kapoeta

Ch'ew Bahir

L. Turkana (L. Rudolf)

Yei
BAHR AL JEBEL
Nagishot

DEMOCRATIC REPUBLIC OF THE CONGO

UGANDA

KENYA

L. Albert
L. Salisbury
Victoria

0   100   200   300 km
0   100   200 mi

Map No. 3707 Rev. 7   UNITED NATIONS
May 2004

Department of Peacekeeping Operations
Cartographic Section

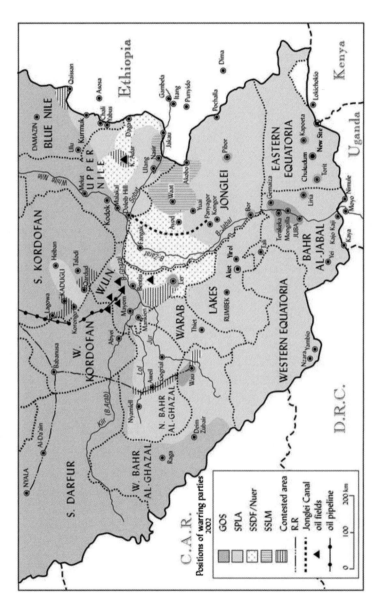

MAP OF SOUTHERN SUDAN

Based on a map in Douglas Johnson, *The Root Causes of Sudan's Civil Wars*. Oxford: James Currey, 2003.

Terms, Abbreviations and Acronyms

Anyanya 1   Common name for the insurgents in the first civil war (1955–1972).

Anyanya 2   Armed groups formed in the South before and after the second civil war started in 1983. Some participated in forming the SPLM/A q.v., while other opposed it. Most of the latter eventually allied with the NIF government q.v.

BYDA   Bahr el-Ghazal Youth Development Association

CMA   Civil/Military Administrator

COC   Convention Organization Committee[1]

DUP   Democratic Unionist Party: One of the major political parties in the North.

EPRDF   Ethiopian People's Revolutionary Democratic Front

FRRA   Fashoda Relief and Rehabilitation Association

GFSCC   General Field Staff Command Council: Interim SPLM/A q.v. military affairs.

IAC   Independent Area Command

IGAD(D)   Inter-Governmental Authority against Drought (and Desertification):[2] Established in 1987.

IRD   Integrated Rural Development

JMC   Joint Military Command: Military council established after the Asmara Declaration in 1995, to co-ordinate military affairs between SPLM/A q.v. and other members of the NDA q.v.

Nasir faction General name for guerrilla groups emerging after 1991 and until formation of SSIM/A in 1995.

NAPEC   National Political and Executive Committee: Replaced NEC q.v.

NC   National Convention: The SPLM/A National Convention q.v. Held in April 1994 in Chuckudum.

NCA   Norwegian Church Aid

NDA   National Democratic Alliance: Umbrella organisation of parties and groups opposing the NIF regime q.v. in Khartoum.[3]

---

[1] The COC is also mentioned in sources as "Convention Organisation Committee" and "Convention Organizing Committee". For the sake of simplicity "Convention Organization Committee" is used throughout, which was the name given in its mandate, 'Communication from The Chairman and C-in-C, SPLM/A to The Chief of Staff, SPLA to be communicated to all GFSCC members and All Units/Ref. No.: Convention/Date: 30/7/1993', p. 1.

[2] IGAD is an interstate forum where both development issues and political/diplomatic questions are discussed. Original members: The Sudan, Ethiopia, Somalia, and Djibouti. Later Uganda, Eritrea and Kenya joined. Changed name from IGADD to IGAD on 21 March 1996.

[33] Originally consisting of northern opposition groups (*Umma* party, DUP q.v., Beja Congress, and others). Agreement in Asmara in 1995 established formal co-operation with the SPLM/A q.v., and John Aarang was appointed to lead the Joint Military Command.

NEC	National Executive Council:[4] Established at the National Convention, as highest political body between NLC q.v. meetings.
NIF	National Islamic Front: Northern political party.
NLC	National Liberation Council: Established after the National Convention as parliament of the "New Sudan".
NGO	Non-Governmental Organisation: 30–40 foreign NGOs q.v. have operated in southern Sudan since the start of OLS q.v., most within the OSL q.v. framework. Cf. SINGO q.v.
NPA	Norwegian People's Aid
NSCC	New Sudan Council of Churches
OAU	Organization of African Unity
OLS	Operation Lifeline Sudan
PMHC	Political Military High Command:[5] Highest political body of the SPLM/A q.v. until its abolition in 1993.
RASS	Relief Association of southern Sudan: Nasir faction's relief wing.
SANU	South African Nationalist Union
SEOC	Sudan Emergency Operations Consortium
SINGO	Sudanese Indigenous NGO q.v.
SPLA	Sudan People's Liberation Army
SPLA United	Name adopted after union of groups opposing SPLM/A q.v. in March 1993. After forming of SSIM/A q.v. it designated only Lam Akol's faction.
SPLM	Sudan People's Liberation Movement
SPLM/A	General term for SPLM q.v. and SPLA q.v.
SRRA	Sudan Relief and Rehabilitation Association: SPLM/A q.v. relief wing.
SSIM/A	Southern Sudan Independence Movement/Army: Name of Nasir faction after Lam Akol broke away/was dismissed in 1994. Headed by Riek Machar.
Umma	Northern political party
UNITA	National Union for the Total Independence of Angola
UNHCR	United Nations High Commissioner for Refugees
USAID	United States Agency for International Development

---

[4] In the period1986–1994 this signified the National Economic Commission, which handled commerce and supplies in rebel-held areas. *Speech* by El Tahir Bior Abdallah Ajak, Secretary of Commerce and Supply at the Civil Society and Civil Authority Conference 1996, p. 1.

[5] Sometimes also referred to as Politico-Military High Command.

Acknowledgements

Guerrilla Government has been made possible with the generous support of several institutions and assistance from numerous people. The Nordic Africa Institute in Uppsala and the Department of History of the University of Oslo supported my combined research trip to Kenya and field visit to the Southern Sudan. The publication department at the Nordic Africa Institute has been patient and helpful in the course of the publication process. Norwegian People's Aid (NPA) has kindly contributed towards the preparation of the manuscript. Logistical assistance from the NPA office in Nairobi and the hospitality and helpfulness of NPA's local stations in Yei and Akot during the field visit were impressive and much appreciated. Norwegian Church Aid lent me office facilities during my stay in Nairobi. The Centre for Development and the Environment (SUM) at the University of Oslo must be thanked for providing me with top-class office facilities.

I wish to thank Endre Stiansen in particular, who did a supreme job as supervisor for my dissertation and who has assisted me greatly in the preparation of this book. I have received valuable comments and useful suggestions on the manuscript from Douglas H. Johnson, Martin Daly, Majak d'Agoot and my fellow Masters students in the History of Africa, the Caribbean and Latin-America seminar group in the Department of History at the University of Oslo. Douglas H. Johnson also provided me with hard-to-find sources, and Gerard Prunier allowed me to read and cite his important manuscript, 'The SPLA Crisis'.[1] I owe special thanks to Matur and John who were *ad hoc*, but nevertheless invaluable, interpreters during the fieldwork at Rumbek and Yirol. Several others have also assisted in different capacities during the preparation of this study, including Øystein Botillen, Svein Olsen, Stein Erik Horjen, Odd Evjen, Gaim Kebreab, Sten Rino Bondsaksen, Stein Villumstad, Jerome Surur, Diress Mengistu and Ezana Getahun.

My friends and my family have given me great support through the whole process. If their patience and goodwill had been an exhaustible resource, I would have spent my ration a long time ago. Despite all this assistance, I fear that the errors were too numerous to be weeded out completely. These, together with the rest of the book's contents, are my responsibility.

---

[1] To be published as a chapter in F. Ireton, E. Denis and G. Prunier (eds), *Contemporary Sudan*, forthcoming.

CHAPTER 1

Introduction

Guerrilla Government is an analysis of continuity and change in Southern Sudanese politics in the period 1990–2000. One event – the 1994 National Convention of the Sudan People's Liberation Movement/Army (SPLM/A)[1] – is the focal point of the study. The Convention was, and to some extent still is, regarded by most members of the SPLM/A as one the Movement's greatest achievements. The National Convention gathered 516 delegates, including representatives of the SPLM/A and civilians representing local constituencies. At the Convention, the birth of the "New Sudan" was announced on behalf of the people of the Southern Sudan, including Southern Kordofan and the Southern Blue Nile. The assembly approved a long list of resolutions, which entailed a radical restructuring of the Movement. It was believed that it would bring radical changes to the SPLM/A and to the Southern Sudanese population as a whole. The National Convention thus became a symbol of the Movement's improvement and reform. The description and discussion of its background, the preparations, the Convention itself and its aftermath provide an analytical frame within which the political history of the Southern Sudan can be presented.

The SPLM/A has been the main rebel organisation in the Southern Sudan since the second civil war in the Sudan (1983–1994), although it suffered a serious setback when, in 1991, three senior commanders tried to wrest control from its leader, John Garang. The SPLM/A's influence over political development in the South has at the national level been matched only by the Government in Khartoum and its armed forces, and at the local level only by chiefs, who derive their power from the old system of "indirect" rule established by the British during the colonial period. An understanding of changes and processes within the SPLM/A is therefore essential for an analysis of the Sudan's contemporary history, and current events, including the continuing peace negotiations, and planning for a post-war Southern Sudan.

This study begins with the attempted coup in 1991 and covers the period leading up to the announcement of the National Convention. The preparations

---

[1] Despite slight variation in the name of the rebel organisation we will refer to it as 'SPLM/A' or the 'Movement' throughout the book, see pp. 21–22.

and the Convention itself are analysed in detail. Thereafter, the book analyses the significance of the Convention and its reforms in light of attempts to implement them. These reforms took place during a turbulent period for the SPLM/A and the South in general, and one aspect of the National Convention's uniqueness was the difficult circumstances under which the Convention and its preparations took place. The conclusion provides a brief summary of events in the period 2000-2004 and presents some thoughts on a future Government of the South Sudan.

In some aspects the conclusions of this study deviate from the official SPLM/A history of the National Convention – its inception, planning and execution as well as the results of decisions it reached. The National Convention was part of a major drive towards democratic reform and establishment of extensive civil administration in SPLM/A controlled areas. The process leading to it was set in motion as early as in 1991, and the resolutions adopted by the Convention were part of a continuous effort to renew the SPLM/A's political programme and, to a far lesser extent, towards re-configuring the organisation. Secondly, the proclamation of the "New Sudan" caused confusion over the distinction between the Movement itself and the emerging civilian government of the New Sudan. This confusion was a result of the SPLM/A leadership's need to counter a possible accusation of establishing an independent state in the Southern Sudan, for which there was little international support. Piecemeal implementation of the Convention reforms resulted from a lack of resources and the SPLM/A leadership's unwillingness to transfer authority to the newly established institutions. Finally, concerning the process of implementing the political and administrative reforms announced at the National Convention, we may discern a difference between results at the central and regional levels and those at the local level. While the attention of international observers has mainly been directed towards the two higher levels, it is in fact only at the local level that significant change can be identified.

Neither the circumstances surrounding the National Convention nor its impact on political development in the Southern Sudan during the 1990s has been closely studied. Detailed scrutiny is justified both by the high esteem in which the Convention is held by the SPLM/A, and by the special circumstances surrounding the event. The background for the Convention was the SPLM/A's ideological *volte-face* during the early 1990s, which coincided with those of the Eritrean People's Liberation Front and the Tigray People's Liberation Front in Ethiopia. With the end of the cold war, African insurgencies with an ideological programme were increasingly rare, and the SPLM/A's new programme for establishing a liberal civil government in a war-zone has, for the period studied, been unique. An investigation into how this political experiment was conceived, developed, and implemented is therefore relevant to the history of African politics in general.

The book's focus on the near-contemporary, and on a subject for which the historian's staple food – official archives – is hard to come by, required a wide-ranging methodological approach. After scrutiny of material obtained during visits to the region and of published work, it was clear that an exploratory approach was needed. But, the book provides data that can be used within a discourse on democracy and the establishment of civil society, and it comments on the continuing debate on the unwanted effects of relief aid in war-zones. Moreover, by concentrating on political processes within a guerrilla movement, the study is relevant to research on theories of insurgencies and politics in civil war environments.

SOURCES

Analysis is mainly based on primary sources and interviews, but our sources also include "grey literature".[2] Concerning the history of the SPLM/A little has been published and material on the SPLM/A National Convention is almost non-existent.[3] There are, however, some publications of relevance.[4] One academic area revolves around causes of the civil war; the reasons for its continuation; what should be done to end it; and how lasting peace could be achieved.[5] There are several positions within these intricate debates; even though most scholars agree that the conflict and its causes are complex, they tend to give

---

[2] "Grey literature" for this study may be arranged in three categories: 1) non-published reports written or commissioned by respective sides of the conflict and foreign agencies involved in, or funding, activities in the Southern Sudan; 2) periodicals and newsletters produced by persons or groups with an informal system of distribution which does not guarantee their preservation in official archives or libraries; and 3) material published only on the Internet. A particularly useful "publication" of the last category is *Sudan Monthly Report*, a comprehensive chronology of events compiled by Sudan Catholic Information Office (SCIO), http://www.peacelink.it/ africa/scio/ previous.html.

[3] Peter A. Nyaba, *The Politics of Libration in South Sudan: An Insider's View*, 2000, gives a personal account of his experiences as a member of the SPLM/A, his defection to the Nasir faction in 1991 and his subsequent return to the SPLM/A.

[4] Two recent publications have made sources for contemporary Southern Sudanese history considerably easier to identify: Terje Tvedt et al., *An Annotated Bibliography on the Southern Sudan 1850–2000*, 2000, and Douglas Johnson's 'Bibliographical Essay' at the end of his *The Root Causes of Sudan's Civil Wars*, 2003. Each of these publications also includes a chronology of events for the period 1972–2002. The vintage 'Select Bibliography' in P.M. Holt and M.W. Daly, *A History of the Sudan: From the Coming of Islam to the Present Day*, 2000, provides a general introduction to the academic field of Sudanese history.

[5] S. Harir and T. Tvedt (eds), *Short-cut to Decay: the Case of the Sudan*, 1994, is a compilation of articles analysing historical processes in Southern Sudan up to 1993. M.W. Daly and A.A. Sika-inga (eds), *Civil War in the Sudan*, 1993, presents a collection of articles which, among other topics, discuss the historical background of the SPLM/A and other rebel groups as well as various militias. An overview of the second civil war from the Nuer people's point of view is provided by Sharon E. Hutchinson in 'A Curse From God? Religious and Political Dimensions of the post-1991 Rise of Ethnic Violence in South Sudan', in *The Journal of Modern African Studies*, Vol. 39 (2), 2001, pp. 307–31.

priority to one factor or another. Some stress the radically different cultures and identities of the North and South,[6] while others emphasise the long history of marginalisation and exploitation of Southerners within successive Sudanese state structures.[7] The SPLM/A's early rhetoric focuses on this aspect, arguing that the Sudan would be a viable state if only the current oppressive regime was changed; northern Sudanese scholars tend to present a somewhat similar version, but here the source of the conflict is the colonial intervention which, through its separation policy, hindered the development of a unified state.[8] In studying the politics of the SPLM/A in the 1990s both perspectives should be included since references to a common identity among Southerners – the main feature of which is its difference from that of Northerners – is actively used as a measure to build alliances and bolster the support for the Movement, and also because one important reason why the war broke out – and has continued – is the Khartoum government's unwillingness or inability to address the grievances and demands from the South and politically and economic marginalised areas in the North.

Another area of academic research is connected to the permanent humanitarian crisis in many areas of the South and attempts to aid the affected population. Relief operations in particular, but also development activities in the Southern Sudan in the period 1989–2000, have received considerable attention.[9] This is partly because of the controversial nature of the operations – pioneering front-line relief conducted by foreign Non-Governmental Organisations (NGOs) – and partly because data and funding are more easily secured for these types of research projects. One sub-category of literature within this field which has been particularly useful for this study is monitor reports from

---

[6] Francis Deng, *War of Visions: Conflict of Identities in the Sudan*, 1995, traces the development of separate Arab-Islamic and African cultures in the North and South, and concludes that they are incompatible and either have to be separated through a loose confederation or as different states, or a new common "national" identity has to be created. Ann M. Lesch in *The Sudan: Contested National Identities*, 1998, follows much the same line of reasoning through a study of Sudanese politics in the period 1969–96.

[7] Douglas H. Johnson and African Rights through their publications might be said to reflect this position.

[8] Mohamed Omer Beshir, *The Southern Sudan: Background to Conflict*, 1979.

[9] Among many: J.M. Burr and R.O. Collins in *Requiem for Sudan: War, Drought, and Disaster Relief on the Nile*, 1995, focus on the efforts of the international aid community in the period 1984–92. Terje Tvedt has written several books and articles using Norwegian NGO efforts in Southern Sudan to illustrate more general theories on NGOs in the international system, e.g. 'The Collapse of the State in Southern Sudan after the Addis Ababa Agreement' in Harir and Tvedt, *Short-cut to Decay*, pp. 69–104, and *Angels of Mercy or Development Diplomats? NGOs and Foreign Aid*, 1998. Wendy James, 2001, "People-friendly' Projects and Practical Realities: Some Contradictions on the Sudan-Ethiopian Border' writes on the more recent topics of refugees and the identity of towns in Eastern Sudan. See also Geoff Loane, 'Literature Assessment of the Wider Impact of Humanitarian Assistance', in G. Loane and T. Schümer (eds), *The Wider Impact of Humanitarian Assistance: The Case of Sudan and the Implications for European Union Policy*, 2000, p. 15–42.

agencies such as Amnesty International, Human Rights Watch and African Rights. The African Rights series of publications on the possible emergence of a civil society in SPLM/A controlled areas, and the role of the Operation Lifeline Sudan (OLS) and the NGOs in this process, have been a very useful source of information and perspectives.

Anthropological studies on the Sudan tend to follow in Evans-Prichard's footsteps and concentrate on the local scene.[10] Political processes at the national level become part of the backdrop rather than dimensions of the life of the people in question. Studies from the civil war explore how conflict affects local societies. They are relevant to this book in helping to appreciate the variations within the territory studied and identify ways in which the war has affected the peoples within the Southern Sudan, but also to understand the structure and local variations of the chiefs' courts and local administration fashioned by the British and retained more or less unchanged until today.

There has been a considerable amount of research on insurgencies and liberation movements.[11] During the 1970s and the 1980s, the ideology of guerrilla movements and liberation armies in Africa, Asia and Latin America held a strong appeal for some segments of Western academia. These movements fought first against oppression from colonial powers, settlers and American imperialism, later against home-grown dictators. Some scholars believed that anthropology, history and political science could be used for a good cause by

---

[10] Edward E. Evans-Prichard is one of the "grandfathers of anthropology" and his books on the Nuer are compulsory reading for everyone with ambitions within this academic discipline. He has published numerous books on the peoples of the Southern Sudan in particular the Azande and the Nuer. See Abdel Ghaffar M. Ahmed (et al.), 2003, *Anthropology in the Sudan: Reflections by a Sudanese Anthropologist*, for a brief presentation and discussion on the works of Evans-Prichard. Sharon E. Hutchinson has received much praise for her massive re-appraisal of Evans-Prichard in *Nuer Dilemmas: Coping with Money War and the State*, 1996, and her focus on historical dynamics and how culture changes over time contributes significantly to Sudanese anthropology. Wendy James has centred her research on the Uduk people of the South Eastern part of the Blue Nile. The anthology of case studies by K. Fukui and J. Markakis (eds), *Ethnicity and Conflict in the Horn of Africa*, 1994, is particularly useful for the understanding of how the civil war was experienced at different locations within the South during the first decade. Studies within the field of Christianity and refugees are also to some extent relevant for this study, see Ch. 3, Notes 79, 82, 83, 84.

[11] This field is expanding both in terms of competing theories and in case studies with more or, sometimes, less innovative approaches. Stephen Ellis, 'Africa's Wars of Liberation: Some Historiographical Reflections', in Konings et al. (eds), 2000, *Trajectories de libération en Afrique contemporaine*, pp. 69–91 presents a brief historical overview of studies of guerrilla movements. William Reno, 1998, *Warlord Politics and African States,* is an example of attempts at developing theories based on a limited set of empirical cases. Examples of comparable case studies are John Young, 1997, *Peasant Revolution in Ethiopia: The Tigray People's Liberation Front 1975–1991*; David Pool, 2001, *From Guerrillas to Government: The Eritrean People's Liberation Front*; Norma J. Kriger, 1992, *Zimbabwe's Guerrilla War: Peasant Voices*; Ismail Ahmed, 'Understanding Conflict in Somalia and Somaliland' in Adedeji (ed.), 1999, *Comprehending and Mastering African Conflicts: the Search for Sustainable Peace and Good Governance*.

making these struggles known to the Western public.[12] The end of the cold war contributed to a blurring of this black-and-white picture. Jonas Savimbi's UNITA, among others, demonstrated that an insurgency could have popular support without having a noble cause. This created problems for pro-guerrilla analysts: "How was a person intent on African liberations to distinguish genuine movements of emancipation from bogus ones?"[13] A question illustrating the limitations of this approach.

Other aspects of civil wars and insurgencies have become more apparent because of their devastating effects on the affected countries' economies and politics. Insurgencies and counter-insurgency strategies have led to suffering and insecurity, inflated government spending on the military and conscription. Unstable states often contribute to regional destabilisation, and halting of development aid from Western countries often ensues. Academic research has therefore shifted from information on movements' good intentions to more pragmatic subjects. This development encouraged new angles in the study of guerrilla wars, bringing up questions about economic aspects,[14] religion,[15] and the effects on relief and development aid in war zones.

This book is a product of this widened scope. Instead of exploring whether the SPLM/A's fight is justified or measuring the suffering of the people in the Southern Sudan,[16] attention is directed towards political processes within the Movement and inside the regions they occupy, focusing on *what* happened and *why* it happened. This is a critical study: it questions the alleged outcome of reforms within the SPLM/A; and the extent to which initiatives taken by its leadership were mainly a result of a new understanding of their situation, or of pressure from internal and external factors instead.

* * *

Written primary sources have been collected in Norway, Kenya and Southern Sudan. Archives of several Western governments, notably those of Norway, the US, Britain, France, the Netherlands and Italy, might hold useful materials

---

[12] Ellis, 'Africa's Wars of Liberation'.

[13] *Ibid.*, p. 83.

[14] P. Collier and A. Hoeffler's paper *Greed and Grievance in Civil War*, 2000, attempts to use economic theories and quantitative methods in an attempt to explain the occurrence of civil wars.

[15] An early example is David Lan, *Guns and Rain: Guerrillas and Spirit Mediums in Zimbabwe*, 1985. Two recent studies relevant for the Sudan: Heike Behrend, 'War in Northern Uganda: The Holy Spirit Movements of Alice Lakwena, Severino Lukoya and Joseph Kony (1986–1997)', in Christopher Clapham (ed.), *African Guerrillas*, 1998; and, Sharon E. Hutchinson, 'A Curse from God? Religious and Political Dimensions of the Post-1991 Rise of Ethnic Violence in South Sudan', in *The Journal of Modern African Studies*, Vol. 39 (2), 2001.

[16] Cf. Millard Burr, A *Working Document II: Quantifying Genocide in the Southern Sudan and the Nuba Mountains, 1983–1998*, 1998.

related to NGO operations and peace negotiations in the Southern Sudan, but searching these archives was outside the scope of this study. Moreover, owing to the topic's recent and sensitive nature it was unlikely that the present author would be able to gain access to much unique material anyway. For similar reasons it was also unlikely that useful material could have been obtained in Khartoum.

In Norway, the archive of the Norwegian NGO Norwegian People's Aid (NPA) was a rich source of primary material. NPA has a policy of taking sides in conflicts, which – in contrast to the neutral approach – this NGO considers to be a more candid as well as effective approach to relief and development. This policy has been controversial in the context of the Southern Sudan, where most international organisations try to avoid being seen as sympathising with any of the warring parties. Nevertheless, NPA's approach has been very beneficial to this project; NPA has sided with the SPLM/A and taken a keen interest in political processes within the Movement. NPA personnel have been given access to internal documents, some of which have been filed in the headquarters archive in Oslo. However useful, material found in these archives was not sufficient; it was necessary to visit Nairobi and the Southern Sudan to obtain the bulk of primary sources.

The most important sources for this book are SPLM/A documents. While centrally placed SPLM/A officials denied the existence of a central SPLM/A archive during the fieldwork, such an archive reportedly exists. This illustrates how difficult it is to gain access to SPLM/A documents. However, they circulate within the NGO environment and are collected in an unsystematic fashion by some NGOs. For this study most of the documentation of political processes within the SPLM/A was obtained through these sources, as were various reports and baseline studies.[17] Relevant material was also identified during the visit to the Southern Sudan, but owing to lack of time and photocopying facilities little of this material could be applied in the later analysis.[18] Unfortunately, it has not been possible to obtain minutes and resolutions from three of four National Liberation Council meetings, nor to acquire sufficient oral accounts to correct this shortcoming. In fact, it has not even been established whether such

---

[17] The manner in which some of the primary sources were obtained poses questions regarding authentication of the material. Authenticity has been determined through an evaluation of documents' contents and appearance in relation to other similar documents, the context in which they are supposed to have been composed and the likelihood that someone would find it worthwhile to falsify the documents. Based on these criteria there is nothing that indicates that the documents referred to in this study were forgeries. The accuracy of the information in the documents and to what extent information has been actively withheld from the accounts are of course different altogether.

[18] The author gained access to local government archives in Yei. The collected material turned out to have little relevance for this book.

minutes exist.[19] However, as will be demonstrated in Chapter 5, it is still possible to reach some conclusions from the one available set of resolutions as well as from other sources that comment on these meetings. The main primary sources are discussed in Appendix 1.

Interviews were conducted in Norway, Kenya and the Southern Sudan. Questions and topics were prepared in advance. The purpose of the interviews was to gather information not available in documents, and to identify variations in the interpretation of events and processes investigated. Some categories of persons consulted were: representatives of the SPLM/A and other rebel organisations; foreign NGOs and donors; local church leaders and representatives of local and regional administrations in the Southern Sudan; diplomats and government representatives. Except for one instance, the interviews were carried out individually. Even if the oral sources are seldom referred to in the text, they have together with the field observation been at least as important as the written material for the understanding of the context for the issues studied here.

Although research in the Southern Sudan was not planned as participatory observation in the strict sense, it was still an important goal to see functioning civil administrative structures and indigenous organisations. Administration offices in three different counties were visited as well as market places and several projects of foreign and indigenous NGOs. Interviews with chiefs of various ranks were conducted. In general, the visit allowed an understanding of the context and challenges of the Southern Sudan that is difficult to achieve through documentary sources. As one historian has put it:

> I believe that an historian should not write about lands he has never visited, for the geographical environment has a great impact upon men and their actions. An appreciation of the land as a factor in the historical process can best be understood by actually visiting the scene of past events. The sense of being there transcends a thousand words, particularly in the case of the dramatic landscape of the Southern Sudan. [20]

The visit to the Southern Sudan lasted only four weeks, and though it included visits to sites in different climatic zones and a considerable amount of travelling, only a fraction of SPLM/A controlled areas was covered. There was not enough time to meet many "ordinary people" and to learn first-hand about their experiences during the last decade of attempted reforms and political changes in a context of civil war.[21] The inclusion of the perspectives of the

---

[19] Considering the new interest in written records within the SPLM/A after the National Convention (NC), and the fact that resolutions exist from one of the meetings, it is likely that at least the resolutions adopted at the meetings were recorded.

[20] Robert O. Collins, *Shadows in the Grass: Britain in the Southern Sudan, 1918–1956*, 1983, p. 459.

[21] Some insight can be gained through a study conducted by Paul Murphy et al., *Planning for Peace in Sudan: A Record of the Perspectives and Recommendations Made by People Living in Opposition Controlled Areas of Sudan on Building and Achieving Peace*, 2001.

people, civilians and military, who supposedly have participated in political processes of the Southern Sudan, is a requirement for future studies on this topic.

A Note on Nomenclature

Adopting an appropriate mode of presentation has been a significant problem. Where it has not been of consequence for the argument, consistency has in some instances been sacrificed to readability. The most basic challenge has involved names and categories. In principle, historical studies should adopt the names used by subjects and organisations themselves. This is straightforward in many instances, but it is more complicated in the case of Southern Sudanese politics during the periods discussed here. Names of groups have changed frequently and different names have been applied to the same person or organisation. This might be noticed particularly in Chapter 2, where the history of the internal split within the SPLM/A in 1991 and its aftermath is discussed. The faction itself later splintered into smaller factions that took new names, most of which included the SPLA acronym. This makes it difficult to present the political and military development of the period simply and accurately. For this reason, John Garang's faction, which for a while was regarded as one of several, is referred to throughout as the 'SPLM/A', and the splinter groups are referred to as the 'Nasir faction' even if this is slightly inaccurate and does not reflect the uncertainty regarding which faction would emerge victorious.

Various names also have various political connotations. When a text refers to John Garang as 'Colonel Garang' and to the SPLM/A as the 'SPLA', this often signals that an opponent of the Movement wrote it. The title 'Colonel' refers to Garang's rank in the Sudanese army, which means that the author in question does not recognise Garang's SPLM/A titles. 'SPLA' alone may imply that there is an army but no liberation "movement" at all. An author sympathetic towards the SPLM/A would use Garang's SPLM/A titles (Chairman and Commander in Chief) or simply 'Dr. John' (referring to his Ph.D. degree) and refer to the SPLM/A as the 'SPLM/A' or the 'SPLM/SPLA' or even only the 'SPLM' (signifying the primacy of the movement over the army). The solution adopted here as a general rule is to omit ranks and titles, and organisations are referred to by the names used by their members at the moment in question, with the exceptions mentioned above. The term 'the Movement' refers to 'the SPLM/A' and they should be regarded as synonymous.

The term 'SPLM/A leadership' also deserves clarification. The term is intended to signify the executive power of the Movement. Our use of this term is another attempt at neutrality. In most cases it refers mainly to the SPLM/A Chairman and Commander-in-Chief, John Garang, but the extent of his personal power cannot be accurately established. Apparently, he reaches decisions in consultation with trusted advisors. It would have been possible to refer by name to the SPLM/A's official executive at different points in time,[22] but this would not reflect actual decision-making within the Movement, which is less formal. The power structure will be discussed at various points in the course of this book, which will also provide insight into the evolving power relations during the period studied.[23] It should also be pointed out that the secondary sources mentioned apply a variety of acronyms. These have been avoided as far as possible with one exception: the 1994 SPLM/A National Convention is shortened to "the NC".[24]

HISTORICAL BACKGROUND

The Sudan is a colonial construct, even if nationalists in Khartoum sometimes try to state otherwise. There is little binding the country together but the shared history of colonial rule;[25] the post-colonial order left borders un-changed and prescribed handing over of the governmental machinery to the Arabic political and economic elite in the capital. Peoples in the periphery both in the North and the South have not been adequately integrated in the state structure and a sense of national belonging exists only to a limited degree. Southerners' sense of alienation from the national centre is rooted in a history of plundering and slave taking by Northerners, by the colonial policy of sepa-ration between the North and the South, as well as civil war and cultural op-pression since independence. Even though this book focuses on the events and processes of the 1990s, it is necessary to briefly discuss the background to the conflict in the Southern Sudan and to follow some historical lines back to pre-vious periods in the Sudan's history giving special attention to the early years of the SPLM/A.

War and Politics in the Sudan before 1983

Southern Sudanese take pride in the Sudan's long history, and the notion of Christian Nuba kingdoms preceding the Islamic conquest of the Sudan has

---

[22] The PMHC, the GSFCC, the NEC, the SPLM/A Leadership Council.

[23] Ch. 3 and Ch. 5.

[24] See list of terms, abbreviations and acronyms above.

[25] Some argue that the Sudan was not part of the British colonial empire since it was ruled in a *pro forma* condominium with Egypt and because it was administered by the Foreign Office in London instead of the Colonial Office. Except for these differences, the administration of the Sudan was very similar to British colonies in Africa where systems of "indirect" rule were intro-duced. Cf. Johnson, *The Root Causes,* p. 21, note 1.

been used in SPLM/A propaganda.[26] The ancient kingdoms of the Sudan had their centres in the North, and the degree to which their influence reached today's Southern Sudan has not been ascertained.

Egypt, the Mahdia and the British (up to 1956)

In the period before the Turco-Egyptian invasion in 1820–21, the South's main contact with the North was through expeditions to capture slaves, raid cattle, and gather ivory and valuable natural resources.[27] The South continued to be "unexplored" during the first two decades of Egyptian rule, and it was not until 1840 that the new rulers managed to navigate up the Nile into what is today regarded as the Southern Sudan.[28] In the wake of exploration, a makeshift administration was put in place and traders of different nationalities established outposts. They met the Azande in the southwest, which was a relatively strong and expansive kingdom. In the northeast, the institution of the *Reth* was recognised by the Shilluk people as the central authority. The Dinka and the Nuer were organised in loose federations of tribes and sub-tribes.

In 1881–85, a religious uprising led by the Mahdi destroyed the Turco-Egyptian regime. The Mahdist state did not manage to administer the South, and this part of the Sudan was not "pacified" until almost two decades after the British conquered the Sudan in 1898, and established the Anglo-Egyptian Condominium. In the period up to 1918 without any close administration, it probably did not make much difference to most Southerners whether it was the Turks, the Mahdists or the British who claimed sovereignty in their territory.[29] The pattern of unequal development in North and South, and difference in the status of the Northern Muslims and Southerners was established long before the British adopted an active policy of differentiation.[30]

---

[26] E.g. the *Vision, Programme and Constitution of the Sudan People's Liberation Movement (SPLM)* is introduced with a historical overview including the following paragraph: "In its history the Sudan goes back thousands of years. Indeed, the history of the Nubian civilization, interwoven with that of Egypt, goes back to 3000 B.C., while the Kushite civilization had reached a high level of development by 1700 BC. The Book of [the] Prophet Isaiah (Chapter 18) talks about the Sudan, as the land beyond the rivers of Ethiopia, describing it as "*spoiled by rivers*" and inhabited by tall, brave and smooth-skinned people that sent ambassadors to Jerusalem. This land is an unambiguous description of the central and Southern Sudan down to Uganda. Southern Sudan still gets flooded (*spoiled by its many rivers*) and is still inhabited by the same smooth-skinned people that [the] Prophet Isaiah described some 2,700 years ago"; Yei and New Cush, New Sudan: SPLM Political Secretariat, March 1998, p. 4 (henceforth referred to as the *Draft Constitution*).

[27] Johnson, *The Root Causes*, pp. 2–4.

[28] P.M. Holt and M.W. Daly, *A History of the Sudan: From the Coming of Islam to the Present Day*, 2000, p. 59.

[29] Johnson, *The Root Causes*, pp. 9–10.

[30] *Ibid.*, p. 8.

The Closed Districts Ordinance of 1922 and the Permits to Trade Ordinance of 1925, which restricted Northerners' movement and opportunities to trade in the South, were introduced as measures to protect Southerners from the perceived threat of cultural dominance from the North. The South was intended to become a protected "garden" and systems of "indirect" rule were established to give the peoples the opportunity to develop along what was believed to be a more "natural" line. Somehow the conversion to Christianity was seen as more "natural" than becoming a muslim and missionaries were allotted zones in which to preach, but also to provide education and medical services. Initially, systems of "indirect" rule were introduced both in the North and in the South but in the South and in Kordofan and Darfur provinces, the British often started by creating tribal authorities before "indirect" rule was established. Once instituted, "indirect" rule was maintained because it was both seen as a way to preserve Southerners' way of living as well as being cost-effective.[31]

Grass Curtain: The First Civil War (1955–1972) [32]

By the time of the Sudan's independence on 1 January 1956, war in the South had already begun. A 1955 mutiny of southern soldiers in the Equatoria Corps at Torit is usually considered the start of the first civil war,[33] even though it was several years before rebel activity had a significant impact. The cause of the mutiny was dissatisfaction with the decolonization process, in which Southerners believed they were losing out; it was widely expected that Northerners would install themselves as rulers of the South: "What was negotiated for the South was the transfer of the colonial structures intact from Britain to the northern Sudanese nationalists."[34] Southern leaders have since argued that de-colonisation was flawed in the sense that Southerners had no influence on the process in general, nor on the future of the Southern Sudan. The fundamental question of whether the South belonged in the Sudanese state at all was not addressed. The Sudan's independence therefore did not lead to much rejoicing in the South.

During the first years, the fighting was not particularly intense. It was only after the military coup led by General Abbud in 1958, which ousted the party based civilian regime in Khartoum, that occasional skirmishes escalated into a full-fledged civil war. This escalation was mainly caused by Abbud's pro-

---

[31] Johnson, *The Root Causes*, Ch. 2.

[32] During the first civil war the South was often referred to as being surrounded by a "grass curtain" since there was so little attention given to it, and one of the Southern newsletters was even called "*The Grass Curtain*", Edgar O'Ballance, *The Secret War in the Sudan: 1955–1972*, 1977.

[33] Johnson, *The Root Causes*, pp. 27–29.

[34] *Ibid.*, p. 22.

gramme of Islamisation, which led to increased repression in the South. Educated Southerners joined forces with the remains of the 1955 mutineers and formed a political front named Sudan African Nationalist Union (SANU), while the armed groups were often referred to as the *Anyanya*[35]. There followed a brief period of unity within the southern opposition, but this broke down later as the Abbud regime was ousted in 1964, and a civilian government was formed in the North. Disagreement over policy towards the new regime split SANU, and in the period 1964–70 various political groups of exiled Southerners with loose connections to armed groups within the Southern Sudan emerged. The first civil war ended as Joseph Lagu, leader of one *Anyanya* group managed to establish a joint military command of the armed groups in the South, with himself as the leader. He opened negotiations with the newly established military regime of Jafar Nimeri in Khartoum. On 27 February 1972 a peace agreement was signed in the Ethiopian capital, and this came to be called the Addis Ababa Agreement.

The Addis Ababa Agreement (1972–1983)

With the peace agreement in place, economic development and the build-up of political and administrative institutions were announced as a priority in the South. Besides peace, the most important result of the Addis Ababa Agreement was the establishment of the Southern Sudan as an autonomous region, with its own parliament and a High Executive Council. It soon turned out, however, that autonomy was quite limited, and it eroded into nothing within the next decade. Manipulation of the Southern politicians and interference from the North caused the regional government to lose legitimacy. Only fractions of the special development budgets for the region were paid out by the central government. The building of the Jonglei Channel was seen as a continuation of the extraction of the South's resources without any benefit to the South. Similarly, following the discovery of oil in the South, Khartoum decided that a refinery would be built in the North instead of the South. An attempt to reduce the number of former *Anyanya* fighters in the newly integrated army was another source of dissatisfaction. In the political field, this period was, therefore, one that started with a hesitant optimism that was soon crushed by broken promises and "agreements dishonoured"[36].

Although national institutions failed to deliver as promised, Western countries poured money directly into Khartoum and indirectly into the South, using international development organisations as proxies. This was the era of

---

[35] The name refers to a certain type of snake venom, *ibid.,* p. 31.

[36] The autobiography of one of the leading southern politicians during this period, Abel Alier, has the title *Southern Sudan: Too Many Agreements Dishonoured*, 1992.

the "integrated rural development" (IRD) approach; large programmes aimed at improving several aspects of life in rural areas that would create a "holistic effect" by which single projects would benefit from each other.[37] The devastation of the first civil war and the lack of priority during the colonial period meant that the Southern Sudan started from scratch with regard to the provision of government services. To the foreign NGOs Southern Sudan was thus both the ideal laboratory for development aid and the ultimate challenge. In particular the southernmost province, Equatoria, benefited from several large programmes where foreign NGOs took over local government responsibility within several sectors,[38] at the same time both undermining the credibility of the regional government and making it possible for the government in Khartoum to escape its responsibilities in the South. This tendency to transfer responsibility for providing services can to some extent be traced to the colonial period, when missionaries had been responsible for much of the education and health services. More recent examples of delegation of government responsibilities to non-state agents, which also had consequences for implementation of the SPLM/A governmental reforms in the late 1990s, are discussed in Chapter 5.

The Start of the Second Civil War

Although the mutiny in the southern town of Bor in 1983 is generally referred to as the beginning of the second civil war, one might still argue, as some of the original *Anyanya* fighters did, that their refusal to accept the Addis Ababa Agreement and choosing to hide along Ethiopia's west border meant that the first war never ended. In 1975–76, they were reinforced by mutineers, but were still no significant threat to the stability of the region. The Ethiopian Derg regime started to support these groups as early as in 1976 as retaliation against Khartoum's support for Eritrean separatists, and Ethiopia became the Sudanese insurgents' material and logistical backbone for 15 years to come.[39] During the period 1980–83, the rebel groups – which were now

---

[37] This kind of programme is discussed more thoroughly in Øystein H. Rolandsen, 'Development Interventions. Illusions and Narratives: The Case of Norwegian Church Aid in Eastern Equatoria 1974–86', MA Dissertation, 2000. One specific IRD-programme in Abyei in the northern parts of the Bahr el-Ghazal has been analysed in detail in D.C. Cole and R. Huntington, *Between a Swamp and a Hard Place: Developmental Challenges in Remote Rural Africa*, 1997.

[38] Perhaps the most informative report, at the empirical and analytical level, on Eastern Equatoria and the services provided by the indigenous NGOs in this period is the 'Agricultural Extension Processing and Marketing Study East Bank Equatoria' conducted by the consultancy firm Huntington Technical Services Ltd. on behalf of the Norwegian Church Aid Sudan Programme, 1984, Ch. 4 in particular is relevant.

[39] Johnson provides an account of how this support started in *The Root Causes*, pp. 59–60. Lam Akol in *SPLM/SPLA* does not comment on this topic directly, but mentions several instances where he and other top leaders were transported in helicopters, which indicates the degree of Ethiopian involvement in the arming and logistics of the SPLM/A.

generally referred to as *Anyanya 2* – became increasingly assertive as the institutions established by the Addis Ababa Agreement started to fall apart. The High Executive Council had no power over political and economic development in the region, Nimeri frequently interfered in the procedures of the HEC, and he often did not even bother to involve southern leaders when important decisions were made. The *Anyanya 2* groups were active in most parts of the South, but in particular in the Upper Nile region and around the newly discovered oil fields. Northern soldiers in the South became more oppressive and targeted civilians as well as guerrillas.

After the mutiny of the Bor Garrison on 16 May 1983, led by Kerubino Bol, only minor skirmishes took place until 1985. Nimeri's provocative actions of introducing Islamic Sharia law in the South and dividing the region into three parts have been seen as the last spark needed, even though these occurred after the mutiny.[40] Several other Southern garrisons mutinied in the months after the one in Bor, and most of these soldiers fled to the Ethiopian border. John Garang was sent by the Khartoum government to mediate, but he joined the mutineers and managed in the course of the next two years to attain leadership of the insurgency. The mutineers decided to call themselves the Sudan People's Liberation Army/the Sudan People's Liberation Movement (SPLA/SPLM),[41] and they published a quasi-Marxist manifesto allegedly to please Mengistu, the leader of the Ethiopian Derg.[42] Attempts were made to join forces with *Anyanya 2* groups, but these often ended with their fighting each other.

Politics in the Sudan, 1983–91, and the First Years of the SPLM/A

A brief overview of political development in the period 1983–91, and in the South in particular, sets the stage for the main discussion of this book, and serves as a point reference for later changes. Some aspects are more important

---

[40] Even if the issue of dividing the Southern Region was discussed before 1983, it was in June 1983 the Addis Ababa Agreement was dismantled by Nimeri and the South divided into three regions. Later, in September the South's exemption from the Sharia penal laws was abolished which was later referred to as the 'September Laws', Gérard Prunier, 'From Peace to War: the Southern Sudan 1972–1984', 1986, pp. 55 and 59.

[41] During the first ten years of the insurgency, the political "movement" existed on paper only. The insurgents were commonly referred to as "the SPLA". Lam Akol gives his version of how the SPLM/A was formed and how Garang managed to become the leader, in *SPLM/SPLA*, pp. 200–9. He did not experience these events himself and parts of his account are biased or inaccurate. According to Lam it was in March 1985 that Garang managed to take full control of the SPLM/A.

[42] Lam Akol describes the process of adopting the Manifesto as the first example of backdating by the SPLM/A: "We now know that even this version of the Manifesto was amended in Tripoli in March 1984 (see later) but, curiously enough, the date of publication to this day still remains to be 31st July 1983", p. 210. See Ch. 3 for other examples of backdating.

than others: political developments in Khartoum, the regional and international setting, and the SPLM/A's early history and political organisation during its first years, all of which form the background for the split of 1991 and subsequent announcement of reforms.

Politics in the North 1983–91

There was almost constant political turmoil in Khartoum during the period 1983–91, partly caused by the civil war. President Nimeri had been considered a master of political manoeuvre but by 1985 he had no more cards to play, and foreign debt had plunged the country into a deep economic crisis. In March, massive public protest led a band of military officers to seize power and form a transitional government. The promise of national elections within a year was fulfilled, and in the period 1986–89 the Sudan experienced a brief return to the parliamentary democracy of the 1954–58 and 1964–69 periods. The new regime was dominated by the power struggle among three major parties, the *Umma* led by Sadiq al-Mahdi; the Democratic Unionist Party; and the National Islamic Front, with Hassan al-Turabi as the central personality. To end the war in the South one way or another, was an important issue in Khartoum. During the spring of 1989, there was finally a breakthrough in peace negotiations, and a peace agreement was expected by July. These expectations were not realised, however, as military officers led by Omar al-Bashir staged a coup on 30 June. A period of confusion followed regarding the new leader's agenda. By 1991, it had, however, become clear that the coup leaders sympathised with the National Islamic Front (NIF) and that Islamic fundamentalism would shape the policy of the new regime.

Sadiq al-Mahdi's government had sought to maintain good relations with Western governments and the US in particular, which was perceived as an important ally and source of financial support.[43] After the coup in 1989, the Sudan's relations with Western countries soon started to deteriorate. This change was partly a consequence of the Khartoum government's strategy of independence from Western and conservative Islamic countries,[44] and also indirectly of its extensive violation of human rights, escalation of the civil war, and its behaviour on the international political scene (most notably supporting Iraq in the Gulf war). Elements of the political elite in Khartoum who were not in power became – as a consequence of arrests and harassment – increasingly estranged from the regime.

---

[43] Alex de Waal, *Famine Crimes: Politics and the Disaster Relief Industry in Africa*, 1997, pp. 94–95.
[44] *Ibid.*, p. 98.

The SPLM/A's Political Structures Prior to the 1991 Split

In the early years of the civil war, the SPLM/A was, although the most important, still one among several rebel groups.[45] During the second half of the 1980s, the Movement merged with some *Anyanya* factions and centred its attacks on government positions. By mid-1989, the SPLM/A controlled several major towns in the South.[46] But while there was progress on the battlefield, the politics of the Movement was in disarray. Tensions rose as John Garang used force and intrigue to bolster his position as supreme leader of the Movement. The most detailed account of the political development of the SPLM/A is found in Lam Akol's autobiographical book *SPLM/SPLA Inside an African Revolution*. He relates how he, as a secret member of the SPLM/A, started an opposition in Khartoum, and how he became a Zonal Commander and an alternate member of the SPLA's Political Military High Command (PMHC) in 1986. Even though his account ends in mid-1991, and the coup he later attempted is never mentioned in the book, the book is obviously an attempt at justifying his subsequent actions. This bias results in his putting all blame for the failings the SPLA on John Garang's incompetence and wickedness. Although it is therefore unreliable, the book still provides useful insights, and is the most comprehensive account of the SPLM/A's internal politics in the period prior to the split in 1991.[47]

In Akol's opinion, the nature of the PMHC was at the heart of the power struggle within the SPLM/A. The PMHC was the highest decision-making body of the SPLM/A, in fact the only one before the National Convention. It had two types of members; ordinary and alternate. In the event of a PMHC meeting the alternate members would not have the right to vote. Akol describes how even as an alternate member he worked tirelessly to organise meetings of the PMHC, and how John Garang's promises to hold such meetings always turned out to be empty.[48] According to Lam Akol, by mid-1991 the PMHC had never formally assembled, and all major decisions within the SPLM/A were made by John Garang and a small number of personal aides.[49] However, when a coup seemed imminent, the PMHC was finally summoned to a meeting in the summer of 1991, which Lam Akol believed to be a trap and refused

---

[45] The most important are listed in Lam Akol, *SPLM/SPLA*, p. 201.

[46] The most important being Torit, Bor and Nasir, Johnson, *The Root Causes,* p. 84.

[47] Peter A. Nyaba, a South Sudanese intellectual, has also written a book about his experiences in the SPLM/A and competing rebel groups. He was, however, not placed in a position where he could follow the decision-making process at the top level of the SPLM/A. The strength of his account lies in what he writes about the split and the internal politics of the competing rebel fractions in the 1990s.

[48] Johnson, confirms several of Lam Akol's statements, in *The Root Causes,* pp. 91–3.

[49] This state of affairs is confirmed by other sources as well as the SPLM/A itself.

to attend. Instead, as we will see, he and Riek Machar launched a coup against John Garang.

Local administrative structures in the South were rudimentary in the period 1983–91. The SPLM/A relied mainly on the old "indirect" rule system for governing the civilian population, and on a small number of civil/military administrators who functioned as the link between local SPLM/A commanders and chiefs. There were also some travelling magistrates who settled cases between SPLM/A soldiers and the local population.[50] By 1990 the Sudan Relief and Rehabilitation Association had established a presence in many areas in the South; both co-ordinating relief operations and taking on functions as local governments.[51]

The SPLM/A was reluctant to co-operate with civilian organisations, domestic and foreign. Despite an overwhelming demand for humanitarian aid in the South, in particular in 1988, foreign NGOs were hardly allowed to establish local bases inside the Southern Sudan. Nor were the southern church organisations popular among the SPLM/A leadership during the early stages of the civil war. However, this relationship improved in 1989 after the establishment of the New Sudan Council of Churches. In 1989 the NGOs too gained access to areas of crisis. These changes can to a considerable degree be attributed to Operation Lifeline Sudan.[52]

Operation Lifeline Sudan and Foreign NGOs Enter the South

In 1989, Operation Lifeline Sudan (OLS) brought a significant number of foreign NGOs back to the Southern Sudan for the first time since the outbreak of war in 1983. The impetus for OLS was the hunger catastrophe in the South in 1988, when perhaps as many as 250,000 people died.[53] The international community was strongly committed to preventing a similar disaster from happening again.[54] Agreements involving the UN, Khartoum and the SPLM/A were signed in March. The OLS was regarded as a great achievement both in terms of alleviating the needs of civilians trapped in war-zones, and as a confi-

---

[50] This system is rather minutely described in M.L. Kuol, *Administration of Justice in (SPLA/M) Liberated Areas: Court Cases in War-Torn Southern Sudan*, 1997.

[51] United Nations Lifeline Sudan, 'An Investigation into Production Capabilities in the Rural Southern Sudan: A Report on Food Sources and Needs', 1990, provides a thorough description of the local relief needs in several areas of the South at the time of writing and also gives a description of local administrative structures.

[52] See Ch. 5.

[53] This is the figure most frequently quoted, but it is still only a rough estimate, e.g. Larry Minear et al., *Humanitarianism Under Siege: A Critical Review of Operation Lifeline Sudan*, 1991, p. ix; Burr indicates that more than 500,000 people died in the Southern Sudan during 1988, *Quantifying Genocide II*, p. 10.

[54] Minear et al., *Humanitarianism Under Siege*, p. ix.

dence-building exercise – a prelude to peace.[55] Relief operations took place between April and August.[56] The foreign NGOs had no established structures in SPLM/A controlled areas and therefore the size of the OLS operation in the South was limited.[57]

In the period 1989–91 it was generally believed that the war was going to end soon, one way or another. With government forces contained in a few garrison towns and the war concentrated on the siege of Juba, the fighting was limited and considerable areas within the SPLM/A controlled parts of the South were even available for long-term development projects.[58] As late as spring 1991, it was possible to imagine that there would soon be no need for OLS-type operations; the first half of 1991 probably provided the best working conditions for relief and development activities in the South since 1984.[59] The belief that peace was imminent was reflected in the informal nature of the OLS: mainly a collection of agreements giving foreign NGOs their blessing for activities in the South and the right to fly the UN flag.[60]

The *ad hoc* nature of OLS activity in this period meant that it could be easily terminated. Actually, this had been the official plan after OLS operations finished in August 1989. Nevertheless, lobbying for a second OLS began before the first operation finished,[61] and the plans were officially presented in March 1990. OLS II commenced in April and the operation was officially ended in October. The results were far less than those of OLS I, mainly because of changes in the domestic political climate, a lack of interest among donors and foreign NGOs, and OLS II's lack of political prestige compared to OLS I.[62] A plan for an OLS III for 1991 was briefly discussed but no agree-

---

[55] Burr and Collins, *Requiem for Sudan: Background to a Conflict*, 1995; Karim et al., *Operation Lifeline Sudan: A Review*, 1996.

[56] *Ibid.*, p. 23.

[57] The first review did not prove that "OLS I averted famine and saved people", *ibid.*, p. 157. Actually, some food delivered during the OLS I operation was delivered by Norwegian People's Aid before OLS I was launched.

[58] Confirmed by the very fact that the United Nations 'An Investigation' report covered most areas of the South with the exception of Equatoria which was believed to have been sufficiently covered by other investigations. As early as 1989 John Ryle in 'SRRA Northern Sobat Basin: Agriculture & Fisheries Rehabilitation Project', recommended agriculture development, fishery projects and support to blacksmiths in the Sobat basin.

[59] Burr and Collins describe in *Requiem for Sudan*, p. 295, how a USAID delegation made an extensive reconnaissance in Southern Sudan during this period, visiting projects vaccinating cattle, nutrition programmes, agricultural extension, several hospitals and clinics.

[60] Part of the arrangement was that aid was given to Khartoum controlled areas as well. However, this agreement worked quite differently from that of the Southern sector. The indigenous NGOs were strictly co-ordinated by Khartoum's Relief and Rehabilitation Committee. In fact, the aid given to the "northern sector" was not far from a bribe to the NIF regime to make them accept the activities in the Southern sector, *ibid., passim.*

[61] *Ibid.*, p. 31.

[62] *Ibid.*, pp. 23–25; Burr and Collins mention that the UN, in order to boost the final result,

ment was reached, and by 1992 "relief deliveries under the OLS had all but collapsed".[63] The 1991 SPLM/A split and subsequent military and political developments turned this situation upside-down. Issues of access and security became increasingly complicated.

Conclusion

Two contradictory themes of the Southern Sudan's history – continuity and instability – are important in the analysis of political changes during the 1990s. Instability had been created and sustained by the antagonism between the region and the centre, but also by the lack of a well-established state-structure. Until the 1920s, much of the South had not been placed under administration, and after that only under a minimal "indirect" rule. The insecurity and destruction during the first civil war meant that by 1972 the people of the South were worse off than at time of the demise of Condominium rule. Thus the challenges facing the regional government and the foreign NGOs in 1972 were tremendous. Then, after only a decade of uneasy peace, the achievements of the Addis Ababa Agreement period were all but reversed during the first years of the second civil war. Therefore, when the SPLM/A officially declared that it wanted to expand rudimentary local administration into a civil government structure in 1991, a war-weary population threatened annually by famine and living in an area with close to no infrastructure did not represent an ideal point of departure for this endeavour.

As a consequence of neglect and, to a lesser degree, design, institutions at the local level had to a surprising degree remained unchanged. By 1983 local institutions partly created by the British policy of "indirect" rule remained largely unaltered, as did most local administrative boundaries.[64] The SPLM/A had to rely on the chiefs and their authority for government at the local level: the chiefs collected taxes, presided over local courts, and provided recruits and labour.

Although the memory of the foreign humanitarian organisations was short, the local population remembered both the colonial period and the peace brought by the Addis Ababa Agreement. Where relief workers in the 1990s saw wilds and ruins, the locals saw what had been, and what they hoped would

---

actually included relief food deliveries in the period December 1989–March 1990 in their calculations for OLS II, which started in April 1990. Karim et al., *OLS Review* state March–December 1990, but it seems that the actual relief activities took place during the period indicated in Burr and Collins, *Requiem for Sudan*, pp. 274–75 and 285.

[63] Mark Duffield, 'Humanitarian Conditionality: Origins, Consequences and Implications of the Pursuit of Development in Conflict', in Loane and Schümer (eds), *The Wider Impact* p. 113.

[64] See Ch. 3 for a discussion of these institutions.

be restored. This point is illustrated by the anthropologist Sharon Hutchinson during her first visit to the eastern parts of the Southern Sudan in 1978–79: "My first reaction was one of amazement. Apart from some clothing, mosquito nets, and the occasional dead radio, there was remarkably little tangible evidence in Nuer cattle camps and villages to betray the passage of some fifty years of war-scarred history."[65] She noticed one change however from Evans-Prichard's descriptions of the Nuer in the 1920s. Instead of conversations revolving around "cows and oxen, heifers and steers, rams and sheep, he-goats and she-goats, calves and lambs and kids", now they were preoccupied by "national political issues, cabinet shake-ups, regional troop movements, and the Jonglei Canal scheme".[66] Correspondingly, there is little tangible evidence left from the events and processes mentioned in this chapter, but they still remain visible in the Southerners' memory.

---

[65] Hutchinson, *Nuer Dilemmas*, p. 32.
[66] *Ibid.*, p. 33.

CHAPTER 2

Out of Ethiopia: A Farewell to Unity

Political reforms within the Sudan People's Liberation Movement/Army's (SPLM/A) were prompted by the drastic changes that took place during 1991 and 1992. The vital logistic and military support the SPLM/A had received from the Mengistu regime in Ethiopia ended; the Movement was torn apart to the point of disintegration; and the end of the Cold War radically changed Western countries' perspectives and agendas as well as the regional political configuration. These changes all pushed the SPLM/A towards liberalisation and reforms. The National Convention of the SPLM/A was announced on 20 February 1993, but the reform process began one and a half years earlier, in the summer of 1991, with the announcement of the first PMHC meeting and the attempted coup in August.

External Changes and Internal Contradictions

After several years of success on the battlefield and of unity within the armed opposition in the South, 1991 witnessed a breakdown of the old order. The SPLM/A's military progress had largely depended on logistic support from Ethiopia and the provision of Soviet arms and equipment.[1] The fall of the Ethiopian Derg demonstrated the Movement's vulnerability to external events. Successive governments in Khartoum had supported the separatist Eritrea People's Liberation Front and Tigray People's Liberation Front (TPLF),[2] the latter of which was the main force behind the EPRDF alliance that took control of Ethiopia in the spring of 1991.[3] These movements repaid their debts to Khartoum by evicting the SPLM/A from their safe areas inside Ethiopia, and immediately stopped support to the Movement. This significantly reduced the SPLM/A's military capabilities.[4] Moreover, the SPLM/A's whole organisational

[1] Gérard Prunier, 'The SPLA Crisis', pp. 2–3, forthcoming in F. Ireton E. Denis and G. Prunier, *Contemporary Sudan*. A shorter version of the manuscript was presented as a paper at the 3rd International Sudan Studies Conference in Boston, 21–24th April 1994.

[2] See pp. 26–27.

[3] Young, *Peasant Revolution in Ethiopia* is the most thorough account of the Tigray rebellion, Chs. 6 and 8 focus on the TPLF's capturing of state power.

[4] de Waal, *Famine Crimes*, p. 149.

structure was dislocated by the loss of rear bases on the Ethiopian border and its political headquarters in Addis Ababa. Approximately 100,000 refugees[5] who had lived in camps in Ethiopia had to flee to southeast Sudan, and many settled around Nasir in the Upper Nile.[6] From the Ethiopian camps, the SPLM/A had diverted food aid from refugees to the army on a grand scale, and when it proved difficult for the OLS and other aid agencies to reach refugees inside the Sudan this source of supplies was drastically reduced.

The Split

On 28 August 1991, Lam Akol, Riek Machar and Gordon Kong, three senior commanders within the SPLM/A, declared John Garang dismissed as Chairman of the Movement.[7] This attempt to seize leadership of the movement changed the civil war in the Sudan for a decade to come.[8] In 'Why John Garang Must Go Now', the trio protested John Garang's "dictatorial" leadership and demanded independence for the Southern Sudan.[9] This repudiated SPLM/A policy, which favoured regional autonomy within a united secular Sudan. Another point of grievance was the assumed dominance of the Dinka tribe within the SPLM/A; Dinka from the Upper Nile region, in particular the district surrounding the town of Bor, were believed to have a disproportionate share of leading positions.[10]

Lam and Riek's focus on ethnicity became more pronounced when their political appeals failed to rally the necessary support.[11] Gordon Kong and Riek

---

[5] Sources present different estimates: Sharon E. Hutchinson in 'A Curse from God?', p. 317, claims that there were as many as 350,000, while Karim et al., *OLS Review,* cite 200,000, p. 157. Douglas Johnson has written a detailed study of the evacuation of the camps, and his estimate is around 130,000–150,000, 'Increasing the Trauma of Return: An Assessment of the UN's Emergency Response to the Evacuation of the Sudanese Refugee Camps in Ethiopia 1991', in Tim Allen (ed.), *In Search of Cool Ground,* pp. 175–76. Given that both aid agencies and rebels benefit from exaggerated figures it is probable that the modest estimates are closer to the fact. In either, this was a tragedy of horrific proportions.

[6] Douglas Johnson, 'The Sudan People's Liberation Army and the Problem of Factionalism', in Clapham (ed.), *African Guerrillas,* p. 63.

[7] *Ibid.,* p. 63.

[8] It has been argued that the loss of Derg support triggered the coup in the sense that John Garang was no longer able to control the sources of supplies. Moving refugees away from the strictly controlled camps inside Ethiopia to relief centres inside the Sudan gave local commanders access to supplies through manipulation of food aid, Johnson, 'The Sudan People's Liberation Army', pp. 63–64; African Rights suggests that the prospect of controlling aid distribution might have been one motive for the attempted coup, *Food and Power: A Critique of Humanitarianism,* 1997, pp. 273–74,

[9] Prunier, 'The SPLA Crisis', pp. 2–3.

[10] Prunier, 'The SPLA Crisis', the dominance of the Bor Dinka as source of friction inside the SPLM/A is discussed in particular on pp. 3, 7–10.

[11] Johnson, 'The Sudan People's Liberation Army', pp. 63–64.

Machar came from the second largest ethnic group in the Southern Sudan, the Nuer. Lam Akol was a Shilluk, a people which mainly lives in northern parts of the Upper Nile region.[12] Since Nuer and Shilluk were in the minority within the SPLM/A, relying on the ethnicity card gave little hope for taking over the leadership of the Movement. The three coup leaders[13] therefore decided to form their own-armed movement, referred to as the 'Nasir faction' or 'SPLA-Nasir'.[14]

It was no coincidence that the rebel leaders drew their support mainly from the Upper Nile region and among the Nuer. The SPLM/A's road to 1989 supremacy in the South had been a history of countless skirmishes with competing guerrillas from this region known as the *Anyanya 2*.[15] Some of these groups were wooed to join the SPLM/A, but the wounds from these fights were far from healed in 1991 and their allegiance to the leadership of the Movement was weak. With the end of Garang's personal control of external supplies, the control over the Nuer commanders was diminished and a second round in the contest for leadership of the rebellion could start. Resentment towards the dominance of the Bor Dinka could have been exploited to broaden the base of the Nasir rebellion. With better preparations, commanders from Western Equatoria and the Nuba Mountains, as well as Dinka from some parts of the Bahr el-Ghazal might have joined the Nasir faction, and the coup would actually have been accomplished instead of causing fracture of the Movement.[16]

During the autumn of 1991, open hostilities broke out between the SPLM/A and the Nasir faction. The latter has been blamed for the fighting,[17]

---

[12] Prunier, 'The SPLA Crisis'.

[13] Lam Akol and Riek Machar were the leaders of the factionalists. While Gordon Kong, a former *Anyanya 2* commander from Maiwut, was less important and based his power on his former *Anyanya 2* units, Douglas Johnson, personal correspondence, 2004.

[14] Nasir is the town in Western Upper Nile where the trio made their announcement of the coup, and which later became their headquarters. John Garang's faction was called 'SPLM/A Torit' after the name of the town in Eastern Equatoria where the SPLM/A had its headquarters during this period. The name changed to 'SPLM/A Mainstream' after Torit was lost in 1992. However, for the sake of clarity, Garang's faction is throughout this book referred to as "SPLM/A", and other factions as "Nasir", "SPLA United", "SSIM/A", etc.

[15] See pp. 26–27.

[16] Johnson, 'The Sudan People's Liberation Army', pp. 63–64. Johnson points out, however, that even if some members of the SPLM/A would have been intrigued by a fight for independence, commanders from the Nuba Mountains and other parts of the Northern Sudan would have stuck with Garang as long as he maintained his unity position.

[17] Often referred to as the "Bor Massacre", this was an attack on Dinka civilians in the area around Bor, Kongor and Jonglei. Cattle were looted and more than 100,000 fled to the Lakes area and to Equatoria. Prunier, 'The SPLA Crisis', p. 12, points out that the timing of the Nasir faction's seemingly unprovoked attack on Bor was "odd". He thinks that the attack might have been masterminded by Khartoum; while Hutchinson, 'A Curse from God?, p. 318, sees it as a retaliation. She maintains that it was Dinka under the command of the SPLM/A who started the fighting during the first weeks of September. Hutchinson has done extensive research on the Nuer and she bases her conclusions on interviews with Nuer chiefs. However, the article appears

which continued for several years with varying intensity, and was at times more violent than the war with the government army. In fact, it was soon clear that the Nasir faction had a tactical alliance with Khartoum, and that the faction's military operations were co-ordinated with Khartoum's offensives.[18] The factional leaders' first public meeting with the Khartoum government took place in the spring of 1992,[19] and it is probable that co-operation pre-dated even the split itself.[20].

During 1992, other SPLA senior commanders broke away from the SPLM/A among them William Nyuon. Some of those that had been imprisoned by Garang for several years managed to escape during the chaos following William Nyuon's defection.[21] They joined the Nasir faction in March 1993. On 26–27 March all the groups opposing the old SPLM/A met in Kongor with a senior southern politician, Joseph Oduho, and signed a joint declaration forming the SPLM/A-United.[22] The link with Khartoum was maintained, and SPLM/A-United concentrated its military operations against the SPLM/A. In October 1993 Riek and Garang signed a declaration in Washington, saying that they would stop fighting each other and, instead, start discussing independence for the Southern Sudan.[23] Agreements notwithstanding, the infighting did not stop. Meanwhile SPLA-United started to fall apart; Riek wanted to end the co-operation with Khartoum, while the other faction leaders disagreed.[24] In February 1994 Riek dismissed Lam Akol. During the summer

---

slightly apologetic regarding the rebel leaders – Riek in particular – for instance claiming that he was forced to side with the government in Khartoum because of lack of supplies, p. 320. Prunier, however, mentions that several of the officers and foot soldiers on both sides were executed in the first months because they were suspected of plotting with the other faction, p. 11. The motive for the Bor Massacre and who fired the first shot – or threw the first spear – will probably remain an open question.

[18] Johnson claims that even the initial attacks by the Nasir faction in the autumn of 1991 were masterminded by Khartoum, in Clapham, 'The Sudan People's Liberation Army', p. 64 and Douglas Johnson, 'The Sudan Conflict. Historical and Political Background', in Loane and Schümer, 2000, pp. 66–67.

[19] Prunier, 'The SPLA Crisis', pp. 12–13.

[20] The Nasir faction denied these allegations for several years, but it is clear that the split was beneficial to the Khartoum regime, and that el-Beshir's government did what it could to encourage the factionalists, Prunier, 'The SPLA Crisis'. Johnson writes "Direct contact between the Nasir commanders and the Khartoum-appointed Governor of Upper Nile State in Malakal ... had already begun by July 1991", *The Root Causes*, p. 96, cf. Johnson, 'The Sudan Conflict', pp. 66–67. Such consultations are not mentioned in either of Lam Akol's autobiographies *Inside an African Revolution* and *SPLM/SPLA: The Nasir Declaration*.

[21] Most important among them were Kerubino Kwanyin Bol and Arok Thon Arok, Prunier, 'The SPLA Crisis', p. 20.

[22] The factionalists stated in their internal magazine *Southern Sudan Vision* that they had invited the SPLM/A as well, and that it was SPLM/A that opposed a re-union of the opposition, No. 29, 5 July, 1993, p. 3.

[23] Prunier, 'The SPLA Crisis', pp. 28–29.

[24] Hutchinson, 'A Curse from God?', p. 320.

the SPLA-United disintegrated, Riek formed his own South Sudan Independence Movement (SSIM/A) in September. Lam moved to Tonga in the Shilluk homeland where he applied the name SPLA-United to local armed groups loyal to him.[25]

Divided, the factionalists ceased to be a threat to the SPLM/A's political hegemony in the South, but the 1991 split had serious military consequences for the SPLM/A. The Nasir faction took control of areas in the Upper Nile and Blue Nile provinces, and a substantial number of SPLM/A foot soldiers and officers stationed there defected to the new faction, hence reducing the size of the army. In addition, the number of bases from which relief supplies could be diverted diminished, and the number of taxable civilians was reduced. Fighting the factions drew the SPLM/A's attention away from the war with the Khartoum. As a result, government forces enjoyed successful dry-season offensives in the period 1992–94,[26] which drove the SPLM/A out of all the major towns in the South, except Yambio in the extreme southwest. During the first offensive, in 1992, the Khartoum government forces did not attack the Nasir faction's towns, deepening suspicion of the faction's collaboration with the North.[27] New bases and supplies routes had to be established. A new political headquarters from where the leadership could participate in regional and international politics, had to be found. The capitals of Kenya and Uganda became the Movement's new political centres, and the southern parts of Equatoria on the borders of Kenya, Uganda and Zaire became the new safe areas of the SPLM/A.

As a consequence of military setbacks, the SPLM/A leadership realised that hopes of a quick assumption of government power had to be abandoned. Instead the Movement had entered into a phase of protracted warfare with no solution in sight, and a new strategy had to be developed. The changed situation on the ground affected the political conditions within the Movement. It became exceedingly difficult to dismiss demands for political and organisational reform by saying that democracy had to wait until victory was achieved. The new element of competition introduced by the split increased this pressure.

The Announcement of the National Convention as Propaganda

The idea of holding a large meeting of SPLM/A members may have been launched internally even before 1991, but, as will be discussed in Chapter 3,

---

[25] Cf. p. 126.

[26] Prunier in 'The SPLA Crisis', provides a detailed account of Khartoum's military gains during this period. The NIF government seemed to be well prepared for the offensives having spent $ 300–400 million on new military equipment in 1991, footnote p. 15.

[27] *Ibid.*, p. 15.

it was only in the spring of 1993 that the decision to hold a national convention was officially announced.[28] Competition between the SPLM/A and the new factions was one reason that the National Convention evolved from a loose idea into an actual plan. The new factions – those led by Riek Machar and Lam Akol in particular – promoted themselves as champions of democracy and, most importantly, of independence for the South; and the "liberal rhetoric of the Nasir faction meant that the Mainstream [i.e. SPLM/A] was obliged to compete, if it were not going to lose the support of most educated Southerners."[29] But it was not only educated Southerners who had to be convinced. The SPLM/A leadership soon realised that they had to prove themselves worthy to those commanders and ordinary soldiers who had remained loyal to them, and they had to compete for the goodwill of the aid organisations. Political and military supremacy within the Southern Sudanese rebellion was at stake.

Lam and Riek challenged Garang politically by establishing leadership councils, publishing their own newsletters, and setting up the aid organisation Relief Association of South Sudan (RASS).[30] RASS competed with the SPLM/A's humanitarian wing, the Sudan Relief and Rehabilitation Association (SRRA) for aid distribution, and RASS was recognised as a counter-part to Operation Lifeline Sudan. Initially the Nasir faction appeared as the best alternative in terms of political visions and their programme gained support from southern intellectuals and foreigners' goodwill. By 1994, as the Nasir faction's inability to put theory into practice had become evident, most of its initial support from these groups was significantly reduced. Yet, in the period 1991–94, many gave the faction the benefit of the doubt and an intense propaganda war developed as the two factions competed for support.[31] Each side focused on documenting and exaggerating the other's attacks on civilians; the SPLM/A condemned the motives behind the attempted coup and the co-operation with Khartoum, while the Nasir faction attacked the legitimacy of the SPLM/A leadership and John Garang.

Even if the political competition between the guerrilla factions degenerated into a propaganda war, it was still necessary for the SPLM/A leadership to achieve something in order to appear convincing to Southern Sudanese and foreigners alike. The National Convention fitted nicely into such a scheme. It was promoted as renewal, a way to leave old practices behind, and it promised

---

[28] See pp. 59–61.

[29] African Rights, *Food and Power*, p. 306.

[30] Almost immediately after the attempted coup, the Relief Association of South Sudan (RASS) was established, and later Lam Akol founded his own FRRA (Fashoda Relief and Rehabilitation Association), African Rights, *Food and Power*, pp. 274 and 281.

[31] This war was fought through the factions' magazines – *The South Sudan Vision* (Nasir), and the *Sudan Up-date* (SPLM/A) – as well as through press statements and "information" given to foreign NGOs, etc. Prunier, 'The SPLA Crisis', provides some vivid examples on pp. 20–22.

the lower ranks of the SPLM/A and representatives from the local population an opportunity to voice their opinions and grievances to the leadership of the movement. Moreover, elections for the top positions were announced, and revision of unpopular policies and laws was promised, together with the establishment of a civil administration.[32] The SPLM/A would demonstrate its legitimacy and multi-ethnic basis by gathering delegates from the whole of the Southern Sudan as well as from areas in the North and from the Diaspora.

Competition Pushes the SPLM/A towards Secession

During the 1980s the SPLM/A took a firm stance for the unity of the Sudan, despite strong separatist sentiments among SPLM/S foot soldiers and the people of the Southern Sudan. This position might be explained by analysing SPLM/A's need to placate foreign supporters and John Garang's personal ambitions. The demands of the Southern Sudanese had been subordinated to what was acceptable within an international and regional context. The explicit separatism of the guerrilla groups in the first civil war, the *Anyanya 1*, was one main reason for their lack of international support.[33] The fear of international isolation because of a policy of explicit separatism was probably well founded; while it would be possible to win support for the fight against suppression from successive Khartoum governments, a struggle to establish an independent Southern Sudan would be met with little understanding by the international community. In particular, the SPLM/A's unity stance seems to have been tailored to please the Mengistu regime. In the 1980s Ethiopia was fighting separatism in Eritrea and might not have wanted to support SPLM/A separatism in the Sudan.[34] However, the need to placate Ethiopia diminished considerably after the SPLM/A was thrown out of Ethiopia. Also, John Garang's ambitions may have gone beyond securing independence of the South, to include taking over the whole Sudan.[35] But, by 1992 it became clear that the 1991 split and the end of Ethiopian support meant that the capture even of the southern capital, Juba, let alone Khartoum, had receded far into the future. Consequently, the SPLM/A's motivation for maintaining the unity policy was reduced, while at the same time the Nasir faction's pro-independence rhetoric required a response.

The independence of Eritrea in 1993 might also have influenced the change in the SPLM/A's position towards self-determination. Suddenly it was

---

[32] The National Convention is discussed in detail in Ch. 4

[33] Johnson, 'The Sudan People's Liberation Army', pp. 56–57. See also pp. 24–25.

[34] Prunier, 'The SPLA Crisis', p. 6.

[35] It is difficult to say whether this really was the case, or was only propaganda from the government in Khartoum.

possible to alter the long sacrosanct post-colonial order in Africa. But the Eritrean secession was significantly different from the case of the Southern Sudan with reference to historical background, size of territory and ethnic composition as well as difference in aims and causes of the rebellions.[36] Moreover, it was expected that the independence of Eritrea would have consequences mainly for Ethiopia,[37] an independent Southern Sudan would be perceived as a potential threat to other countries dependent on the Nile, notably Egypt, and it would border several countries, hence complicating regional politics.

At the same time, however, other factors pulled the SPLM/A in the opposite direction. During the late 1980s the SPLM/A had managed to expand to what it called the "Western, Eastern, Blue Nile, Ingessana and other marginalized areas", and notably into the Nuba Mountains.[38] If the Movement started to fight for an independent Southern Sudan that did not include them, the SPLM/A would quickly lose support among the people and fighters in these areas.

Another group, which tried to forestall secessionism, was the northern politicians of the National Democratic Alliance (NDA). The NDA needed the Southern rebels' firepower in the struggle against the NIF regime, and they presumably trusted that co-operation with the SPLM/A would check secessionist tendencies in the South.[39] The NDA and SPLM/A began co-operation as early as March 1990. Considerable political differences gave way gradually to a common understanding. After the SPLM/A split, the NDA continued to support John Garang. They condemned the Nasir faction because of its position in favour of secession and its close link to the NIF regime.[40] Yet, the NDA's leaders and the SPLM/A had difficulties because the NDA was not willing to discuss a secular constitution.[41] A major breakthrough in co-operation between the NDA and SPLM/A had to wait until a meeting in Nairobi in April 1993, when the NDA, including the DUP and *Umma* party, agreed on establishing a secular constitution after the NIF regime had been removed.[42]

The issue of self-determination was, however, still a problem, and the new co-operation was threatened as early as in October 1993, when Garang and

---

[36] Johnson, 'The Sudan People's Liberation Army', pp. 70–71.

[37] However, although a bit unexpected Eritrea has also become a complicating factor in regional politics.

[38] Prunier, 'The SPLA Crisis', pp. 14–15. On the Nuba Mountains in particular, see African Rights, *Facing Genocide: The Nuba of Sudan,* 1995, pp. 60–103.

[39] Prunier, 'The SPLA Crisis', pp. 1 and 10.

[40] *Ibid.,* pp. 16, 18–19. Ann Mosley Lesch, *The Sudan*, p. 188. Johnson gives a more or less corresponding account of the development of relations between SPLM/A and NDA in *Root Causes, passim.*

[41] Lesch, *ibid.,* pp. 187–89. A secular constitution has been the most consistent demand of the SPLM/A.

[42] *Ibid.,* p. 190.

Riek signed the above-mentioned Washington declaration, calling for self-determination. The leaders of the NDA opposed this policy, since an independent Southern Sudan would tip the balance of power in the North further towards the NIF, and leave moderate Northerners politically marginalized.[43] The *Umma* and DUP had in any case always opposed separatism when they had held office themselves.[44] But, the SPLM/A needed co-operation with the Northern opposition just as much as it needed the support from Southerners, so the Movement could not take a very strong position in favour of self-determination. The effect of competition from the Nasir faction strengthened the separatists' position within the SPLM/A. John Garang found himself in the contradictory position of needing to champion self-determination in order to compete with the Nasir faction for support among Southerners, while simultaneously denouncing separatism in order to maintain co-operation with the NDA.

The Split Affects Peace Negotiations: Abuja I, Abuja II and the IGADD

The fate of various peace initiatives in the period 1992–94 is another example of the strong effect of the split on politics in the South and the SPLM/A in particular. Immediately after the NIF coup in 1989, there seemed to be an opening as the new regime signalled that it might give up the claim on the South in order to stop the war. Whether this was a serious proposal is not clear, and it was flatly rejected by John Garang, who was riding a wave of military victories.[45]

Peace talks in the wake of the split did not have any direct effect on politics in the Southern Sudan, but the way in which they were conducted was symptomatic of the difficulties facing the SPLM/A. The first comprehensive peace initiative was launched by the Organization of African Unity (OAU), which facilitated two rounds of peace talks in the Nigerian capital, Abuja, in May–June 1992 (Abuja I) and April–May 1993 (Abuja II).[46] The political and military events behind the split affected the parties' positions. Unlike previous

---

[43] *Ibid.*, p. 188.

[44] Cf. M. Kevane and E. Stiansen, discussion on the opening up of the separatist discourse within the Sudan political opposition during the 1990s, 'Introduction: Kordofan Invaded', in M. Kevane and E. Stiansen (eds) 1998, *Kordofan Invaded: Peripheral Incorporation and Social Transformation in Islamic Africa*, pp. 1–7.

[45] John Garang, 'First Statement by John Garang to the Sudanese People on 10 August 1989; Following the Military *Coup d'etat* of 30 June 1989', in Mansour, *The Call for Democracy in Sudan*, pp. 253–54. Cf. Burr and Collins, *Requiem for Sudan*, pp. 212–13.

[46] S. Wöndu and A. Lesch have written a book on the peace talks analysing the transcripts from the talks, *Battle for Peace in Sudan: An Analysis of the Abuja Conferences 1992–1993*, 2000. Wondu was a member of the SPLM/A delegation at the peace talks, which makes the book a rich source for studying these events. Prunier gives a somewhat more critical analysis of the peace talks in 'The SPLA Crisis', pp. 16–18, 24–25.

peace negotiations, where the Khartoum regimes and the SPLM/A negotiated on equal terms, the NIF leaders regarded the Abuja talks as a chance for the Movement to conceded defeat in an honourable way, instead of suffering a humiliating defeat in the field.[47] Negotiating from strength, Khartoum insisted that the Nasir faction had to be invited as well.[48] This move amplified the impression of unevenness between the parties at the negotiation table – on the one side a national government and on the other disunited local rebel groups. The SPLM/A was not ready to discuss negotiated surrender, and nothing new emerged from the negotiations except a common declaration on self-determination from the two Southern factions.[49] Failure at the negotiation table and military setbacks were closely linked. The SPLM/A's predicament led Khartoum to believe that the Southern factions would opt for a settlement if it offered some kind of recognition and personal incentives for the leaders.[50] Khartoum miscalculated both the SPLM/A's strength and its leadership's commitment to the cause; the Movement refused to surrender and continued the military campaign.

When the OAU initiative failed, the member states of the Horn of Africa Intergovernmental Authority on Drought and Desertification (IGADD) established a Standing Committee on Peace in Sudan on 7 September 1993, which had a more permanent character than the OAU-initiative. Four IGADD-sponsored negotiation sessions were arranged during 1994. The negotiations managed, through a Declaration of Principles, at least to establish a framework for subsequent negotiations, but the parties were far from any peace agreement.[51] The IGADD initiative was launched at a time when Khartoum claimed that the SPLM/A had become irrelevant because of its military setbacks.[52] And indeed, that the SPLM/A had to suffer the humiliation of negotiating together with the Nasir faction, was partly a result of the SPLM/A's inability to prove that they were "the only true" representatives of the Southern people.[53] Success on the battlefield could remedy this to a certain extent, but it

---

[47] This is mentioned in the comments on Abuja II, *ibid.*, p. 25.

[48] Prunier, 'The SPLA Crisis', p. 16.

[49] It is, however, unclear whether this was the policy of the SPLM/A at this time since John Garang was not a part of the delegation and was still, officially, committed to unity. It is more probable that this was an unauthorised proposal from William Nyoun, the head of the delegation, and that this was one of the reasons for his defection later that year, Prunier, 'The SPLA Crisis', pp. 16–17, 19–20.

[50] *Bedden Falls Resolutions*, p. 1; Prunier, 'The SPLA Crisis', p. 24; African Rights, *Food and Power,* p. 155.

[51] There were four sessions during 1994: Prunier, 'The SPLA Crisis', pp. 38–39. Lesch, *The Sudan*, pp. 179–85.

[52] Lesch puts it this way: "The government felt no need to accommodate the SPLM politically since the SPLA could not mount a serious military challenge", *ibid.*, p. 187.

[53] The SPLM/A could have refused to participate, but then it would have appeared unwilling to negotiate peace something which – given the Movement's predicament – it could ill afford,

is reasonable to assume that the announcement of political and organisational reforms was partly motivated by the need to demonstrate a qualitative difference between the SPLM/A and the other factions, in order to gain the status of the *real* people's liberation army.

In short, the split, together with the fall of Mengistu in Ethiopia, caused military setbacks that brought the SPLM/A close to collapse. This changed the SPLM/A leadership's perspective on the war from that of aiming at ending it quickly to the prospects of a long-term war with no end in sight. This in turn affected its political strategy. The need for change was amplified by the political and ideological competition with the Nasir faction. The discussion on John Garang's legitimacy as leader was brought into the open, and external pressure urged the SPLM/A leaders to prove that the Movement in fact represented and fought for the people living in the Southern Sudan. Moreover, the debate on a united Sudan versus self-determination for the South put the leadership of the SPLM/A in an awkward position, but the need for a change of policy in this regard became evident as well. Altogether, the split resulted in a strong impetus for change in the SPLM/A, at a time when, for different reasons, the foreign NGOs and the UN were trying to pull the Movement towards internal change and local administration reform.

The Dilemmas of Aid and Insurgency: Who Governs Whom?

The split and the changing regional and international circumstances affected relations between foreign humanitarian organisations and the warring parties as well. Of particular interest is whether Operation Lifeline Sudan (OLS) contributed significantly to the SPLM/A leadership's decision to arrange a national convention. The literature on humanitarian activities and agencies during the civil war is not well integrated into studies of the general political development in the South.[54] These agencies' main objective is well known – to execute successful relief operations. As such agencies try to reach this goal some secondary objectives emerge – to gain access to areas where relief operations are to be executed, and to ensure a satisfactory level of security for the operations. It is in attempting to achieve these secondary objectives that OLS and the foreign NGOs' operation in the Southern Sudan entered the arenas of national and local politics. Therefore, before these organisations' role in the political development of the South during the 1990s is assessed, the issues of access and security must be briefly addressed in order to comprehend the dynamics of these agencies' relations with Khartoum and the rebel organisations.

Prunier, 'The SPLA Crisis'.

[54] Geoff Loane, 'Literature Assessment'.

Access

In the early 1990s, the main obstacle to relief operations was lack of *access* to aid beneficiaries. In the Southern Sudan, physical and logistical obstacles such as lack of airstrips and roads might deny access, but more often than not it was caused by diplomatic hindrances and insecurity.[55] The novelty of OLS I in 1989 was exactly the high level of access to war zones in the South granted by both the Sadiq government in Khartoum and the SPLM/A. Even if the latter at times could decide to close off parts of the South, it was mainly the government in Khartoum that was reluctant to grant access, in particular to SPLM/A-held areas. Khartoum had little actual influence over the areas, but the areas were formally a part of the Sudan. Without permission from Khartoum, foreign NGO operations in SPLM/A areas were illegal and represented a violation of the country's sovereignty.

For Khartoum, giving access to SPLM/A areas was not only a problem of indirectly admitting that part of the Sudan was outside its control, but relief operations would also be a potential source of supplies for the SPLM/A and represented some sort of an international recognition of the Movement. Besides, to deny starving people food aid could be seen as rational from the Khartoum government's point of view. An aspect of its counter-insurgency strategy was to kill or displace civilians in contested areas,[56] and in this way limit the basis for recruitment and taxation for the SPLM/A, and quell the will to rebel. Allowing aid to reach these people and having foreigners present to observe the strategy at work would in consequence be counter-productive. Access to war zones and SPLM/A-held areas was therefore an object of constant negotiation between the UN and Khartoum. The focus of negotiation was most often flight permits, since many locations could not be reached by land or water transport. The airstrips and zones where relief flights were allowed changed rapidly, and the access obtained was more often than not a result of diplomatic pressure

---

[55] Burr and Collins discuss in detail the issue of access for aid operations in western parts of the Sudan in the 1984–88 period, and later also the south, *Requiem for Sudan, passim.* David Keen argues that denial of access was a part of a plan for artificially creating famine, where local and national elites benefited economically and politically, *The Benefits of Famine: A Political Economy of Famine and Relief in Southwestern Sudan, 1983–89,* 1994. The issues of access and security for OLS in the period 1989–96 are discussed in detail in Karim et al., *OLS Review,* pp. 23–61.

[56] Supplying and encouraging raids by local militias have often been an important part of this strategy, in particular the period 1984–88. The Baggara Murahaliin raids on the border between Kordofan and Bahr el-Ghazal were particularly vicious, see for instance Alex de Waal, 'Some Comments on Militias in the Contemporary Sudan', in Daly and Sikainga, *Civil War in the Sudan.* Since the early 1990s, local militias have been used as an element in the GoS scorched earth strategy in the Nuba Mountains and in Upper Nile and it has continued up to 2003, Human Rights Watch, *Sudan, Oil and Human Rights,* 2003. Moreover, since mid-2003 *Janjawiid* militias mobilised and armed by the GoS have been deployed in an attempt at quelling the rebellion in Darfur, Human Rights Watch, *Darfur Destroyed: Ethnic Cleansing by Government and Militia Forces in Western Sudan,* 2004.

from the UN and Western countries rather than of the actual needs of target groups.[57]

We have already seen how, during OLS I in 1989, the size of humanitarian operations inside the Southern Sudan grew rapidly. In the early 1990s, the humanitarian situation worsened. Following the fall of the Derg in May 1991, the influx of refugees from Ethiopia to remote areas in the eastern Upper Nile created a humanitarian crisis. The split within SPLM/A aggravated the situation by increasing insecurity and, at the same time, increasing the need for assistance. The foreign NGOs' access to the areas diminished after government forces took back most of the towns held by the SPLM/A factions, and, after 1992, access to other parts of the South had to be repeatedly negotiated with Khartoum and the rebel factions. Although the operational environment became more difficult, the split gave OLS administration and the associated foreign NGOs a strong incentive to intensify relief and development activities.

Despite their success in battle and in exploiting political division in the South, the NIF government was willing to accept a continued OLS presence in the South. The NIF needed international goodwill after siding with Iraq in the Gulf War. They feared an international intervention similar to the one in Somalia in 1992.[58] As a result OLS recovered from the 1990–91 crisis and entered a phase of growth and institutionalisation. The OLS programme changed from an annually negotiated agreement among Khartoum, the SPLM/A and the UN, to a permanent administration. It also became clear that the division between a Northern sector, operating out of Khartoum, and a Southern sector stationed in Nairobi was to be retained. The warring parties even signed an agreement in 1994, which formalised the tri-partite principle of the OLS operation. While the NIF government in the North maintained a hostile approach towards the relief operations, it was in OLS's and foreign NGOs' best interest to encourage the SPLM/A to establish a more explicit claim for the right to administer the areas under their control. A quasi-autonomous region in the South would make the humanitarian apparatus less dependent on approvals from Khartoum.[59]

---

[57] Karim et al., *OLS Review, passim.*

[58] *Ibid.*, pp. 42–43. Khartoum's recent successes and the setbacks for the SPLM/A might have led the NIF regime to believe that it was soon going to win anyway, and it could afford to be generous; other reasons for allowing OLS activities are discussed in Michael Medley, 'Humanitarian Assistance in Sudan: A Chronological Analysis of Shifting Mandates', in Loane and Schümer (eds), *The Wider Impact*, pp. 179–80.

[59] The dispute over the Memorandum of Understanding in 1999–2000 shows however that OLS and the foreign NGOs did not want the SPLM/A to use its quasi-governmental power to regulate the relief and development activities within their territory. See pp. 131–32.

Security

The high level of insecurity was a continuous threat and hindrance to OLS activities and the local security level determined the types of activities in which the UN and the foreign NGOs' could engage in different areas. Relief distribution was possible in most of the Southern Sudan,[60] while long-term development activities in education, health, water and agricultural projects tended, before 1997, to be concentrated in southern and western parts of Equatoria, where a high level of security could be provided.[61] After 1991, the main source of insecurity was fighting between the factions combined with the NIF regime's increased military assertiveness. Eastern Equatoria and most of the Upper Nile and Bahr el-Ghazal had by mid-1993 become chronically unsafe. The need to improve this situation became one of the main reasons that humanitarian organisations deemed it necessary to influence political developments in the Southern Sudan.

One of the unique features of OLS, as a UN operation in a war zone, was that it did not include a military force protecting the operation. It relied solely on agreements with counterparts and their willingness to adhere to them.[62] This meant that operations were vulnerable. The government in Khartoum declared that the reason for frequent and unpredictable flight bans was that it could not guarantee the safety of relief flights; OLS planes did not have their own escort, so flights were stopped owing to exorbitant insurance costs.[63] Insecurity caused by fighting and unruly rebel commanders made some areas inaccessible for long periods. During the mid-1990s, the insecure operational environment created by fighting between the southern factions and the increased presence of government forces in the South became a serious hindrance to the implementation of relief and development operations. What the humanitarian organisations needed was security for aid personnel and non-interference from the warring parties. As a result, the UN organisations and the foreign NGOs reached the conclusion that they needed to change the warring factions' attitude towards the civilian population and relief aid activity. This desire was prompted by their new agenda: the promotion of democracy, civil society and human rights was the universal recipe for improving societies in the third world.

---

[60] After 1993, the areas with the highest level of insecurity were serviced by the World Food Programme, rather than foreign NGOs, Karim et al., *OLS Review*, pp. 68–69.

[61] *Ibid.*, pp. 78–80. Factors such as inadequate co-ordination of foreign NGOs' activities and the wish to service the different factions equally also influenced the distribution of NGO programmes.

[62] *Ibid.*, pp. 33 and 37. As a result of lacking protection in the South, OLS had to develop a security monitoring system that made it possible to evacuate expatriate NGO personnel with a few hours notice, pp. 52–53.

[63] *Ibid.*

Another reasons for the high level of insecurity was that the goodwill and resources of the foreign NGOs became one of the prizes competed for in the rivalry between the southern factions. From the factions' point of view, aid was a resource that could be used in warfare. The question was how to balance the use of this resource against both the danger that humanitarian organisations might withdraw, and the need to maintain good relations with Western countries.[64] Aiding guerrillas was not the stated goal of relief and development interventions. Quite the contrary, most foreign NGOs would do almost anything to avoid being accused of fuelling the war or siding with one of the factions. This meant that more often than not, attempts at diverting or abusing relief assistance had a negative impact on relief operations themselves, as well as on the relations between the international humanitarian organisations and the guerrilla factions. This too would have consequences for the aid organisations' willingness to engage in activities in the different factions' areas. Thus, the split seems to have had two distinct effects on aid organisations' working conditions. First, intensification of the conflict increased the need for resources and made it more difficult to identify culprits when irregularities occurred; second, increased competition meant that in the worst case, an aid organisation could close down projects in one faction's area and move to another.

Aid Fuelling the War

Having identified two of the humanitarian organisations' motives for promoting political reforms and the policy of self-determination for the SPLM/A,[65] we turn now to what kind of leverage the foreign NGOs and OLS had. In short this was the resources that could be diverted through their projects, and the potential for creating good or adverse publicity. Which was more important – the supplies rebel factions received from sympathetic countries or captured in battle, or the food and resources diverted from relief operations or "mobilised" from the local population – is still difficult to establish. What is certain is that the cut-off of supplies from Ethiopia made whatever could be obtained from the local population and the aid organisations much more important.

Relief and development aid and the humanitarian organisations themselves could be exploited and manipulated in several ways. The most usual was to use relief aid as alternative sources of supplies, mainly of food, but also of medicines and various equipment. These activities were so common that a certain amount of loss caused by diversion to armed groups was considered normal by

---

[64] This is not to say that all individuals within the rebel organisations were making such calculations all the time, and never considered the welfare of civilians, but, rather, that as organisations their decisions were mainly utilitarian not altruistic.

[65] A third was the need to have the SPLM/A facilitate creation of local partners. See pp. 78–79.

the foreign NGOs.[66] Supplies could be obtained by stealing them from the foreign NGOs directly or from their contracted transporters.[67] Sure to cause confrontation with the relevant aid agencies, this method was in general avoided, except by local warlords allied with Khartoum who did not plan to build relations with the humanitarian organisations.[68] Food aid could also be diverted in more subtle ways, where the Southern Sudan's inaccessibility and the aid organisations' inadequate monitoring and secondary distribution mechanisms could be exploited so that theft would go mostly undetected. Diverting food aid had been easy before the exodus from Ethiopia. In the relief camps there, food from aid organisations was distributed through the SRRA to refugees as well as to SPLA recruits trained in camps nearby.[69] The Mengistu regime assisted this scheme by setting strict limits on UNHCR personnel's freedom of movement within the areas.

After 1991 the most common way of diverting food aid was through the factions' relief wings. Food was transported by aid agencies to certain points, and the SRRA, FRRA or RASS had responsibility for distributing food to the needy. These relief wings were nominally independent, but as integrated parts of the respective movements they would skim off food and give it to the army.[70] This could also be done by distributing food to women who had husbands or sons living at home who were members of one of the armed groups, or by taking supplies indirectly from civilians through taxation. Civilians could be forced to move in order to change the sites for the aid distribution, or they could be deliberately starved in order to attract food aid.[71] The civilians could be used as human shields in the fighting, by placing them near important military targets or at the borders between factions' areas of control. In this way, the opposing faction would lose credibility if it attacked.

Foreign NGO workers were also assets in themselves. Most importantly they could be taken hostage for different types of ransoms.[72] The risk of being

---

[66] Aid workers refer to "the realities of war", Duffield et al., *SEOC Review*, pp. 85–86. Even local churches took advantage of relief food they were supposed to distribute, and used it to pay church employees or handed it out as encouragement for attending services, *ibid.*, p. 88.

[67] The extent of these activities during the period is not known.

[68] Kerubino Bol is the most typical example of the latter category. In the period after the SPLA – United fell apart his troops were systematically attacking relief distribution points and foreign NGO camps, and as a consequence of those actions he managed to almost close down the humanitarian operations in the northern parts of Bahr el-Ghazal, African Rights, *Food and Power*, p. 283.

[69] African Rights provides an interesting description of different aspects of life in some of Africa's largest refugee camps, *Food and Power*, pp. 73–81.

[70] See pp. 73–75 for more information on the SRRA.

[71] African Rights mentions the breakaway commander William Nyuon, who supposedly deliberately starved a camp of displaced children in order to attract relief food, which was subsequently seized by guerrilla soldiers, *Food and Power*, pp. 283–84.

[72] For instance, Lam Akol's SPLA United demanded to be recognised as an OLS partner, while

kidnapped or killed by accident meant that there were few aid workers present. The humanitarian organisations' property could be used to serve the goals of the warring factions; vehicles and radios might be commandeered or stolen.[73] This strained relations between the agencies and factions, as well as limiting the size of the programmes. For example, it was impossible for food aid programmes to have trucks inside the Southern Sudan for transporting food from airstrips to target groups, because there was a high risk that the trucks would be stolen together with any stored fuel. The result was that only people able to walk to the airstrips could receive aid.

The foreign NGOs' status as outside observers could also be taken advantage of. For instance, a representative of Norwegian People's Aid captured on video the devastation caused by the Nasir faction's attacks on Dinka civilians in the Gemmiza region north of Bor in the autumn of 1991.[74] Partly because of this video, all factions blamed the Nasir faction for the subsequent killing and looting of civilians. This film was distributed within the foreign NGO network and contributed to cooling some of the early enthusiasm for the Nasir faction and its liberal rhetoric.

To deny competing factions the benefits brought by humanitarian organisations was another aspect of the power struggle. Publicising other factions' errors and wrongdoing was one way of doing this, but direct attacks on areas of relief activities also occurred. The split itself contributed to an increasing level of distrust between the SPLM/A and the OLS organisations. John Garang claimed that the UN organisations and most of the foreign NGOs supported Khartoum, or gave more aid to the North than to the South. He charged that the leaders of the Nasir faction had been encouraged by foreign NGOs in planning the coup attempt in 1991 and given free flight.[75] The NIF regime too sought to exploit aid activities to influence competition between the factions. In 1992, after the suspected link between Khartoum and the Nasir faction became official, Khartoum's game of giving and withdrawing flight permits was effectively employed to assist the Nasir faction against John Garang's faction. OLS organisations were denied permission to fly to SPLM/A-held towns, while they were allowed to go to Akobo, Waat and Nasir in the Nasir faction's area of control.[76] Thus by the early 1990s OLS and the foreign NGOs were, however reluctantly, significant actors within the Southern Suda-

---

Kerubino Bol wanted money and cars, African Rights, *Food and Power,* pp. 281 and 283.

[73] E.g., Duffield et al., *SEOC Review,* p. 61, mention that the Save the Children Foundation (UK)'s vehicles for secondary distribution of relief food had been commandeered by the warring parties.

[74] Burr and Collins, *Requiem for Sudan,* p. 301.

[75] *Torit Resolutions,* pp. 9–10; Johnson, 'The Sudan People's Liberation Army', p. 65.

[76] Burr and Collins, *Requiem for Sudan,* p. 308; Prunier, 'The SPLA Crisis', p. 16.

nese political context, and they had a clear interest in attempting to change the practices and policies of the rebel factions.

OLS and the Foreign NGOs' Role in the Formulation of SPLM/A Political Reforms

OLS and the foreign NGOs' first attempt at directly influencing the political situation in the South was prompted by an incident in late 1992, when three aid workers and a Norwegian photographer were killed in Eastern Equatoria.[77] All foreign NGOs, with the exception of NPA and World Vision, withdrew in protest, demanding that the murders should be investigated properly.[78] The UN conducted an investigation, but for what seems to have been diplomatic reasons the results were kept secret. The foreign NGOs demanded that the security situation to be improved before they returned. The new humanitarian agenda seemed to provide the solution: make the warring parties commit themselves to human rights protocols, assist them in establishing civil administration, and provide economic incentives for the establishment of non-state organisations.

These concepts were realised through a programme of funding the first indigenous NGOs (SINGOs),[79] through capacity-building projects, and most importantly through development of the so-called Ground Rules. The first version of the Ground Rules was agreed upon in early 1993 and aimed at improving security for OLS and foreign NGO personnel. OLS and the foreign NGOs stated that before they resumed work in the South the warring parties had to endorse the rules. These "established the inviolability of aid workers and their property, including free access to radios".[80] This first set of rules were therefore limited in scope, but they demonstrated a will to use whatever influence the OLS operation had to enforce a change in behaviour of the armed factions in the South. As we shall see, the Ground Rules were later widened to include important humanitarian principles and a framework for extending the OLS mandate to include the monitoring of rebel factions' violence against civilians.[81]

For aid organisations the ideological motivation for encouraging a civil society was supported by the practical need for local partners. This need resulted from the insecurity and inaccessibility of the Southern Sudan, which made it difficult to maintain a large contingent of expatriate personnel in the field.

---

[77] de Waal, *Famine Crimes,* p. 147.

[78] Karim et al., *OLS Review;* de Waal, *Famine Crimes,.*

[79] Sudanese Indigenous NGOs.

[80] Karim et al., *OLS Review,* pp. 51–52.

[81] Discussed in particular in *ibid.,* pp. 53–56.

Ideally, the foreign NGOs wanted local NGOs and community groups as working partners. Before the first SINGOs were established in 1993 this was difficult to accomplish, and even after this liberalisation the situation was only slightly improved. The aid organisations did not trust the factions' own relief arms, mainly because they were seen as incompetent and mere fronts for guerrilla groups. The churches were not perfect aid distributors, either. To some extent religious foreign NGOs took matters into their own hands and established local church and community groups, and put pressure on the SPLM/A and Nasir faction to initiate local democratic and administrative reforms. The practical need for local, "neutral" partners was fuelled by an ideological conviction that local NGOs and community-based organisations would also contribute towards a liberalisation and development of society as a whole. But were OLS and the foreign NGOs in a position to bargain with the Southern factions, notably the SPLM/A?

The Power of the Aid Organisations vis-à-vis Southern Factions

What power did the OLS administration and the foreign NGOs have in the Southern Sudanese political setting, and what influence over political processes within the SPLM/A? At the operational level, inside the Southern Sudan, the guerrilla factions had the last say in the never-ending discussion on access, security and abuse of the humanitarian organisations and their assistance. Although the humanitarian organisations could use withdrawal as a threat, they were extremely reluctant to do so. At the ideological level and in political debates, however, the aid organisations had other advantages. Just as it was important for the warring parties to show willingness to participate in all peace initiatives – in order to demonstrate the will to find a peaceful solution – it was also necessary for them to demonstrate their humanitarian inclination by asking for help from the UN and foreign NGOs to alleviate civilian suffering. The SPLM/A's need to prove its legitimacy and its dedication to improving the living conditions of civilians was a matter of some priority.

As we have seen, cessation of supplies from Ethiopia made other sources more valuable, but competition caused by the split made it necessary to be more careful in exploiting these. One way of assessing the aid organisations' influence over the guerrilla factions might be to discuss relations between these factions and the benefactors of relief assistance and development projects, who were first and foremost the civilians. The first question should then be whether the survival and well being of civilians was important to the SPLM/A? For the period before 1991, the answer is mostly negative. The SPLM/A got their supplies from Ethiopia, and from what they could extract from civilians. Civilians could be used to attract food aid that could be diverted – such as in the instance of refugee camps in Ethiopia supported by the UNHCR – but the improvement of the lives of the civilians themselves was at best something to be postponed until after the planned victory.

The situation changed in 1991, when the Nasir faction brought in the element of competition, and when the supplies from Ethiopia were cut off. The use of civilians to attract the foreign NGOs was still important, but their location was now inside the Southern Sudan, in the middle of the theatre of war, which brought the foreign NGOs much closer to what was happening on the ground. Hence, aid workers could get a more realistic impression of the civilians' situation, and what was causing their predicament. In order to maintain working relations with these organisations, the SPLM/A and to some extent the Nasir faction needed at least to appear to show interest in the welfare of these people. Moreover, competition between the factions increased the importance of good relations with the aid organisations. Some educated Southerners and officers were genuinely committed to the welfare of the people; if the military leaders' actions caused OLS and the foreign NGOs to withdraw from their territory, those supporters might defect.

Conclusion: External Pressure for Reform

Prior to 1991, havens in Ethiopia and material support from the Derg had allowed the SPLM/A to ignore external criticism. Political developments within the region and the Sudan itself in the period 1991–93 weakened the SPLM/A and made the Movement more receptive to the opinions of both southern Sudanese and foreigners. The fact that the Movement did not collapse after Ethiopian support dried up demonstrated that it had not been totally dependent on that support. Since the support from Ethiopia had been channelled through Garang, thus bolstering his power within the SPLM/A, the end of Ethiopian support created a favourable climate for a coup.

The split was the most important factor behind the decision to organise the National Convention, since it forced the SPLM/A leadership to address the problems publicised by the opposition. The political impact of the split is illustrated by the Movement's change in its professed aim – from unity to self-determination – and by changes in the configuration of the peace negotiations. Initiation of the process of liberalisation was an answer to the challenges from the Nasir faction, and the convention became an important part of this strategy. As suggested by African Rights, a programme of liberalisation and increased accountability was of common interest to both the guerrilla factions and the international humanitarian organisations,[82] and even more for the SPLM/A than the other factions, since it had more to lose.

---

[82] African Rights, *Food and Power,* Ch. 12.

CHAPTER 3

The Threat of Becoming Irrelevant: Reforms and New Local Institutions

This chapter deals with developments within the Sudan People's Liberation Movement/Army (SPLM/A) and the institutions in areas controlled by the Movement in the period 1991–94. The first part examines attempts at initiating reforms through meetings of the Political Military High Command (PMHC) and how the decision to hold the National Convention was made. The SPLM/A's predicament in this period compelled its leadership to demonstrate vigour and willingness to execute reforms to impress the Sudanese intelligentsia and international supporters, both current and potential. The most important change at the central level was that the PMHC actually started to meet, and started issuing formal resolutions. These resolutions announced reforms and official stances on internal and external political matters, but, oddly enough, made no mention of the Convention. The pretext for the Convention will be investigated briefly as an illustration of the nature of the political environment in the period 1991–94. Since the reforms adopted by the PMHC seem to have had little impact at the local level, we may ask what their purpose was. If it was really to restructure the movement, why were results not forthcoming?

The second part of this chapter is concerned with the local levels of the SPLM/A's structure and how the movement related to the local population and agencies operating inside their territories. The most significant local entities in this period were the Movement's local administrative structure, often represented by Civil/Military Administrators (CMAs); the SPLM/A's relief wing, the Sudan Relief and Rehabilitation Association (SRRA); the international humanitarian organisations; the church organisations; and the traditional structures inherited from the colonial period.

Deciding to Hold a Convention

The SPLM/A's formal political structure remained weak in the period 1991–94. Three meetings of the PMHC were the only venues for formal political decisions. These decisions were released after the meetings as sets of resolutions. For this study, it has been possible to obtain documentation from two of these meetings, at Torit in September 1991 and at Bedden Falls on 7–9 August 1992.[1] This documentation consists of only two sets of resolutions, without any indication of how the meetings were held and how decisions were made. However, combined with other contemporary documents issued by the SPLM/A, by competing factions, and by the UN/NGOs, these allow tentative conclusions on how and for what purpose the reforms were developed.

Most of the resolutions consist of statements concerning the SPLM/A's policy on various current topics, e.g. regional political development and peace talks. Some address the issue of political liberalisation and institutional reforms. But while the Torit meeting was unequivocally positive towards reforms, the tenor of the Bedden Falls meeting appears far more hesitant. In any case, the adoption of these resolutions was not followed by significant efforts towards implementing them, and one is obliged to ask why reforms were announced if they were not supposed to be implemented? Part of the answer is the propaganda effect that such promises could achieve, but to comprehend the full picture it is necessary to look for other reasons as well. Arguably, there was a genuine desire among most of the SPLM/A leadership to initiate change, and the resolutions resulted from attempts to find a consensus on how to execute these reforms. Through the PMHC meetings, ideas could be shaped and support canvassed.

The Torit Meeting

Without directly saying so, the Resolutions of the Torit meeting were partly a response to Lam Akol and Riek Machar's 'Why John Garang Must Go Now' statement.[2] The meeting had in fact been announced before the attempted coup, but was delayed because of it. Lam Akol had in particular been pushing for a formal PMHC meeting, but when it was finally held he and Riek Machar refused to attend because they were convinced that they would be incarcerated if they turned up.[3] The meeting finally took place in September 1991. This

---

[1] The third meeting was at Isoke. It has not been possible to identify any documents from this meeting. It is assumed that this meeting did not present any major diversion from the general thrust of the SPLM/A's policy in this period. A reference in the press statement from 20 February 1993 that most of the members of the PMHC had been consulted on the decision to dissolve itself, hardly implies an official PMHC meeting. No official Resolutions were ever issued by this meeting.

[2] The Torit meeting was attended by nine of the 13 PMHC members: John Garang, William Nyoun Bany, Salva Kiir, James Wani Igga, Daniel Awet, Kuol Manyang, Martin Manyiel, Lual Diing Wol and Galerio Modi. Yusuf Kuwa could not come, while the other three absent were Lam Akol, Riek Machar and Gordon Kong. This information is attached in a one-page document to the Torit Resolutions with the heading "Attendance".

[3] African Rights, *Food and Power,* p. 273. The threat was real enough since opponents such as Arok Thon Arok and Kerubino Bol had already been locked up on suspicion of conspiring against Garang, Johnson, *The Root Causes,* p. 92.

meeting produced *The SPLM/SPLA Torit Resolutions*, dated 12 September 1991,[4] the principal policy document issued by the Movement prior to the National Convention.

This meeting was important for several reasons, not least, the fact that it actually took place, the first PMHC in the SPLM/A's history.[5] Several working groups were set up to present reports to the next PMHC meeting.[6] The Torit meeting therefore represents a significant step towards formalising the Movement's political structures.[7] Torit Resolution No. 7, point 6 states that civilians could become members of the SPLM/A without going through military training.[8] Previously, every member was a soldier who at any time could be commanded by persons of higher rank, regardless of position within the political structure. Therefore, this resolution was reckoned as a significant step towards reforming the Movement's militaristic culture.

Some of the reforms later claimed to be great achievements of the NC, were actually first presented at the Torit meeting. Most significantly, Resolution No. 7 prescribes establishment of autonomous local administrative units, at levels of "county", "payam" and "village".[9] It is explicitly stated that the civil administration at the local level would be separate from the military, but the "Front Commander" – the military head of the area – was given overall authority to arrange things as he saw fit. Resolution No. 15 concerned "Human Rights and Civil Liberties", and affirmed the SPLM/A's commitment to non-discrimination, freedom of worship, and protection of prisoners of war.[10] 'Self-determination' is also mentioned, which is described as different from any regional autonomy arrangements similar to the Addis Ababa Agreement.[11]

---

[4] The *Torit Resolutions* are also found in 'Appendix 2' in Mansour, *The Call for Democracy*, pp. 282–91.

[5] Prunier refers to an interview with Lam Akol in 1993, 'The SPLA Crisis', p. 9, and Akol writes the same in his book, *Inside an African Revolution*. Furthermore, the present author is aware of no attempts by the SPLM/A leadership to claim that there were any official PMHC meetings before 1991.

[6] These groups were: the Commission to Organise and Develop Public Administration (CODPA); the National Economic Council; a panel of judges, former army officers, and others to revise existing laws and draft new ones; a New Sudan Institute for Legal Affairs to train chiefs to act as judges; a committee to revise the SPLM/A manifesto; and a committee from the High Command to draft the powers, procedures, rules and code of conduct governing the Politico Military High Command and lower organizational echelons of the Movement down to payam level", *Torit Resolutions*, pp. 10–11.

[7] The importance of this depends on the extent to which PMHC members could discuss freely and influence the content of the resolutions.

[8] *Torit Resolutions*, p. 6.

[9] *Ibid.*

[10] *Ibid.*, pp.11–12.

[11] *Ibid.*, p. 4; Cf. Prunier, 'The SPLA Crisis', p. 10.

Support for self-determination – which would definitely have been a sudden and radical change in SPLM/A policy – is not elaborated upon.

The *Torit Resolutions* give the impression that the SPLM/A was trying to make comprehensive changes. Declarations of good intentions and the announcement of reform committees indicate at least that these were wanted, and that the announced institutions had not existed before.[12] The fact that elaborate plans for reform were presented within a fortnight after the Nasir declaration demonstrates that they were already under development before the split. It is, however, difficult to avoid viewing the *Torit Resolutions* in light of the attempted coup. The document tries to remedy almost all the points of criticism from 'Why Garang Must Go Now' – the lack of civilian structures, the unclear chain of command, and lack of democratic debate.[13] In sum, the *Torit Resolutions* demarcate an important change in the Movement's rhetoric, away from militarism and uncompromising unity of the Sudan, and towards a stated desire to separate the military wing from the administration of areas under the SPLM/A's control and a hesitant support for the goal of self-determination for the South.

The Bedden Falls Meeting

The Bedden Falls PMHC meeting took place in the wake of the Abuja I negotiations (May–June 1992),[14] where William Nyoun as representative of the SPLM/A signed a joint declaration with the Nasir faction calling for self-determination. In the *Bedden Falls Resolutions* the PMHC meeting is referred to as an emergency meeting. The emergency seems to have been that Garang needed to clarify the SPLM/A's position on the Abuja negotiations. A collective PMHC declaration would put more weight behind policy statements than if Garang had issued them alone. The *Bedden Falls Resolutions* represent at best a slowing down of the process towards extending the civil administration. In Resolution No. 7: "On Civil Administration", it is evident that a programme of improving the civil administration was seen as less important than pressing military issues. The PMHC expressed concern at the effect of "many officers and soldiers [having] been absorbed by the civil administration. This has had [an] adverse effect on military operations."[15] The resolution therefore called for the "majority of officers, NCOs [Non-Commissioned Officers] and men who are physically fit [to] be relieved of civil administration assignments and re-

---

[12] Prunier, *ibid.*, p. 11.

[13] *Ibid.*, p. 2.

[14] See pp. 42–43.

[15] *Bedden Falls Resolutions*, p. 6.

placed by civilian members of the Movement."[16] Although, the reason given for this decision was "so that civil administration becomes truly civilian",[17] there were probably few educated, physically unfit civilians left who could take over the positions of those re-assigned for military duties. Most educated Southerners who were not already trained as soldiers and officers had by 1992 fled abroad or to the North, and were living either in refugee camps or in Western and neighbouring countries. Indeed, the resolution appears to have been motivated by unwillingness to allocate any significant amount of personnel to civil institutions.

Resolution No. 7 also states that "The SPLM/A Ad hoc Committee on Political Work and Organization commences its work immediately so that further steps are taken for the establishment of SPLM organs at the Village, Payam, County and I.A.C. [Independent Area Commander] levels."[18] Where resources and manpower to implement these reforms were going to be found is not mentioned. The resolution gives the impression of a reform that was well under way, or, at least, did not await any approval from a future national convention.

The Significance of the PMHC Meetings

Although the PMHC meetings symbolised greater formality of SPLM/A structures, they still represented only a small step forward. At the local level the announcements had little effect.[19] More than anything else, the PMHC meetings seem to have been part of the propaganda war against the Nasir faction. The meetings give the impression of being occasions for approving John Garang's current policies, and giving them more authority and legitimacy. It is also worth noting that the two sets of resolutions make no mention at all of the upcoming National Convention, despite Garang's later claim that it had been planned since before 1991; on the contrary, the resolutions give no impression of any imminent national convention. The two PMHC meetings are, however, still related to the National Convention. There is a clear link between the *NC Resolutions* and some of the resolutions from the Torit and Bedden Falls meetings; not all the decisions reached at the Convention reflected a sudden change of policy. Ironically, the meetings may also have contributed to the decision to convene the National Convention, in the sense that a lack of results from the PMHC meetings compelled the SPLM/A leadership to stage a more momentous event.

---

[16] *Ibid.*, p. 7.
[17] *Ibid.*
[18] *Ibid.*, pt. 7.2 .
[19] See pp. 79–80.

Announcing the Convention

The paucity of written sources to the internal politics of the SPLM/A has made the date for the Movement's decisions on holding the National Convention difficult to ascertain. But the time for the official announcement of the planned Convention should be possible to pinpoint. This date is significant in itself, more important however, it is relevant for an analysis of the reasons for holding a National Convention in the first place. Curiously enough, there is no consensus on the date for the announcement of the upcoming National Convention. African Rights' date is 20 February 1993, John Garang himself has referred to both June 1991 and September 1992. Garang explained in his opening speech to the delegates at the National Convention:

> This Convention was first called in June 1991 following the collapse of the Mengistu Regime and the changing regional and international situation. The former Political Military High Command (PMHC) called for [a] Convention in June 1991 in order to review and analyse the impact of these changes on our Movement and adjust ourselves accordingly. But this was frustrated by events which you all know and which I need not go into in these opening remarks. Again, when conditions improved and the imperative of holding the national convention remained as urgent as ever, we announced in mid-1993 that we would hold the convention before the end of the year, but the enemy for the first time in ten years launched a wet season military offensive which it continued into this dry season.[20]

What Garang was saying here was that changes were under way in mid-1991, and that the split – referred to as "events which you all know" – together with later military set-backs, were the main reasons that the Convention was postponed. But, as we have seen, official policy documents produced by the SPLM/A in the period between August 1991 and early February 1993 reveal no plans for holding a convention. Also, the SPLM/A's plight had yet to reach its nadir and the situation was certainly not improving in mid-1993 as Garang claimed.

In his speech quoted above, Garang said that the Convention was announced in June 1991. There are, however, several reasons to believe that a national convention of the sort that materialised in April 1994 – with several hundred delegates, radical restructuring of the movement, election of leaders, etc. – was not among the plans of the Political Military High Command (PMHC) in mid-1991. It has not been possible to locate any records of a PMHC meeting in June 1991, and there is no trace of any other document from that time calling for a national convention. Moreover, the *Torit Resolutions* do not mention any NC. If the National Convention had been announced in June 1991, it should at least have been mentioned in the Torit Resolution

---

[20] *Proceedings*, p. 10.

No. 7 on civil reforms, and decisions made at the PMHC should have been presented as subject to the approval by the up-coming convention. The *Bedden Falls Resolutions* are also silent about any plans for a convention. It only points out that the Nasir faction had not fulfilled its promises of holding one, and concludes that elections are impossible in wartime.[21] John Garang repeated these points in a speech on 10 February 1993, only ten days before what seems to have been the first official reference to the National Convention. Since plans for holding a convention were not reflected in any official documents from the Movement in the period following the alleged announcement, we may assume that the PMHC did not in fact announce such plans in June 1991.

The first mention of the National Convention in an official SPLM/A document occurred on 20 February 1993 at the end of a five-page press statement.[22] "In implementation of the *Bedden Falls Resolutions* of the Political Military High Command, the Chairman/C-in-C, CDR/DR. John Garang, has ordered the conveying of an SPLM National Convention not later than 16 May, 1993."[23] Since the *Bedden Falls Resolutions* do not mention a national convention, and in fact reflect a rather negative attitude towards spending scarce resources on organisational reforms it seems odd that Garang referred to this document when announcing the intention to hold the National Convention.

The *decision* to hold the convention – as opposed to the day the plans were made public – may have been reached between 10 and 20 February 1993. In the speech of 10 February 1993 mentioned above,[24] Garang comments on human rights, Sharia law, the Abuja I and II peace talks, and the military situation. If the final decision to organise the National Convention had been made, one might expect it to have been mentioned in this speech, but it was not. It is possible that a plan for the National Convention had already been discussed, but that the SPLM/A leadership had not yet decided to make it public. But in the 10 February speech, Garang attacked the Nasir faction's promises of elections and conventions: "Our conditions of war simply cannot allow them to hold elections in the same way that the same conditions have not enabled us to hold elections."[25] If the leadership of the SPLM/A had by 10 February already decided to hold a national convention where the leadership would be elected, Garang would probably not have dismissed elections as infeasible. Therefore, it is possible to conclude with considerable confidence that the final

---

[21] *Bedden Falls Resolutions*, p. 3.

[22] *SPLM/SPLA Press Release*, Kampala, February 20 1993, p. 5. The other four pages were dedicated to a clarification of the SPLM/A's position regarding a message that President Bashir wanted to deliver to John Garang in connection with preparations for the Abuja II negotiations.

[23] *Ibid.*, pt. b, p. 5.

[24] "Briefing Notes on Sudanese Conflict by Dr. John Garang De Mabior".

[25] *SPLM/SPLA Press Release*, p. 6.

decision to organise the National Convention was made as late as mid-February 1993, not in June 1991 or August 1992.

What was the motive for "back-dating" the announcement – that is, claiming it to have been made earlier than it had? The reference to the Bedden Falls meeting in 1992, which was made in the press statement of February 1993, was probably intended to attribute the decision to organise the Convention to a formal PMHC meeting. This would give more formality and legitimacy to the Convention than would Garang's personal decision. The second back-dating, referring to June 1991, was probably intended to diminish the impact of the criticism from the Nasir faction, by implying that the attempted coup in August 1991 had, instead of prompting reforms, caused delays in planning the National Convention.

Why Did the SPLM/A Want a National Convention?

If the brief notice at the end of a press statement was the first official mention of the National Convention, why was this announcement made in February 1993, anonymously, and in a press statement on a totally different topic? Why was there suddenly a perceived need for a national convention?

In the quote from Garang's opening speech, "the collapse of the Mengistu Regime and the changing regional and international situation", are referred to as the reason for organising the Convention. These factors had indeed profoundly affected the SPLM/A's ability to wage guerrilla war, and there was obviously a need to reassess and draw up a new course. But there are reasons to doubt that these were the main explanations for the decision to organise the convention. First, the format of the forum was not appropriate for the type of policy debate John Garang called for. It was not to be expected that several hundred delegates, mainly drawn from different parts of the "liberated" South, who had not before been aware of, and certainly had not influenced the forming of, the SPLM/A's foreign policy, would be in a position to reach informed decisions on these issues. Second, the *Proceedings* of the National Convention reveal that policies towards Ethiopia, regional issues, and the international approach of the SPLM/A were not the main focus of the meeting. Therefore, the reason for the Convention must be sought beyond official statements from the Movement, and in a context of the political and military situation in which the SPLM/A found itself.

By referring to a meeting between Donald Petterson the US ambassador to the Sudan, and John Garang, African Rights tries to link the announcement to US influence:

> Garang was encouraged to adopt definite measures of liberalisation. On 20 February, the
> SPLA issued a press release announcing preparations to convene a National Convention.[26]

But Garang's meeting with the ambassador took place eight days after the announcement, on 28 February.[27] Yet, even though the ambassador's visit was
not the reason for the announcement, African Rights is correct in pointing to
the SPLM/A's concern for its external image and expectations and pressure
from Western countries and foreign organisations as important reasons for the
announcement of reforms. The process of internal reform, which was set in
motion by the attempted coup in August 1991, must also be taken into account. Also, from 1993 onwards was a period when relations between Khartoum and the new governments in Ethiopia and Eritrea began to deteriorate;
the radical Islamist agenda of the NIF government was at odds with the West-
oriented approach of the latter countries' governments. To position itself as a
democratic alternative for the support of these governments was therefore poli-
tic for the SPLM/A.

It remains possible that the SPLM/A leadership did not know exactly what
they wanted of the National Convention at the time of its announcement. If the
National Convention was mainly intended for public relations, then the un-
usual method of announcing it might be explained; the Convention might
have been planned to exhibit firm control over the areas the Movement occupied, and to confirm the SPLM/A's legitimacy. This need to prove that "the
elephant was not yet dead" is to some extent reflected in the Movement's military priorities as well. Displays of military potency demonstrated that the
SPLM/A was not defeated, as evidenced by the commando attack inside Juba in
June 1992[28] and the brief re-capture of Torit in June 1993.[29] In the opening
speech at the NC, John Garang stated:

> The mere fact that we are able to hold this convention at this particular time when the
> NIF regime has launched its biggest dry season offensive in 11 years, billed the mother
> of all dry season offensives, sends a clear and frightening signal to those who beat the
> drums of war in Khartoum. It reminds them that the SPLM/SPLA is very much alive,

---

[26] African Rights, *Food and Power*, p. 307.

[27] Petterson, *Inside Sudan: Political Islam, Conflict and Catastrophe*, 1999, p. 53. Petterson writes
that the idea of making this trip to Kenya, Uganda and the Southern Sudan came to him as he sat
on the plane back to Khartoum after visiting the USA. He left Khartoum almost instantly and
did not even obtain permission from the US State Department to go. The circumstance of this
decision means that the 20 February SPLM/A press statement was not prompted by this visit.
Furthermore, he does not mention that he brought up issues of liberalisation and reform during
the talks. Rather, he seems to have been much more concerned with finding a way to bring Garang and Riek Machar together.

[28] Bona Malwal wrote that the attack was staged in order to show "the elephant was not yet
dead". Prunier, 'The SPLA Crisis', p. 18, quoting Malwal's *Sudan Democratic Gazette* (May
1992).

[29] Tvedt et al., 'Chronology', in *An Annotated Bibliography*, p. 902.

kicking and very dangerous ... This Convention frightens and shakes Turabi, Beshir and the NIF to their toes because it unambiguously signals that their dream of defeating the SPLM/SPLA is just that, a dream![30]

Thus, regardless of whether the NC was planned as a demonstration of force in a difficult period, it was most certainly used for this purpose. And as we shall see, the planning process indicates that the scope of the Convention changed over time.

An explanation for why the decision was reached precisely in February 1993 might be found in the hypothesis that the National Convention resulted from the reform process set in motion by the split and the PMHC meeting at Bedden Falls in 1991. The *ad hoc* committee mentioned in the *Bedden Falls Resolutions* delivered its report to Garang early in 1993, and it recommended the organisation of a national convention. This recommended action may have stemmed from the experiences of the Advisory Council in the Nuba Mountains in September 1992.[31] This idea is supported by the fact that another important announcement was made on the same page: to replace the SPLM/A's highest decision-making body, the PMHC, with the General Field and Staff Command Council (GFSCC), consisting of 61 members, with effect from 21 February. This council was presented as an interim government until a proper one was elected at the National Convention. The members were not named;[32] no schedule for meetings was given; no details of its mandate were mentioned in the press statement. Whether this reorganisation had any real consequences is therefore difficult to say.

It is reasonable to conclude that if the *ad hoc* committee presented its recommendations in February 1993, a national convention and plans for re-organising the PMHC into the GFSCC were included.[33] However, even if there are good reasons to doubt the official version of the background for the Convention and other more plausible motives and explanations can be found, the secretive nature of the SPLM/A leadership and the lack of documentation concerning the decision to hold the National Convention means that the exact circumstances of its conception are difficult to establish.

It may even be the case that the announcement reflected a longer planning process within the movement, and that decisions later heralded as major achievements, such as the separation of civil and military authority and the

---

[30] *Proceedings*, p. 10.

[31] Cf. Chs. 4 and 5. African Rights, *Food and Power*, pp. 312–14.

[32] Only 18 members are mentioned in the list of NC participants in the 'Delegates to the National Convention', in *Proceedings*, pp. viii–ix.

[33] Garang's above-mentioned reference to the *Bedden Falls Resolutions* in his speech of 20 February could be to the *ad hoc* committee instead of to the announcement of a National Convention. This would make it easier to understand why he chose to refer to this meeting rather than to e.g. the Torit meeting.

establishment of local government structures, were only public announcements of decisions made privately at preceding PMHC meetings.

The Local Administration: Did It Exist?

Information about how and to what extent the SPLM/A administered the areas under its military control is scarce, however, in particular for the period before 1994.[34] The significance of the National Convention partly hinges on the degree to which the convention resulted in changes in SPLM/A controlled areas. Such an analysis necessitates an investigation into how these areas were governed before implementation of the Convention's resolutions. In connection with this book, interviewees were asked what kind of administration there was in SPLM/A areas before the National Convention. Few could elaborate on this. Yet, it was possible to detect that there had been a universal dissatisfaction with the pre-1994 system. A typical response was:

> During the times of the Civil-Military Administrator there were some difficulties. The army was in charge. They would use military language and sometimes there would be misunderstandings. They were not skilled in civil administration.[35]

There are two main accounts of the SPLM/A's administration in the period 1983–94. Rakiya Omaar and Alex de Waal,[36] fronting the advocacy group African Rights, present SPLM/A structures as minimal and partly blame international food aid for this lack of development. SPLM/A government structures in the Nuba Mountains are seen as an exception.[37] Douglas H. Johnson represents the other interpretation. He claims that there was a comprehensive and uniform administration of SPLM/A areas, where representatives of the

---

[34] Academic studies on the political processes within the SPLM/A mainly come from two sources. The London based African Rights group who in the period 1995–97 researched the effects of humanitarian aid on the establishment of local political institutions and civil society in the Southern Sudan, particularly the Nuba Mountains. Its findings were published in several overlapping publications (see Bibliography). The other source is the historian Douglas H. Johnson, who draws on his own research, and partly from the African Rights publications, even if he disputes some of their conclusions. To date, his most comprehensive discussion of the development of the SPLM/A in the period after 1991 is 'The Sudan People's Liberation Army', in Clapham, *African Guerrillas*, in particular pp. 62–71. His recent book, *The Root Causes of Sudan's Civil Wars*, does not add significant new information or perspectives concerning internal political development of the SPLM/A or the administration of areas under the Movement's control, except for a detailed comment on the difference in the administration of the West Equatoria and the East, pp. 85–87, 108–109.

[35] Interview with Chief Kon, Aluakluak Yirol County, 4 March, 2002.

[36] He later left African Rights and founded a new organisation, Justice Africa in 1999.

[37] This interpretation is consistently expressed through African Rights books and reports, which publish the results of members' and associates' fieldwork in the Southern Sudan and the Nuba Mountains in the first half of the 1990s.

Movement worked closely with the chief structure. The reason why little is known about this structure is, according to Johnson, lack of documentation.

The level to which these interpretations contradict each other is reflected in the fact that they do not even agree at the level of basic definitions. For example, opinions differ regarding the meaning of the SPLM/A "having an area under its control" in the period before 1989. African Rights claims that "control" meant little more than "rendering a place unsafe for the Sudan Government, and making it available to rebel fighters for movement, recruitment and requisitioning."[38] Johnson states that after "the current war began the old structures [of "native administration" from the Condominium period] were retained in many important respects, but, in all those rural areas which it occupied, a civil/military administration was created within the military structure of the SPLA."[39] Nevertheless, the main problem here is not of conflicting views about administration of the SPLM/A areas, but that both accounts pay insufficient attention to changes over time and variances within those areas.

The timeframe of this study has not allowed the collection of sources necessary for substantial tests of the accuracy of these different accounts. Our own account of political and administrative development within SPLM/A controlled areas is therefore presented through a historiographic review of secondary literature contrasted with some new material.

The African Rights Interpretation

African Rights maintains that the local SPLM/A and SRRA apparatus for administering and assisting the local population in SPLA controlled areas was insignificant before Operation Lifeline Sudan I was initiated in 1989. Alex de Waal states:

> The SPLA put military victory before political mobilization: the political philosophy of its leader, Dr. John Garang, was to capture state power and then use it as an instrument for social transformation from above. In the meantime the SPLA made no attempt to deliver social reforms or welfare. At its best its administration represented benevolent paternalism, at its worst it was violent and extractive. SPLA military tactics created food shortages in many areas (by requisitioning food, labour, and livestock) and exacerbated them in others.[40]

According to African Rights, the first OLS period (1989–91) represented an opportunity lost, since the new flow of resources could have been used by the SPLM/A to expand and consolidate its control over the captured territory and its population. This did not happen. Instead the relief aid impeded the devel-

---

[38] African Rights, *Food and Power,* p. 263.

[39] Johnson, 'The Sudan People's Liberation Army', p. 67.

[40] de Waal, *Famine Crimes,* p. 96.

opment of local accountability by the SRRA and local commanders. In "1989–91 the SPLA lacked a strong concept of civil administration, anyway. The impact of relief aid did not destroy an enlightened policy; it only helped to retard the formation of one."[41] Thus, African Rights focuses on shortcomings and negative consequences, but without descriptions of the system criticised, making it difficult to evaluate its claims.

Regarding the period between 1991 and its last publications on political development in the Southern Sudan in 1997, none of African Rights' associated publications comprehensively analyses SPLM/A administration below the central level. However, African Rights has been very much interested in developments in the Nuba Mountains, and there it found the SPLM/A administration genuinely concerned with the welfare of the local population,[42] who, through the chiefs and village councils, had real influence on decision-making processes.[43] African Rights believes that the reason for the Nuba administration's inability to provide social services was a dearth of resources as consequence of the war, and isolation of the SPLM/A occupied areas in the Nuba Mountains, not the political system.[44] African Rights also claims that the reforms in other SPLM/A controlled areas, most importantly the idea of holding a National Convention, were inspired by experience in the Nuba Mountains.[45]

When trying to explain this – to them – abnormal development among the Nuba, African Rights identified two factors, the democratic inclinations of the rebel leader in the Nuba Mountains, Yousif Kuwa, and the fact that there were no international aid agencies present.[46] The latter is seen as significant because international aid agencies would have given the SPLM/A an alternative supply of resources, which would have made co-operation with the local population less important. This analysis then implies that bad leaders and too much aid retarded political development elsewhere.[47]

The African Rights account of local politics and administration in the Nuba Mountains is the most comprehensive of its kind for the period before 1994. The SPLA entered the area in 1987, but only as taskforces; a permanent presence was not established before 1989. Then the SPLM/A worked through local chiefs and village councils. From 1991 on chiefs were elected and administrations were established "at County, Payam (sub-district), and village levels,

---

[41] African Rights, *Food and Power,* p. 268.

[42] African Rights, *Facing Genocide.*

[43] *Ibid.,* pp.

[44] *Ibid.,* p. 314.

[45] See p. 89–90.

[46] African Rights, *Food and Power*, pp. 313–14.

[47] African Rights, *Facing Genocide,* states "In contrast to every other senior commander in the SPLA, Cdr Yousif has placed the emphasis on political mobilisation and the establishment of civil administrations", p. 315.

elected committees meet and wield real power."[48] The next step was taken in September 1992, when an advisory council for the Nuba Mountains met Kuwa in order to decide if they would continue the war. After that, this council met every year and made important decisions. An executive was formed and attempts were made to set up schools, health centres and courts, but these were severely limited by lack of resources. Abuses and looting by local SPLA soldiers were also an impediment. The African Rights' account of these developments is brief, and it is difficult to evaluate its claims for the councils' powers. Two questions that must be asked in this regard are: Were these structures essentially new, and were they unique?

Douglas H. Johnson's Interpretation

Douglas H. Johnson states that the lack of information from the period prior to 1994 is the reason we do not know much about the political and administrative system during this period, not the absence of a system *per se*. Johnson – and the SPLM/A – claim that there were well-ordered structures in the areas under the Movement's control and that the main problem was that they were too authoritarian. Johnson argues that others have been looking for the wrong things – church organisations and trade unions – when they conclude that there were no civil institutions in SPLM/A controlled areas. Instead, the role of the chiefs and their courts should be studied more closely.[49] According to Johnson, establishment of an administration based on the old chieftaincy structure was common for the SPLM/A when they entered a new area. As early as 1984, the SPLM/A started "establishing a civil administration which regulated the election of chiefs and the functions of chiefs' courts."[50] Courts were established as early as 1985.[51] Police posts, an inter-tribal conference in 1990, and "firm and coordinated action by commanders" kept local raiding in check.[52]

As a historian, Johnson draws historical lines from the SPLM/A administration back to the colonial period when the system of indirect rule was established. Johnson explains that local government structures from the Condo-

---

[48] African Rights, *Food and Power*, p. 313; African Rights, *Facing Genocide*, p. 315.

[49] Johnson, 'The Sudan People's Liberation Army', pp. 66–67.

[50] *Ibid.*, p. 66.

[51] In his discussion of the SPLM/A's court system in the 1985–94 period Johnson refers to an account of the personal experiences of one of the SPLM/A mobile magistrates, M.L. Kuol, *Administration of Justice*. Kuol later presented a more systematic account of the same topic in his M.Phil dissertation, 'The Anthropology of Law and Issues of Justice in the Southern Sudan Today', 2000.

[52] Johnson, 'The Sudan People's Liberation Army', p. 66

minium period remained unchanged until the outbreak of the current war.[53] Within the pre-war structure the chief had judicial and to some extent executive responsibilities and reported to a government representative at the lowest administrative level. The changes wrought by the SPLM/A were to put a Civil/Military Administrator (CMA) as the supervisor of the chiefs' structure and that chiefs were placed within the military structure.[54] This change gave SPLM/A commanders considerable power over election of local chiefs and gave the chiefs paramilitary tasks such as recruitment of soldiers. Johnson also discusses the inadequacy of a judicial system wherein it was difficult even to get copies of the 1983 Penal Code.

With reference to a personal account by a former magistrate who worked as a judge and mediator in the SPLM/A areas, Johnson writes that the organisation of chiefs' courts dates as far back as 1984.[55] He explains that the Movement placed the chief at the bottom of its administrative and judicial hierarchy, as the link between the population and the rebel army. This sustains Johnson's larger argument, that the civil population was organised and administered by local administrators long before the 1994 National Convention.[56] He goes on to describe how the SPLA Zonal Commanders had overall responsibility for civilian administration in their areas, and that they appointed the CMAs, who had the responsibility for collection of taxes, while judicial officers oversaw the court system.[57]

Johnson takes his argument one step further in stating that

> it is within the framework of a functioning civil administration throughout SPLA controlled territory that one can find the answer to the overall success of the SPLA in securing and holding on to large sections of the rural civil population (that is, maintaining a civilian base), despite the overwhelmingly military nature of the movement, and despite the political and military upheavals of the years after 1991.[58]

Consequently, not only does he contest the African Rights' claim that there were no structures; he considers the structures to have been essential for the SPLM/A's survival in the 1991–94 period. Johnson makes use of the example of Riek Machar as proof: as a SPLM/A commander, Riek Machar was known as a just and efficient administrator, but he was unable to demonstrate the same abilities when he established his own movement. According to Johnson this is explained partly by the fact that administrative collaboration between commanders within the SPLM/A structure ensured a uniform system that kept

---

[53] *Ibid.*, p. 67.
[54] *Ibid.*
[55] *Ibid.*, p. 66.
[56] *Ibid.*, p. 67.
[57] *Ibid.*
[58] *Ibid.*, p. 65.

individual commanders in line. Because the manpower base in the Nuer area was much smaller than in SPLM/A controlled territory, the number of competent potential administrators was limited.[59]

The Two Interpretations Compared

The pictures of local structures in SPLM/A controlled areas that emerge from the African Rights' publications and Johnson's accounts appear to contradict each other. This appearance is mainly created by their different points of departure and their different interpretation of facts. Johnson wants to demonstrate that areas under the control of the SPLM/A were not characterised by anarchy, and that – through the CMAs – there was a systematic exchange between the movement and the local population, mediated by SPLM/A-appointed magistrates and the chiefs. Johnson's formal outline of the CMA-chief structure concurs with a survey of local government in the Southern Sudan produced by Rohn, Adwok Nyaba and Maker Benjamin, which describes the CMA structure in more detail.[60] Prior to 1992 SPLM/A areas were organised into large units comprising several of what are now called counties under the administration of a Civil/Military Organiser, who had several Civil/Military Administrators under him. He also supervised a number of Assistant CMAs who were responsible for payams, who in turn oversaw a set of village administrators, who were the direct link to the chiefs and civilian population. In 1992 the larger districts were divided into Independent Area Commands but, according to the report, civil administration did not change much until after the NC.[61]

For Johnson important proof that this system really existed and functioned as intended is that it managed to curtail raiding and feuds within SPLM/A areas of control. But he does not discuss whether it is fair to have expected more from the CMA administration. After all, its main duties were to extract taxes and maintain law and order. Provision of services and the facilitation of markets and economic activities were not in their job description. This was a system strictly geared towards the military effort, wherein the chiefs' main task was to provide what was needed (recruits, porters, grain, cattle, etc.) in addition to their local conflict resolution capacity. Security and rudimentary justice are not important in the African Rights version. It asks to know to what extent the SPLM/A improved or worsened the situation of the local population – did

---

[59] *Ibid.*, p. 70. Riek Machar's success as an administrator in the period prior to the split is also mentioned in Hutchinson, *Nuer Dilemmas,* pp. 148–49.

[60] Rohn, Adwok Nyaba and Maker Benjamin, 'Report on the Study of Local Structures in Maridi, Mundri and Yei Counties, West Bank Equatoria, South Sudan', 1997, p. 10. Other sources also mention the CMAs, e.g. Karim et al. in the *OLS Review* state that their responsibilities were "collecting taxes from the civilian population and supervising the court system within their jurisdiction, under the authority of the SPLA Area and Zonal Commanders", p. 83.

[61] Rohn, Adwok Nyaba and Maker Benjamin, 'Report on the Study of Local Structures', p. 10.

the SPLM/A provide food, education and health care or did it actively or passively deny these? African Rights is less interested in the chiefs' structure and in the SPLM/A's ability to police its territory. The fact that they taxed the population, forced youths into the army, and used internally displaced people as bait for obtaining relief food, marks the movement as predatory.

Although Johnson does not explicitly state that the SPLM/A controlled areas were under a uniform and extensive local administration in the period before the National Convention it is important for him to gainsay the claims of African Rights that what few structures existed were not for the benefit of the civilian population. Criticising those who charge that the SPLM/A is too centralised, he claims that the SPLM/A is in fact "built up of semi-autonomous commands, whose autonomy grows with their distance from the main seat of operations."[62] He mentions inadequacies within the administration of justice, in particular the administration of the death penalty. He mentions that the SPLM/A was seen as an army of occupation in Yei, but does not discuss what consequences this would have for relations between the Movement and the local population – compared, for example, with Bor or Yirol, two of the SPLM/A's core areas. In *The Root Causes of Sudan's Civil Wars* Johnson expands a little on this topic in discussing differences between SPLM/A policies in Western and Eastern Equatoria. Overall, Johnson's account gives the impression of harmony and common interest between the SPLM/A and the local population.

Thus, while Johnson tries to analyse the SPLM/A in a historical perspective, mainly focusing on the differences and similarities between local civilian government structures and administration of chief courts, African Rights seeks to measure the effect of relief aid in civil wars. However, until more research is done on representative localities, and until former CMAs are interviewed systematically, definite conclusions about the nature of the SPLM/A's local administration in the period prior to the National Convention cannot be reached.

* * *

Even though available sources do not allow an independent analysis of the SPLM/A structures and the relation to the civilian population some issues might be raised. Based on the overall development of the Movement one might expect that the establishment and consolidation of local administration could to some extent be divided into periods. In the period 1984–89 installing a standard system of Civil/Military Administrators was presumably the main task as new areas were brought under the Movement's military control.[63] It is there-

---

[62] Johnson, 'The Sudan People's Liberation Army', pp. 71–72.

[63] There seems however to have been an established practice to frequently rotate the SPLM/A cadres from one position to another, often as a promotion. This might have limited the CMA-system's ability to improve over time.

fore hard to imagine a standardised local administration in the SPLM/A controlled areas during this period. The period 1989–91 was quite different:
most of the Southern Sudan was consolidated under SPLM/A rule and there
was relative peace. The aid organisations started to work in earnest in the South.
These changes should have had important consequences for the tasks assigned
to the CMA apparatus and for relations between administrators and the local
population. For example, trade was suddenly feasible, and precarious trade
networks emerged. These activities had to be facilitated and administered.
Johnson made a survey of this, mapping how goods moved from government
controlled Abyei all the way across SPLM/A areas to Yambio and Uganda.[64]
The survey also shows how these achievements were undone after the split in
1991,[65] when almost the whole of the South experienced fighting and a high
level of insecurity.

Other factors that changed over time and should have affected the nature of
the local civil administration were internal displacement, insecurity and distance to fronts. Since 1983 most of the Southern Sudanese population has had
to flee their homeland or accommodate displaced people for longer or shorter
periods. The result of displacement or an influx of refugees was that the
CMAs' tasks and authority vis-à-vis the military commanders would change,
and this would also influence the SPLM/A's relations with the local population. Insecurity probably had an important effect on the degree of autonomy
granted to the civilian structures and the chiefs.[66] High insecurity leads to
stricter military control. Distance from the front might have influenced how
many soldiers and aid agencies that were present, which again had consequences for the level of taxation and the type of aid projects operating in an
area. All these factors formed parts of the background of each local community's unique history of the civil war and its exchange with external actors –
Sudanese as well as foreign. Therefore, the network of local administrators
probably worked differently in 1987, in 1990 and in 1993, and there might
have been considerable variations from place to place. Local administration
reforms adopted by the PMHC after 1991 (explained in the discussion above
on the *Torit Resolutions* and the *Bedden Falls Resolutions*), and re-emphasised in
the *NC Resolutions* clearly indicate that an extensive, well-oiled, government
machinery was not in place in the early 1990s. This does not mean that there
was anarchy, but that the nature of local administration probably varied considerably, and was shaped by local circumstances and personalities.

---

[64] Johnson, 'Destruction and Reconstruction in the Economy of the Southern Sudan', in Harir
and Tvedt (eds), *Short-Cut to Decay*, pp. 136–41.

[65] *Ibid*, pp. 141–42.

[66] Cf. discussion on structural constraints, pp. 133–38.

The Role of Local Institutions in the South
in the Period 1991–94

Many places in the Southern Sudan became isolated during the 1991–94 period by government offensives and fighting between southern factions. In such areas only CMAs and local chiefs remained. What was in the early 1990s called the 'hunger triangle',[67] the area bounded by Ayod, Waat and Kongor, was an extreme case. This area was a no-man's land between two factions, suffered widespread famine and was almost inaccessible to NGOs and other non-Sudanese. In other places, such as Western Equatoria and the area around Waat, the level of security was acceptable, and extensive relief and development activities took place.[68] Other local institutions present in these areas were connected to relief activities.

The Chiefs

In the Southern Sudan, the Anglo-Egyptian Condominium administration established a system of indirect rule in which a hierarchy of chiefs were granted considerable judicial powers as well as responsibility for taxation and labour mobilisation, which made them mediators between colonial administrators and the local population. The chiefs were organised in most cases so that at the top there was a paramount chief who answered to the British District Commissioner. Under him was an executive chief for each village, who again had headmen who answered for sub-sections within the village. This structure is in many places of the South intact even today.

Whether this system was uniform and universal is debatable, but common features included a hierarchy of chiefs and headmen, and the inheritability of positions within the chiefs' extended family. In some places selection of a new chief appears to have been subject to some sort of public approval.[69] The executive chief and the paramount chief had courts where they heard cases, mainly civil ones. The chiefs also participated in mediating disputes between tribes and sections of tribes. The chiefs mobilised people for public works, and were often given the task of distributing relief food and assessing needs. It

---

[67] African Rights, *Food and Power,* p. 277.

[68] This was particularly the case in Nasir faction areas where relief was handled by RASS. OLS and many of the foreign NGOs associated with OLS tried to demonstrate impartiality in the conflict between the SPLM/A and the Nasir faction, and so initiated a series of projects in the Nasir area. The amount of project activity was beyond the capacity of RASS, which lacked accountability and was ridden with cases of misuse of relief funds, Karim et al., *OLS Review.*

[69] E.g. Chief Kon explained in an interview that his older brother had been chief before him, but had to resign and leave the post to Kon because the people were dissatisfied with the way he carried out his office, Aluakluak Yirol County, 4 March, 2002.

seems that when all other structures collapsed, the chiefs' institutions remained and gained more influence. In some areas the elders – who often enjoyed more authority than the executive chief and the headmen – balanced this power.

Sudan Relief and Rehabilitation Association

The official date for the founding of the Sudan Relief and Rehabilitation Association (SRRA) is disputed, but the most widely accepted version is that it was founded at Itang refugee camp in Ethiopia in 1986.[70] During the next few years, the SRRA's role was rather unclear:

> At this time [until 1989] SRRA barely existed inside Sudan [*sic*] and there was considerable ambiguity as to whether it was an indigenous NGO, an instrument of the SPLA civilian administration or simply an external fund-raising instrument for unspecified purposes.[71]

The uncertainty was somewhat reduced with the commencement of Operation Lifeline Sudan in 1989. The SRRA settled into the role of the Movement's liaison with the international NGOs operating in SPLM/A controlled areas, and the SRRA established a presence at several locations inside the Southern Sudan. The SRRA's limited autonomy resulted partly from the fact that most of its personnel were temporarily re-assigned SPLM/A officers drawn from the security unit.[72] Johnson gives the following description of relations between the Movement and the SRRA: "Throughout OLS the SRRA often gave the impression that it was the procurement department of the SPLA, at least as food and medicines [were] concerned."[73] He does not explain this further. Attempts at increasing the SRRA's autonomy and accountability were made through grants from several foreign NGOs, OLS and the Sudan Emergency

---

[70] Duffield et al., *SEOC Review*, p. 96. However, Karim et al., *OSL Review*, p. 81, and African Rights, *Food and Power*, p. 87, give the date as 1984. Moreover, the present author has found a SRRA document called 'The Constitution of Sudan Relief and Rehabilitation Association' which was supposed to have been signed and sealed "by the Sudanese refugees at Itang in their meeting held on 2nd of September 1984". The document has, however, been tampered with in that the SRRA's letterhead with a Nairobi address has been added, and it cannot have been entirely produced in 1984. The issue is quite unimportant since the work done by the SRRA before 1986–87 was insignificant, African Rights, *ibid.*

[71] Duffield et al., *SEOC Review*, p. 98.

[72] Johnson, 'Destruction and Reconstruction', p. 133. The *SEOC Review* confirms this observation, but differentiates between intelligence officers (GIS) and SRRA personnel, saying that the former were often attached to the latter. Moreover, the *Review* comments that it was the SPLM/A officers' ability to speak English that was the main qualification for transfer to the SRRA, Duffield et al., *SEOC Review*, p. 98.

[73] Johnson, 'Destruction and Reconstruction', p. 133. *The SEOC Review* from February 1995 states that the SRRA was "completely under the control of the SPLA leadership", p. 98.

Operations Consortium to the SRRA's Nairobi administration, but without significant effect.[74]

The SRRA operated on two rather separate levels. The central level focused on interaction with NGOs and the OLS structure in Nairobi. The local level consisted of SRRA officers stationed inside SPLM/A controlled areas. The central level lacked resources to coordinate the field level, and the latter was more or less cut loose to work closely with local SPLM/A structures. The SRRA staff's importance within the local contexts varied, however, and changed over time. Prior to 1991 the local SRRA did not function properly, and often the OLS administration and NGOs had to negotiate directly with local commanders.[75] African Rights gives this description of local SRRA officers in the early years:

> The SRRA officials were all named from amongst the soldiers anyway and retained their military rank. They received no salary and usually no instruction from the head office. Without supplies, they had nothing to do except other military duties. If aid did materialise, the first human needs to be served would naturally tend to be those close to the [SPLM/A] army.[76]

Thus local SRRA officers were to facilitate the reception and distribution of external aid. They were not supposed to take any initiatives on their own.

In places with weak CMA structures the SRRA staff could also end up as the link between civilians and the SPLM/A. In other places local SRRA officers managed to be the nexus between the local community and local SPLA commander on the one side, and the UN organisations and the foreign NGOs on the other.[77] In some cases the SRRA officer doubled up as a CMA: as SRRA officer he was responsible for assessing need and distributing relief food, while as CMA he was also collected taxes, often in kind (livestock and food) from the

---

[74] The reason for this failure was partly the lack of a clear plan for how this money was to be used. E.g. in addition to buying cars and providing fuel, the SEOC paid school fees for senior SRRA officials' children, funeral costs and family support. For three years an annual sum of £50,000 was paid "to support [the] general budget", Duffield et al., *SEOC Review*, p. 99; A similar account is given in African Rights, *Food and Power*, pp. 323–25.

[75] Karim et al., *OLS Review*, p. 81; Norwegian People's Aid Oslo's co-ordinator for the Sudan programme explains plainly the inadequacies of the SRRA both in Nairobi and in the field by 1988 in a confidential report from 7 November 1988, 'Report from Kapoeta Oct. 17th, 18th and Meetings with SRRA in Nairobi the Following Week', NA-04-7, Box 00207860. Another report from the Dutch NGO Interkerkelijke coördinatie commissie ontwikkelingsprojecten (ICCO) provides a detailed analysis of the interaction between the SRRA HQ, and the indigenous NGOs, in particular the NPA, attached to a letter from Sjoerd van Schooneveld, 8 May to NPA att. Arne Oerum [sic], (NPA Archive, 831-SUD-07). The report states that in 1990 there was general dissatisfaction with all levels of the SRRA organisation. However, it also gives voice to the SRRA personnel and explains their reluctance to allow strict monitoring as their wanting to be allowed to manage their own business: "several times SRRA staff referred to monitors as 'international policemen'", p. 3.

[76] African Rights, *Food and Power*, pp. 88–89.

[77] Duffield et al., *SEOC Review*, p. 99.

same population.[78] This practice of giving with one hand and taking with the other was often difficult for the aid organisations to accept.

Church Organisations

In the period before 1993, the only organisational structure at the local level worth mentioning – except for the chieftaincy structure and SPLM/A institutions – was provided by the churches. The number and size of local congregations varied considerably. Local churches traced their origin to the establishment of colonial rule in the Southern Sudan through the Anglo-Egyptian Condominium in 1899, which opened up the region to the establishment of permanent missions.[79] Various denominations were given separate zones for their missionary activities, and in the first decades were given sole responsibility for providing education in the South.[80] This was an important component in the colonial government's Southern policy, whereby through isolation Southerners were 'protected' from the Muslim Northerners.[81] This policy was abandoned after independence and the missionaries expelled in 1964, but Islam has not been able to rival Christianity in the South and the geographical division between different churches remains. This made it prudent to form an ecumenical co-ordination body, the Sudan Council of Churches. After the second civil war broke out the council, with its headquarters in Khartoum, was unable to communicate effectively with local churches in the South. This resulted in the establishment of the New Sudan Council of Churches (NSCC) on 8 February 1990,[82] with the Roman Catholic Bishop Paride Taban as its first leader.[83] It is reported – not only in spite of the war, but possibly because

---

[78] Karim et al., *OLS Review,* p. 83.

[79] Several attempts were made to establish Catholic missionary stations during the 19th century, but they did not survive the Mahdist revolution in the 1880s, and missionaries started more or less from scratch in 1899. Andrew Wheeler provides a brief overview of the history of missionaries in the Sudan in 'Gateway to the Heart of Africa: Sudan's Missionary Story', in F. Pierli et al., *Gateway to the Heart of Africa,* 1999. Marc R. Nikkel has thoroughly researched the history of missions and Christianity among the Dinka from the 19th Century up to 1993 in, *Dinka Christianity: The Origins and Development of Christianity among the Dinka of Sudan with Special Reference to the Songs of Dinka Christians,* 2001.

[80] Holt and Daly, *A History of the Sudan,* p. 108.

[81] See p. 24.

[82] African Rights, 'Great Expectations: The Civil Roles of the Churches in Southern Sudan', 1995, pp. 25–28. The NSCC issued the following statement in 1991: "The concern for all God's people in Sudan has united us. This is why we formed the New Sudan Council of Churches. The war has separated the church into different areas. But we feel united with our brothers and sisters in the North as we feel united with you. We have formed the NSCC to strengthen the churches to better serve the suffering people in the SPLA/M-held areas." 'New Sudan Council of Churches Press Release', in connection with second executive committee meeting, September 18, 1991, Nairobi, Kenya, p. 2.

[83] Edward Nordrum, *Biskop Paride Taban – Fredskjempe i Krig,* 2002, p. 26. The Catholic Church is cooperating very closely with the other churches through the ecumenical networks.

of it – that there has been a massive growth in the number of conversions to Christianity among Southerners since the outbreak of the second civil war.[84]

The immediate impetus for the establishment of NSCC came, however, from the SPLM/A. Before 1989 the SPLM/A had been accused of hostility towards the churches,[85] but this changed after the NIF coup and the beginning of OLS. Permission to establish NSCC was expected to benefit the Movement in several ways. First, as a sign of tolerance, NSCC could help to improve the SPLM/A's standing among the Western donor countries, and increase their willingness to grant aid to the Southern Sudan. Second, NSCC would be a convenient way of channelling this aid. Finally, as a way of bolstering resistance against the Islamic north, NSCC could strengthen the Christian identity of the South.[86] However, the SPLM/A needed to balance these benefits with its scepticism towards the churches; the Movement had seen church organisation, NSCC in particular, as a potential threat and competitor for the position as the legitimate spokesperson of the Southern people.[87]

There have indeed been instances of local priests contesting the supremacy of the SPLM/A. One example is the so-called "Exodus" of 1990, when Bishop Seme Solomona and Father Peter Dada organised a massive flight from Yei just before it was taken by the SPLM/A.[88] They then established a community in the border town of Kaya, which soon grew to 30,000 people. When the

---

[84] The anthology *Land of Promise: Church Growth in a Sudan at War* edited by Andrew Wheeler presents several case studies which focus on this growth. Wheeler provides an interesting summary of the research done on church growth in this period in the article, 'Introduction: Church Growth – But How Deep Are the Roots?', pp. 7–38. Different factors have been mentioned when this growth is analysed: i) forced Islamisation, which has a counterproductive effect; ii) that churches can provide education; and, iii) dissatisfaction with the old religions, Hutchinson, *Nuer Dilemmas,* pp. 312–15. Much research remains to be done on these phenomena. For instance, Wheeler appears reluctant to discuss the role of relief aid and the fact that many local churches have been used as counterparts in the delivery of aid. As will be mentioned later, it appears that some have used this type of aid to increase their congregations. Some claim that relief aid has had an effect as a symbol of power associated with the Christian god: "foreign humanitarian aid (particularly arriving by air) is a particularly dramatic intervention. Although the aid does not reach everybody, and is rarely a major factor in peoples' [sic] survival, it suggests the existence of a tremendous external power capable of helping people. The relief deliveries are taken to indicate benevolence, but the factors which determine their time, place and magnitude are inexplicable". African Rights, 'Great Expectations', p. 9.

[85] African Rights, 'Great Expectations', p. 7.

[86] *Ibid.,* p. 10.

[87] This animosity has continued even if there have been some improvements. E.g. in August 2001 the NSCC held a large meeting in the Kenyan town of Kisumu for Sudanese leaders both within the Southern Sudan as well as the Diaspora. This included educated Sudanese as well as chiefs. A dispute developed between the NSCC and SPLM/A, wherein the latter felt that the NSCC was assuming a position of leadership for the South. The SPLM/A claimed that they had not been properly consulted and that the meeting should be held within an SPLM/A controlled areas. Consequently, several chiefs in SPLM/A controlled areas were not given permission to travel to the conference.

[88] The story is relayed in Wheeler, *Land of Promise,* 'Introduction', pp. 30–31.

SPLM/A military setbacks threatened the security of Kaya, the two churchmen wanted to move to Uganda while the SPLM/A authorities preferred that they move to a different place inside the Sudan. On 3 August 1993 the church leaders led the 30,000 people to Koboko in Uganda, unhindered. When Yei and Kaya were recaptured in the 1997 offensive, Bishop Seme and Father Peter convinced the people to return to Yei. This appears to have been an exceptional case, and one may assume that local SPLM/A commander had the final word in most local disputes.[89]

Relief aid was a new factor with the potential of altering the balance between local church leaders and SPLM/A authorities. When the OLS administration and the International NGOs – in particular the religiously based ones – found the SRRA wanting as a counterpart, they turned to NSCC and the local churches. Relatively independent from the SPLM/A-SRRA structure and with a considerable local network, the churches appeared to foreign aid organisations as better suited to become local partners for relief and development work. The churches claimed "a historical commitment to peacemaking, to justice, to the relief of human suffering, and to speak out on behalf of the poor and forgotten,"[90] and their ability to provide social services such as education and health care had been established during the beginning of the Condominium period. To extend their scope to development aid and, in particular, to relief distribution was seen by the humanitarian organisations as a sensible expansion of the churches' activities. Given the large amounts of food and money involved in relief activities, this strategy could potentially have increased the significance of the local churches and NSCC considerably.

Attempts at using NSCC and local churches as aid institutions were not as successful as anticipated. These organisations, with the possible exception of NSCC,[91] were not originally meant for this kind of task, and they encountered conflicting expectations. As a review of these aid activities pointed out: "Local churches in South Sudan are primarily religious and pastoral institutions. They are not tightly structured relief mechanisms."[92] At the central level NSCC had a weak structure and unskilled personnel which created the same accountability problems as the SRRA had, albeit on a smaller scale. The NSCC also had the same problems as the SPLM/A and SRRA when it came to local

---

[89] The size of the congregation, the local SPLM/A commander's religious position, the place's degree of isolation, are some of the factors that might influence this relationship.

[90] African Rights, 'Great Expectations', p. 2. As will be discussed later, preservation of the church organisation and increasing the congregation might at times have been more important than this credo.

[91] The NSCC handling of relief aid caused friction among member churches and in 1994 a "special consultative committee of Church leaders was established to authorise allocations on a case-by-case basis", *ibid.*, p. 26.

[92] Duffield et al., *SEOC Review*, p. 92.

co-ordination. Worse, NSCC had no local offices, but relied on local churches to perform planned activities.[93]

The churches were expected to perform better than the SRRA mainly because of the church leaders' perceived higher moral standard. That expectation was not always fulfilled. In an assessment of the relief food donated through the Sudan Emergency Operations Consortium (SEOC), a description was given of a system by which aid was distributed so that local churches got 30 per cent of the food, and the SRRA the rest. But, instead of giving their share to famine victims, the churches distributed it to lepers and theological students, and as salary for clergy and church workers. In addition, the *SEOC Review* reports that "relief food has also been used by churches as means of increasing congregations."[94] These institutions were not meant to be relief NGOs. Pretending to be was to some extent incompatible with expectations of both the mother church and the local congregation.

Sudanese Indigenous NGOs and Other Newly Introduced Local Institutions

In early 1993 the SPLM/A allowed the establishment of the first Sudanese indigenous NGO (SINGO). Several more sprang up during the next years. These organisations – ideally an important component of a modern Southern Sudanese civil society – were also yet another attempt at creating local counterparts for foreign NGOs and international donors. None of the parties involved thought this necessarily a negative development. Just as the SPLM/A had encouraged NSCC, so the opening up for local NGOs was partly motivated by the prospect of attracting more development aid to SPLM/A controlled areas and improving the Movement's reputation in the Western world. SINGOs helped the SPLM/A to create alternative opportunities for dissatisfied SPLM/A officers and educated Southerners, who otherwise might have defected to one of the other factions. The activities of the SINGOs were almost entirely funded by foreign NGOs and international donors, thus making it possible for leaders of the SINGOs to secure salaries they could not have had from Southerners' membership fees. The foreign humanitarian organisations hoped that they had finally found local counterparts that could meet their exact needs. However,

---

[93] African Rights, 'Great Expectations', p. 27.

[94] Duffield et al., *SEOC Review*, p. 88. The review analyses shortcomings of the local churches from the Western donors' point of view. African Rights, 'Great Expectations', pp. 20–23, tries to analyse the meaning and impact of relief aid from the local churches' and local population's point of view. A typical conclusion was that the "Western technocratic conceptions of aid tend to overlook its social implications, and those who acquiesce to the demands of relatives and neighbours may be labelled as 'corrupt'. Foreigners prefer the imagery of a 'suffering Church' dispensing relief to the poor and outcast without any reciprocal benefits at all", p. 22.

there was but a few SINGOs that managed to initiate projects in the period before the National Convention, and their projects were rather small.

There were other types of local organisations established to facilitate the aid and development work, but which had little influence on political development locally.[95] Remnants from the local agricultural cooperative structure established, mainly by foreign NGOs, during the period of the Addis Ababa Agreement still existed in the early 1990s, in particular in Equatoria.[96] African Rights describes well-organised co-operative systems in Maridi and Yei,[97] which sent representatives to local CMAs demanding tax-cuts and price controls.[98] Owing to lack of sources it is difficult to evaluate the importance of these institutions.

What Happened to the Early Reforms?

The limited source material available on political development in the period 1991–94 provides no indication of results from the reforms announced after the two PMHC meetings. Johnson has a point when he says that the lack of data does not necessarily mean that nothing happened. Yet, the lack of evidence does not mean that there *were* results, let alone that there was radical change. After all, some investigations were conducted, which to some extent included the nature of the local administration before 1994 – the *SEOC Review*, the *OLS Review*, Johnson's and those of African Rights, as well as reports from foreign NGOs working on the ground. When they report no reforms and changes at the local level in the period 1991–93, it is reasonable to assume that the effects of the announced reforms were meagre.

This conclusion is supported by our analysis of the two sets of PMHC resolutions. The *Torit Resolutions* announced drastic reforms and establishment of a local administrative structure, which should indicate that this was not already there. Then, a year later, the *Bedden Falls Resolutions* demanded that civilians should replace all soldiers tied up in civil administration. Does this mean that there had been drastic changes during the year between the Torit

---

[95] The most important of these were Joint Relief Committees that were supposed to assist the SRRA, CMAs, local commanders and the foreign NGOs to co-ordinate relief activities. Local committees were also established in refugee camps and in some villages as a way of under-cutting the power of local chiefs to decide who was going to receive relief aid, African Rights, 'Imposing Development: Aid and Civil Institutions in Southern Sudan', 1995, pp. 25–30.

[96] *Ibid.,* pp. 30–32.

[97] African Rights reports that there were 56 co-operatives with 8611 members registered in Maridi County in May 1995, *ibid.,* p. 31.

[98] *Ibid.,* African Rights comments, "elected representatives [from the co-operatives] would appear to be accountable to their constituents in a definite way … It is still a very young system, but if it works, it could be the strongest model of a democratic institution in the South Sudan".

and Bedden Falls meetings? Or, had increased military pressure meant that resources must be drawn from wherever possible? It might even be that statements in the *Bedden Falls Resolutions* were meant to soothe hardliners within the military, who complained about wasting resources on civilian administration. The sources do not provide sufficient evidence to conclude one way or another, but since discussions at the National Convention and *NC Resolutions* repeat the same need for a local administration that was described in the *Torit Resolutions*, we may assume that in most places the new policy had not led to significant changes.

Rather, it was the foreign NGOs' need for local counterparts that led to the introduction of new institutions on the ground. The SRRA was strengthened; the churches were allowed to form NSCC; local churches were tested as relief distributors; the SPLM/A permitted the establishment of SINGOs and other local committees. In the period between the split in 1991 and the National Convention in 1994, it seems that the Movement was catering to the foreign NGOs instead of to the local population, and that the declarations of reforms were mainly meant to counter allegations from the Nasir faction.

The split had the effect of increasing pressure on the SPLM/A to apply liberal rhetoric, but, at the same time, through the military disruption caused by the split, decreasing its ability to implement the very reforms they announced. By early 1993 something had to be done. The announcement of the NC might have been a way to compensate for failure, and to win the support of the local population for one large effort. Moreover, the ability to convene a seemingly democratic meeting with representatives from the whole of the Southern Sudan, the Nuba Mountains and the Ingessana Hills, from the North and from the Southern Diaspora, would prove once and for all to the world that the SPLM/A was in a different league from the other factions. Its grip on the South had to be tightened as it became clearer that the war would drag on. The NC could serve many purposes simultaneously. Whether these insights were available in February 1993 is, of course, a different question altogether.

CHAPTER 4

What Was the National Convention?

The Sudan People's Liberation Movement/Army's National Convention (NC) was held in Chukudum Eastern Equatoria, on 2–13 April 1994. It was the first meeting of its kind in the Southern Sudan since before the war, and for the members of the Movement the Convention has become an important symbol of reform and liberalisation. The fact that hundreds of people were willing to travel for several weeks on foot on perilous roads illustrates the importance vested in the meeting.[1] The NC has mainly received positive treatment in scholarly writings. Peter Nyot Kok writes, "The National Convention (April/May 1994) was the first serious step towards democratic rule".[2] African Rights and Douglas Johnson both see the Convention as part of the Movement's liberalisation. African Rights describes the Convention as a symbol of alliance between the SPLM/A and OLS and the foreign NGOs: "[for] the advocates of a reformed, liberalised and institutionalised SPLA/SPLM ... this was a fine moment".[3] Johnson is mainly concerned with how the NC formalised the chiefs' position within the SPLM/A administrative structure:

> Entrenching the position of customary law was one of the reforms enacted at the SPLA's first national convention at Chukudum in April 1994. A new hierarchy of customary courts from village to county level was recognized, strengthening the role of the chiefs in matters of appeal.[4]

These interpretations are not mutually exclusive, but they endow the Convention with separate meanings.

Prunier presents yet another, more critical interpretation of the NC:

> Although it was trying to revamp the SPLA's image in the general public, both at home and nationally, the Chukudum [National] Convention had also been a display of old style command politics, complete with "pre-selected" delegates, Dinka ethnic over-representation, "prepared" motions and enthusiastic unanimous re-elections of the old

---

[1] Eight people died, three of them delegates to the NC, when a car bringing delegates from Pageri to Chukudum crashed, 'Introduction and Background', *Proceedings*, p. ii.

[2] 'Sudan: Between Radical Restructuring and Deconstruction of State Systems', *Review of African Politics and Economy*, No. 70, 1996, p. 560. Also Ann Mosley Lesch, *The Sudan*, gives a positive account of the NC, pp. 200–201.

[3] African Rights, *Food and Power,* p. 308.

[4] Johnson, The Sudan People's Liberation Army', p. 69.

surviving main SPLA Political Military High Command (PMHC) leaders to their "new" leadership positions.[5]

Prunier dismisses the Convention as a show for external consumption that did not represent any significant change. Our own research favours that view: the process of adopting resolutions (here referred to as the *NC Resolutions*), and the elections at the Convention were *pro forma*; the delegates only to a limited degree represented the people of the Southern Sudan. It would, however, be an over-simplification to say that the purpose of the NC was merely to impress "the general public", if only because together with the start of the rebellion in 1983 and the attempted coup in 1991, the SPLM/A – and Southerners in general – have come to regard the National Convention as one of the seminal moments in the Movement's history.

The importance vested in the National Convention after the fact, justifies close scrutiny of the event. However, the available sources do not yet allow the writing of the Convention's definite history. Our findings are based on incomplete documentation and are really an assessment of available information, which can be used as a point of departure for further investigation; the conclusions may be regarded as hypotheses which need to be tested against other types of sources.[6] Despite incomplete sources, it is evident that during the period between when the Convention was announced and when it was held, the NC was transformed and its scope grew considerably. Initially the SPLM/A leadership announced that they wanted a party congress, but ended up claiming that they had organised a national convention on behalf of the people of the "New Sudan". By closely examining the preparation process, the debates at the Convention and the *NC Resolutions*, we may better understand what the Convention was intended to be, how it was planned and how the plans were executed.

PREPARING FOR THE NATIONAL CONVENTION

For a study of the National Convention and its outcome, the question of how the Convention was prepared is almost as important as what actually took place at the NC itself. The shape and content of the NC were by no means predetermined when it was announced in February 1993. The SPLM/A had never before organised anything similar to the NC;[7] there was no precedent.

---

[5] He refers to several interviews with SPLM members as background for his analysis, Prunier, 'The SPLA Crisis', p. 33.

[6] Most importantly, extensive interviews with delegates and persons involved in the preparations for the NC and the execution of the arrangement itself.

[7] African Rights argues a link between the experiences from the Nuba Mountains in the early 1990s and the changes in the SPLM/A at a central level, but the meeting in the Nuba Mountains was altogether on a different scale, see pp. 66–67, 89–90.

Yet, when the delegates arrived at the NC, someone had invited them, had decided what they were going to discuss, and had formulated drafts of the proposals to be voted on. In the opening speech to the NC, John Garang stated:

> You have in front of you the documents of the COC [Convention Organization Committee]. These are proposals of the COC. This Convention is Sovereign. You can reject all these proposals and bring your own agenda, you can modify them, adding new items, while deleting others; it is completely up to you.[8]

However, the *Proceedings* show that the pre-determined framework for the National Convention was adhered to and that very few significant changes were made. Furthermore, although Garang gave the COC the credit for having prepared the Convention, one of its members maintains that the COC was only a technical committee that had no power to set the NC's agenda.[9] Investigations suggests that the COC played an important role, but that they did not act alone; that the planning process did not follow the pre-established plan; and that changes made as preparations progressed radically changed the final outcome.

The Planning Process for the National Convention (February 1993–April 1994)

On the basis of available material, what can be established about preparations for the National Convention and who participated in these? The only published fact concerning this issue has been that Yousif Kuwa was in charge.[10] We have seen that the probable date for announcement of the National Convention was 20 February 1993,[11] and that the content of the announcement may have been based on recommendations made by the "SPLM/A *Ad hoc* Committee on Political Work and Organization" established at the Bedden Falls PMHC conference.[12] The announcement stated that the Convention would be held no later than 16 May – the date of the SPLM/A's 10th anniversary; and that it would be organised by a "preparatory committee" headed by James Wani Igga. The National Convention was delayed, however, because, as

---

[8] *Proceedings*, p. 24.

[9] Interview with Martin Okerruk, 26 March 2002.

[10] Lesch writes that the NC "was organized by Nuba commander Kuwa", *The Sudan*, p. 201. Kuwa's name is spelt in many ways. The version used in this book is the same as in an extensive interview conducted by one of Kuwa's friends on his deathbed, Nanne op't Ende, *Interview with Yousif Kuwa Mekki*, London 12–13 February 2001, http://leden.tref.nl/-ende0098/ articles/interview NotE.htm.

[11] See pp. 59–61.

[12] *Bedden Falls Resolutions*, p. 7.

John Garang said in the opening speech, it had been subordinated to other pressing issues.[13]

The activities of James Wani and his committee are not documented, and nothing can be said for certain now regarding their preparations for the Convention. It might be assumed that James Wani's preparatory committee drafted the message dated 30 July 1993 from John Garang to all units of the SPLM/A where the COC was appointed and received its mandate (hereinafter referred to as the *Mandate*),[14] but there is no direct evidence to support or refute that assumption. This message provided loosely defined terms of reference, which laid a basis for the Committee's subsequent planning. The *Mandate* outlines topics to be discussed and gives general criteria for the composition of the delegations and overall size of the Convention.[15] Therefore terms for the preparations for the NC, and, ultimately, the outcome of the Convention itself, were to some extent determined before the COC was established. The important point here is that the thoroughness of the *Mandate* indicates that before the COC was established, someone in the SPLM/A leadership had given serious thought to how the National Convention would be organised and what it would achieve.

The Convention Organization Committee consisted of 35 senior SPLM/A cadres, all with military rank,[16] of which the most important members will be presented below. At the time of appointment, some members were stationed inside the Southern Sudan as well as in Nairobi and Europe. Commander Yousif Kuwa was assigned the task of heading the Committee. The COC had five sub-committees: the Steering Committee; the Secretariat; the Administration and Security Committee; the General Logistics Committee; and the Finance Committee.[17] The Steering Committee was the most important, as it was responsible for drafting the agenda and co-ordinating the work of the other committees.[18] The Finance Committee was given the task of raising funds. Most Steering Committee members were assigned to one of the other committees as well, thus ensuring control and communication between the Steering Committee and the other sub-committees. This elaborate planning structure demonstrates that the SPLM/A leadership at this stage of the process already wanted the National Convention to be well prepared and consequential.

---

[13] *Proceedings,* p. 10.

[14] Communication from The Chairman and C-in-C, SPLM/A to The Chief of Staff, SPLA to be communicated to all GFSCC members and All Units/Ref. No.: Convention/Date: 30/7/1993.

[15] *The Mandate,* pp. 4–6.

[16] The fact that all had military ranks is not particularly surprising considering the fact that, until 1991, military training was required for membership of the SPLM/A. Presumably, the COC members had all been members of the movement for more than two years.

[17] *The Mandate,* pp. 2–3.

[18] *Ibid.,* p. 3.

There are reasons, however, to believe that it was not foreseen that the Convention would be as momentous as it became. This fact does not support Prunier's hypothesis that the Convention was organised only to impress an external audience. While this hypothesis might correctly describe the SPLM/A leadership's original plans in February 1993, by July 1993 these had changed. The differences between the circumstances in February and those when the *Mandate* was issued, suggest a change in the intentions of the SPLM/A leadership. The former, a brief mention at the end of a press statement about the Abuja II peace talks, suggests that the Convention was indeed meant for public relations purposes and was not considered particularly important. The later announcement is different, in the sense that it was addressed to SPLM/A units, and that the message itself was dedicated to preparations for the upcoming National Convention. This is the first indication of a tendency towards continuous expansion of the scope and size of the Convention. Instead of choosing an easy, cheap, hastily and superficially planned gathering for the 10th anniversary, the leadership invested extra time and resources in the project.

After the COC was appointed, some members held five meetings in Nairobi during August in order to work out an agenda for the NC and to establish quotas for the delegations. These deliberations are recorded in five sets of minutes (henceforth referred to as the *Minutes*).[19] Some of the discussions taking place during these meetings were intense, but still often concerned with more trivial aspects of the topics under discussion. It has not been possible to identify minutes from later COC meetings in Nairobi, if there were any. The fifth of the COC's Nairobi meetings was held in order to inform the members about the establishment of two sub-committees which where going to work on different aspects of the agenda. These sub-committees consisted of seven members each, who were more or less the same people as those who had attended the COC meetings during the previous weeks. The Nairobi sessions culminated in a new message from John Garang, sent to the whole of the SPLM/A on 30 August, where the composition of the delegations and an agenda for the NC were announced. There are significant differences, which will be discussed

---

[19] The minutes consulted may not be the complete series, but in the present author's opinion they suffice to establish a picture of the COC's activities. The *Minutes* relate to five meetings in August 1993 which preceded the 30 August message from John Garang in which he presented the results of the COC's work. For the preparations during the period after 30 August, the documentation is scarcer. The most significant sources are two sets of minutes from COC meetings in Nimule; articles in the *SPLM/SPLA Up-date*; one request for funding from the foreign NGOs sent by the COC's financial committee; and, the *Agenda* document prepared by the COC in Nimule. This documentation, however incomplete, provides an insight into the preparation process and gives access to some of the debates within the COC concerning the shape of the NC.

below, between the conclusion reached in the COC meetings and the message sent out by John Garang.

The source material reveals a hiatus between late August and October 1993, when the COC re-emerges in Nimule in Eastern Equatoria. Here the COC gathered for another series of meetings during October and November, where a new political agenda for the NC was hammered out. The results from these meetings were presented in a fifty-page long *Agenda for the First SPLM/SPLA National Convention and Recommendations of the Convention Organizing Committee (COC)* (later referred to as the *Agenda*). The *Agenda* can be read as minutes from the COC meetings. Sections of the document are introduced with almost identical wording, saying e.g., "This is a summary of proposal arrived at by the COC Members in their sessions of 12–13 October in the COC HQS."[20] In this way the *Agenda* refers to several COC meeting sessions in Nimule in the period 9–21 October and one on 11 November.[21]

The *Agenda* only provides the results from the discussions, but one might expect that the debates were as intense as those revealed in the minutes from the Committee's Nairobi meetings and the NC's *Proceedings*.[22] Since important policy questions were worked on, it is unfortunate that the *Agenda* does not provide a list of those who attended these meetings. Were there more people present at these meetings than in Nairobi, or did a small number of COC members continue to make decisions on behalf of the whole Committee? One indication might be the attendance list for the November meetings where seven people attended the first meeting and ten persons attended the second.[23] However, these two meetings were concerned with minor technical issues, in which fewer members might have been interested. And since the Nairobi *Minutes* give the impression that the entire COC was supposed to convene after the members in Nairobi had arrived in Nimule,[24] it is probable that most Committee members were present at the meetings that drafted the *Agenda*. It has proved difficult to reconstruct the COC's activities between December 1993 and April 1994 when apparently 23 specialised *ad hoc* committees were re-

---

[20] The *Agenda*, p. 3.

[21] *Ibid.*, pp. 1, 3, 11, 13, 17, 21.

[22] On page 5, three alternatives for the size of the SPLM/A National Liberation Council are presented which might reflect either the COC's inability to reach consensus or that they wanted feedback from the rest of the SPLM/A. The latter alternative is less probable since this is the only instance of alternatives in all the fifty pages of the *Agenda*.

[23] The meetings took place on 2 and 18 November. The minutes from these meetings are very brief.

[24] In the discussion on whether the COC meetings in Nairobi had a quorum, Yousif Kuwa is credited with the following opinion: "the majority of the members are in the liberated areas and this meeting should determine when the members should move to the liberated areas where *the necessary quorum can be got*" (emphasis added), pp. 2–3. This indicates that it was expected that the meetings inside "the liberated areas" would include more participants.

viewing different parts of the *Agenda*.[25] The *Agenda* (with the alterations suggested by the *ad hoc* committees was the point of departure for the discussions of the resolutions at the NC.[26] Except for the deliberations in these committees and the practical preparations that took place immediately prior to the Convention, there were apparently few other planning activities after December 1993.

In his message of 30 August, John Garang announced that the National Convention would be held during the two first weeks of October. This proved impossible, and the Convention was postponed once more. There might have been several reasons for this delay. First, by the beginning of October the COC had by no means finished its preparations, and the schedule for them may have been adjusted when other factors made the original date unfeasible anyway. Second, the delay could have been necessitated by logistical problems since a majority of the delegates had to travel on foot, and those coming from places as far away as the Nuba Mountains spent up to three months on the road. Obviously, the one month between the announcement in August and the planned start of the Convention was not enough time for all of the delegates to be selected, to consult with their constituents, and to travel to southern Equatoria. The issue of travelling time had been discussed in the COC before the announcement, but it seems that the Committee had unrealistic estimates about the speed of travelling.[27]

The reason that the SPLM/A leadership were in such a hurry to organise the National Convention was that Khartoum's dry season offensive was expected to start in October.[28] By then, most members of the Movement would be preoccupied, and would have no time for attending meetings. By mid-September, it must have become evident that it would not be possible to hold the NC in early October, and that the Convention had to be delayed once more, lest it be hindered by dry season military activities. This was probably

---

[25] The *ad hoc* committees are first mentioned in the *Minutes* (4) where Malok reports that Garang had agreed that "SPLM members... who are well versed or knowledgeable in certain technical fields" be included in "specialised sub-committees to prepare leading papers on the main issues on the agenda for the convention", p. 1. The resolutions from the PMHC meetings mention *ad hoc* committees, but it is unclear whether some of these were included in the new *ad hoc* committees. The *Proceedings* mention the *ad hoc* committees, which presented a report named "Ad-Hoc Committees' View Points on the suggested agenda of Convention Organizing Committee (COC) for the 1st. National Convention, 1994", p. 81. This title suggests that these *ad hoc* committees performed some kind of revision of the *Agenda* drafted by the COC. This assumption is supported by the subsequent comments in the *Proceedings*, which directly relate to the *Agenda*, pp. 81–92. The *Mandate* mentions that the agenda should include "reports from the Ad Hoc Committees and other Specialised Committees" and John Garang's message on 30 August explicitly mentions 23 *ad hoc* committees, p. 4.

[26] The *Proceedings*, p. 81.

[27] COC members believed that one month would suffice, (1), pp. 8–9. But some of the delegates spent more than a hundred days on the road, Johnson, *The Root Causes*, p. 92 (note 2).

[28] Statement by Elijah Malok, *Minutes* (1), p. 9.

the reason it was delayed for six months, until April 1994. By then, the rainy season would have started, fighting would be less intense, and the venue would be less vulnerable to attacks from government forces.

In any case, even if almost one and a half years elapsed between the first announcement of the National Convention and the actual opening of the Convention, it was during the period July–November 1993 that the political content and general framework for the NC was developed. Delays in preparations were not used to perfect the concept of the NC or to broaden the scope of the process. What might initially have been intended as a brief show to improve the SPLM/A's standing developed into something close to a genuine debate about the future of the Movement and its relations to the people of the Southern Sudan. A statement by one of the most outspoken members of the SPLM/A leadership, Mario Muor, during one of the COC meetings in Nairobi, emphasised the importance of allocating sufficient time for preparations: "the convention is a two-edged sword because it may improve or it may destroy the Movement." He insisted that the convention must have consequences for the Movement, and not merely be "a political platform for public consumption." Therefore, "the convention should not be done in a hurry and should be given time to allow preparations to take place."[29]

The Role of the Convention Organization Committee

As an *ad hoc* institution within the SPLM/A the Convention Organization Committee was unprecedented in terms of size as well as scope. However, the real test of its importance is the extent to which the Committee was allowed to fulfil its mandate – whether the COC was allowed to reach independent decisions that were not subsequently altered. The available documentation leaves much to be desired for investigating these issues, but it is still possible to discuss some aspects of the Committee's activities and to reach preliminary conclusions. The Nairobi meetings were mainly concerned with practical issues and the organisational framework for the Convention, while the meetings at Nimule focused on political issues. It is therefore sensible to differentiate between the COC meetings in Nairobi and those within the Southern Sudan, for which there is less source material than for the Nairobi deliberations. These differences suggest that conclusions about the Nairobi meetings will not necessarily be valid for those in Nimule. Here, our main concern will be with the Nairobi meetings, while the results of the meetings inside the Southern Sudan are discussed later.

---

[29] The *Minutes* (1), pp. 9–10.

The Members of the COC

Several senior members of the SPLM/A were appointed to the COC steering committee, and it is reasonable to assume that many of them were members of the General Field Staff Command Council (GFSCC).[30] The criteria for membership of the Committee are not mentioned. The heavy representation of top leaders and the explicit and official mandate implied that the decisions made by the COC would have a certain authority. It is interesting to investigate the degree to which individual members contributed to the discussions, and to estimate members' relative influence during the meetings. According to the *Minutes*, only a fraction of the Committee's official members attended the Nairobi meetings, and even fewer contributed significantly to the discussions. The active members were almost identical to the first six persons listed in the announcement of the COC. This list was arranged by rank, which suggests that seniority was a factor and that junior members might have thought – or been told – that it would be inappropriate for them to participate.

What can be concluded from the contributions made by the COC members who actively participated in the discussions? In several publications from African Rights, the Chairman of the COC, Yousif Kuwa, is portrayed as a bold and far-sighted leader who had managed to initiate important political reforms in the Nuba Mountains.[31] African Rights argues that "[t]he SPLA's democratisation actually began in the Nuba Mountains."[32] However, the African Rights account does not explain in which way these reforms triggered political change within the rest of the SPLM/A.[33] A more compelling clue to the alleged influence of Kuwa and the experience of the Nuba Mountains is the following comment in the *Proceedings*: "In the process of convention preparation, Cdr Yusif accepted to disagree with his staff but refused to be disobeyed. It was that quality of allowing free views to be expressed but knowing when to channel them into required resolutions, that made the Convention to succeed."[34] Kuwa is described as both an innovator and a liberal leader.[35] The

---

[30] The GFSCC was an intermediate solution replacing the PMHC in the period between the announcement of the upcoming National Convention on 20 February and the actual NC, see note 81.

[31] E.g. African Rights, *Food and Power*, pp. 312–13 and *Facing Genocide,* pp. 314–29.

[32] African Rights, *Food and Power*, pp. 312–13.

[33] Quite the contrary, African Rights say that this was "unknown even to many in the SPLA high command". Not even in Kuwa's opening speech at the NC were the previous experiences mentioned, nor in the more informal COC meetings. It is therefore difficult to establish how and to what degree the Nuba Mountain experiences were important for the decision to hold a NC, and for the political reforms initiated at the Convention. African Rights, *Food and Power*, pp. 312–14.

[34] The *Proceedings*, 'Introduction and Background', p. x.

[35] In one obituary he is even mentioned as the person who "[ushered] the Movement [The SPLM/A] into the Era of Democratization", *Commander Yousif Kuwa Makkie – The Man,*

Minutes confirm that there was considerable debate during the meetings and that Kuwa contributed to the discussions. But his comments focused on formalities and the agenda, seldom on more substantial matters. It also appears that he even tried to avoid discussing difficult aspects of the agenda for the Convention: no one questioned why certain items should be included or excluded, and what exactly they were supposed to entail. When the composition of the delegations was brought up, Kuwa also said nothing about the process of selecting representatives or about the ratio of civilians to members of the Movement.

Perhaps most importantly, the question of exactly what the National Convention would be and what it was supposed to achieve, was not discussed. In fact, it seems that Kuwa tried to avoid these questions. When Michael Nyang almost sparked off a general debate by suggesting that the COC should "address ourselves to how the convention can solve some of our present problems in the Movement"[36] Kuwa interrupted that this was exactly the purpose of the Committee's activities.[37] Considering all the tedious discussions of detail revealed in the *Minutes*, it is difficult to agree with the COC Chairman on this point. Nyang's suggestion was either too provocative or too uninteresting. Instead, harmless questions about the venue, when the COC should move to the Southern Sudan, who could be considered "elder statesmen", etc., produced lengthy discussions.[38] It is possible that the more general issues had been postponed until the October meetings at Nimule, and that this was the reason the Nairobi meetings did not address them. Yet, if the Convention was regarded as important, preparing the list of delegates and the agenda were important topics that should have prompted discussion. An interesting aspect of the Nairobi meetings is therefore why certain issues were avoided. Documents from the Committee meetings may not do justice to Kuwa's efforts,[39] but on the basis of the available material, it appears that his contribution has been overrated.

In the *Minutes*, Elijah Malok, the COC's secretary, on the other hand, appeared to be in charge even when Kuwa was present. Malok definitely contributed most to the discussions, and he also participated in most of the COC's consultations with John Garang.[40] In the fourth meeting in Nairobi, Kuwa

---

http://www.mathaba.net/africa2020//sudan/kuwa.htm, p. 1.

[36] *Minutes* (3), p. 9.

[37] *Ibid.* (3), p. 9.

[38] *Ibid.* (2), pp. 12–13.

[39] Joseph Garang, the COC secretary, wrote the *Minutes*. It has not been established whether they were subject to approval from Kuwa.

[40] A committee consulted Garang on the number of Independent Area Commands, and on the number of districts within SPLM/A controlled areas, *Minutes* (4), p. 1. Malok communicated Garang's approval of the COC's proposed agenda and list of delegations, *ibid.* (2), pp. 2–4.

stated that Elijah Malok had taken over the COC's chairmanship, and this is confirmed in the minutes from the fifth meeting, wherein Malok asked Pagan Amum to step in as chairman when he himself was absent.[41] In Kuwa's absence, Malok's tendency to dominate was even more pronounced.[42] In the COC meetings, Malok gives the impression of being a pragmatist not overly concerned with popular representation at every stage of the decision-making process. For instance, in the discussion on whether the 1983 Manifesto should be re-printed in the *SPLM/SPLA Up-date* so that members could prepare suggestions for revision of the Manifesto at the NC, he argued that revision was going to be undertaken by a special committee.[43] Heading the NC secretariat and participating in all the important meetings during the Convention, he continued to play a dominant role throughout. Malok is mentioned by Prunier as one of Garang's closest associates,[44] and his proximity to the chairman was proved several times during the preparations. It appears, however, that he was not acting as Garang's mouthpiece, and that the opinions he presented were mainly his own.[45]

Mario Muor, Secretary General of the Sudan Relief and Rehabilitation Association (SRRA), was the second most active person in the planning meetings. Even when he voiced strong opinions, he did not appear to be in direct opposition to the SPLM/A leadership. Differing from Elijah Malok, Muor argued for broad representation of the civil population at the Convention. Mario Muor was indeed the Committee member who displayed the strongest interest in defining the delegation categories and finding a fair system of distributing the delegates. He was the first to suggest a method for allocating delegates to the military units and to the districts, laying the basis for further discussion. Muor himself was apparently not present at the Convention, for he is not listed among the delegates.[46]

---

[41] *Minutes* (5), p. 3.

[42] It is unclear whether the chairmanship in question was of the whole COC, or if Malok was given responsibility for the preparation work in Nairobi, as Kuwa moved into the Southern Sudan to lead preparations there (*Minutes* (4), p. 2; cf. *ibid.* (5), p. 3). The latter is probable, since it is likely that Kuwa wanted to be inside the Southern Sudan where preparation of the Convention's political content was to take place. This interpretation, that Kuwa continued his leadership, is supported by the *Proceedings* where Kuwa is still referred to as leader of the COC, which would probably not have been the case if he had quit almost a year earlier.

[43] *Minutes* (3), p. 8. In the same discussion he stated that the people needed guidance in their deliberations at the NC, lest they run out of time, *ibid.*, p. 10.

[44] Prunier, 'The SPLA Crisis', p. 8, mentions other COC members among Garang's closest advisors: Deng Alor, Nhial Deng and Kuol Manyang.

[45] Malok is generally known to be very loyal to Garang, but he is also regarded as strong-willed and a man of integrity. This characteristic was confirmed by the impression he gave during our interview in Rumbek, 1 March 2002.

[46] He is only mentioned once in the *Proceedings* from the NC, and then in the list of elected NLC members.

Other members of the COC who contributed frequently to the discussions were Deng Alor, Niahl Deng, Lawrence Lual, Pagan Amum, and to a lesser extent, the deputy chairman, Kuol Manyang.[47] Their comments do not reveal any particular predisposition. The Committee members were not alone in participating in preparations for the Convention. Ambrose Riiny Thiik was neither a member of the COC nor officially a senior leader of the SPLM/A,[48] but his opinions had considerable impact on the legal aspects of the reforms decided on by the NC, and he was head of the Convention's Election Commission. The elite nature of the SPLM/A leadership and the lack of communication facilities seem to have excluded most ordinary members, as well as the people of the Southern Sudan at large, from contributing to the planning of the NC.

As for John Garang, it was he was who decided that the NC would be held, and he established the COC. On the basis of the available source material, it is difficult to measure his influence on the planning process itself: it seems that he had the power to make major alterations to suggestions from the Committee. The available source material also does not reveal to what extent senior leaders outside the COC were involved in the planning process, and whether they influenced it. The possibility of James Wani Igga's contributing at the first stage of the planning has already been mentioned. Second in command Salva Kiir was active during the debates at the NC, but there is no trace of his participation in planning the Convention.

The Role of the Nairobi Meetings

What was the status of the Convention Organization Committee's meetings in Nairobi? How did the Committee interact with the SPLM/A leadership? These questions can be tentatively answered by examining the Committee's mandate, the *Minutes*, and how the SPLM/A leadership responded to its recommendations. Even if the *Mandate* allowed the COC some leeway, the document outlines the framework for the National Convention in rather specific terms. To what extent the COC was allowed to alter the *Mandate* is uncertain, and the minutes from the first Nairobi meeting reveal confusion. The first issue discussed at length was whether the fourteen members present represented a quorum, since the Committee consisted of thirty-five members in total. Malok explained that most of the twenty-one absent members were "deep inside the

---

[47] With the exception of Lawerence Lual, these men are still among the most influential within the SPLM/A.

[48] He came to the SPLM/A during the early 1990s. Before that he had been a judge and politician in GOS controlled areas, 'Ambrose Riiny Thiik: A Born Rebel', *Horn of Africa Vision* (4) Vol. 2, 1999, p. 26.

liberated areas", and therefore could not be present.[49] Different ways of defining the group were discussed, but in the end they decided, "this meeting should be considered as the COC meeting and not the steering committee meeting although the fourteen members present do not constitute the required quorum."[50] This decision prompts several questions. What exactly were the quorum requirements? As long as the Committee had quorum requirements, how was it possible for a minority of its members to ignore them and make decisions on behalf of the majority? Why did fewer than half the members attend? Was the Committee's work purely informal – so it did not matter what they decided upon? Or were those present the members with real power, while the others were only nominal representatives who were not supposed to contribute?

First, it appears that COC members regarded the meetings in Nairobi as less important than those that would take place inside the Southern Sudan, and therefore a quorum was not required. But through their drafting of the National Convention's agenda and defining the delegations, the Nairobi meetings did indeed have significant influence on the NC's design. Second, since it is hard to establish how many people attended the later meetings, it may be that this no-quorum practice continued. However, the quorum debate reveals that the Committee did not have a clear idea of the status of the meetings themselves nor of their decisions.

The SPLM/A's lack of efficient structures for decision-making and policy implementation meant that it could not be taken for granted that conclusions of the COC's meetings would be acted upon. Some members even feared that discussions during Committee meetings would be censored. During the discussion on the size of delegations, Acuil Malith, in his sole recorded contribution, complained that Elijah Malok "would only give a summary of the points discussed and not to [sic] endorse the proposal as proposed by Cdr Mario Muor."[51] Malok assured Malith that Muor's suggestion would be adopted since a majority agreed upon this.[52] As we shall see, the COC was in constant consultation with the SPLM/A chairman, and, consequently, changes were made to the Committee's conclusions that significantly changed the NC's design. This indicates that even if the COC meetings in Nairobi had an impact on the forming of the NC, the Committee was in reality not authorised to make independent decisions.

---

[49] *Minutes* (1), p. 3.

[50] *Ibid.* (1), p. 4.

[51] *Ibid.* (2), p. 7.

[52] There are, however, no records in the minutes of any voting, so majority support for Muor's position appears to have been Malok's assumption.

Drafting an Agenda

The COC began discussing the agenda for the NC at its third meeting in Nairobi. The *Mandate* required that the following topics be included:

– Report of the Chairman and Commander-in-Chief, SPLM/SPLA, covering the ten years of the existence of the Movement.
– Position papers, debate and resolutions on Main [sic.] themes of the Convention, including reports from the Ad Hoc Committees and other Specialised Committees.
– The SPLM [1983] Manifesto: Debate, Amendments and Passage.
– Any Other Business as shall be determined at the passage of the Draft Agenda for the Convention.[53]

The COC was allowed to suggest new topics. Elijah Malok maintained that the topics directed by John Garang should suffice, which indicates his limited ambitions for the NC as an assembly; the only addition he proposed was the establishment of a group to revise the laws of the Movement.[54] Mario Muor disagreed, and proposed four new items for the agenda, the two most controversial being the drafting of a constitution for the SPLM/A and the restructuring of the army and civilian institutions.[55]

Apparently, his proposals were well received. However, instead of discussing why the Movement needed a constitution the Committee debated whether a draft constitution should be prepared before the National Convention, or if only the *concept* of a constitution should be discussed. In Muor's opinion the latter would be sufficient, and the others finally agreed.[56] The *Proceedings* from the NC, however, do not mention any discussion of the concept of a constitution, recording instead the establishment of a Constitutional and Legal Affairs Committee, which was given the task of looking into the concept of a constitution. Exactly why the concept of a constitution was not discussed during the NC is uncertain, but it might be related to the ambiguous status of the Convention itself – as a convention for the SPLM/A or for the people of the Southern Sudan – and the unclear division between the SPLM/A and the re-defined "New Sudan".

At its third meeting the Committee agreed on the following agenda (additions to the above are marked with italics):

– Report of Chairman and Commander-in-Chief, SPLM/SPLA.
– Reports of Ad hoc, other Specialised Committees and *Directorates*.

---

[53] *Mandate*, p. 5.
[54] *Minutes* (3), pp. 6–7.
[55] *Ibid.* (3), p. 7. The two other topics were reconciliation and peace initiatives with Khartoum.
[56] *Ibid.* (3), p. 11.

- *Review of the SPLM/SPLA Manifesto.*
- *Discuss the concept of SPLM/A constitution.*
- *Restructuring of political, civil and military institutions.*
- *Discussion of SPLM/SPLA foreign policy.*
- *SPLM/SPLA strategy for the peaceful resolution of conflicts in the Sudan.*
- *Unity and reconciliation within the SPLM/SPLA.*
- *Review of the Penal and Disciplinary Laws of SPLM/SPLA.*
- *General strategy and conduct of war.*
- *SPLM/SPLA Policy on Relief.*
- *Revenue generation.*
- *Human Rights and Social Justice.*

Then at the fourth meeting, on 24 August, Elijah Malok informed members that John Garang had "endorsed the [COC's] recommendations and the agenda for the convention."[57] This was confirmed when the agenda was officially announced on 30 August, indicating that during the Nairobi meetings, the members of the COC had had the opportunity to suggest significant additions to the agenda. Nevertheless, the agenda that was officially announced on 30 August was substantially different from the Committee's suggested agenda in the sense that several items had been added, as can be seen below (additions and alterations to the above are marked with italics):

- Report of Chairman and Commander-in-Chief, SPLM/SPLA.
- Reports of the *23* Ad hoc, other Specialised Committees and Directorates.
- Review of the SPLM/SPLA Manifesto.
- Discuss the concept of SPLM/A constitution.
- *Democratization* and Restructuring of political, civil and military institutions.
- SPLM/SPLA strategy for the peaceful resolution of conflicts in the Sudan, *and Review of other conflict situations in Africa.*[58]
- *Consolidation of Unity and Reconciliation within the SPLM/SPLA and the population in the liberated areas.*
- *Code of Conduct, Public Accountability and Elimination of Corruption and Misuse of Power.*
- General strategy and conduct of war *and establishment of security in the liberated areas.*
- *Popular participation and Mobilization of population in the both [sic] liberated areas and in NIF Government occupied towns to support and participate in the liberation struggle.*

---

[57] *Minutes,* (4), p. 1.

[58] The last part of the sentence appears to be inserted as a substitute for the "Discussion of SPLM/SPLA foreign policy" theme in the previous agenda.

- *Mobilization of Sudanese living [sic] abroad to fully support and participate in the liberation struggle and to contribute materially, intellectually and organizationally to the Movement and to the formation of the New Sudan.*
- *Review of SPLM/SPLA membership in the National Democratic Alliance (NDA), and the role of the NDA in the liberation struggle and in the formation of the New Sudan.*
- *Revenue generation for prosecution of the war and struggle for just and peaceful resolution of the war.*
- SPLM/SPLA Policy on Relief, *rehabilitation, social services and development in war conditions.*
- *SPLM/SPLA post war economic policy.*
- Human Rights and Social Justice.
- *Women participation in the liberation struggle.*
- *Any other items that may be proposed by the delegates during discussion and adoption of the agenda.*[59]

While the COC's proposed thirteen items for the agenda, the new one had eighteen. Although it suggested additional items, the COC's agenda focused on the SPLM/A as an organisation. The six new items, however, changed the whole concept of the Convention and broadened the scope considerably. The manner in which the agenda for the National Convention was developed illustrates how the COC could influence the planning process, but was not able to monopolise it.

A closer look at the agenda signed by John Garang on 30 August reveals that, unlike the Convention Organization Committee's version, it appeared more suitable for a convention for the people as a whole than the Movement. New topics were included: fighting corruption and misuse of power, security in SPLM/A controlled areas and popular participation and mobilisation of people in the whole of Sudan as well as abroad. Rehabilitation, provision of social services and development were added to the relief agenda, as was the participation of women in the "liberation". Perhaps the most symbolic of these changes was the expansion of item number seven: in the COC's version it was only "unity and reconciliation within the SPLM/SPLA" that was to be discussed, while in the new agenda this became "Consolidation of unity and reconciliation within the SPLM/SPLA and the population in the liberated areas."[60] The word "democratization" was also added.

---

[59] This item resembles to the last on the original agenda proposed in the *Mandate*, but now it is the delegates that can bring up new items, instead of the undefined organ that was going to pass the draft agenda.

[60] Whether economic constraints were significant when deciding the size of the NC cannot be established from the available sources. Even the cost of the NC is difficult to estimate. The finance sub-committee presented a budget of US$ 600,000 to potential donors. It is probable that the real cost was less than that. NPA's Resident Representative, Helge Rohn, commented that "the budget is at times quite unrealistic, but the total costs will still be considerable" (present

It is therefore clear that the scope of the NC was substantially altered in the period between the writing of the two documents,[61] and that the decision to change the National Convention from a party meeting to an organisational meeting for the "New Sudan", can be traced to late August. What had happened between the last Nairobi Committee meeting and the official announcement? The COC itself may have amended its own proposal, but it is more likely that someone in the SPLM/A leadership was responsible for the alterations. As long as the COC had been given the task of preparing the Convention, there is no straightforward answer to why these changes were made, and we can only conclude that important decisions regarding the NC were made outside formal COC meetings in Nairobi, which in turn indicates both the limited importance of these meetings and the extent of informal decision-making within the SPLM/A. Thus, the drafting of the agenda for the National Convention illustrates both that Convention Organization Committee members influenced the planning process, and that important decisions were also made outside the Committee.

Delegate Selection

Resolution 1 of the National Convention begins, "We, the people of the New Sudan, represented by this convention ... ."[62] Did the Convention have the right to make this claim? Arguably, a minimal criterion for representing a people – at least in the manner assumed in the *NC Resolutions* – would be election or appointment by constituencies, proportionally derived. Thus how delegations were composed and delegates selected[63] is essential to the discussion of the *NC Resolutions'* legitimacy, and of that of the Movement's leadership.

---

author's translation), fax Helge Rohn to NPA Oslo, 'SPLA/SPLM National Convention', 13.9.93, 30-SUD-01, NPA Archive Oslo, p. 1. The NC received support from numerous foreign NGOs: Oxfam UK, Oxfam America, and USAID. NPA contributed as well, *ibid.* Some embassies (the American and French in particular) contributed. The SPLM/A leadership also contributed $ 10,000, *Minutes* (4), p. 2.

[61] The limited scope of the plans for the NC prior to the 30 August announcement is reflected in one of Elijah Malok's statements at the beginning of the first COC meeting, "we [the COC members in Nairobi] should be in Nimule as from 25 August 1993 to enable the movement to hold the convention in early September", *Minutes* (1), p. 7. Given this tight deadline he suggested, the convention Malok had in mind could only have required a minimum of preparation and the time proposed would have been insufficient for people from most parts of SPLM/A controlled areas, suggesting that Malok thought the Convention could do without participation from the all of the SPLM/A controlled areas.

[62] *Proceedings*, p. 180. In his speech at the end of the Convention Garang concluded that delegates represented the people of the Southern Sudan: "The National Convention as you have seen here comes from a broad base from all the five regions and in each region everyone is represented. We can say that this Convention represents the will of the people of the five regions", *ibid.*, p. 201.

[63] In order to reflect the lack of information regarding this process, 'selection' is applied as a neutral term to describe the processes of deciding who would be delegates for the NC.

The lack of organisational structures defined in an orderly manner within the SPLM/A, combined with limited information about the civil population in SPLM/A controlled areas, proved to be a major obstacle for the COC's planning. Documentation of procedures for selecting the delegates to the NC is inadequate as a basis for drawing definite conclusions regarding their popular mandate. Our investigation provides additional insights into the decision-making culture of the SPLM/A and its suspicion of representative democracy at that time.

Defining the Delegations

Three different lists of delegations appeared during the period August 1993 – April 1994. One was drawn up by the COC during its Nairobi meetings, another was transmitted by short-wave radio by John Garang on 30 August, and a third list, of those who attended the National Convention, was included in the proceedings. When compared, these lists reveal important differences. In order to explain this, one might suppose power struggles and strong wills pitted against each other over the size and composition of delegations from different segments of Southern Sudanese society – inside the Sudan as well as in the Diaspora. The available sources do not support such an explanation. Rather, the delegations for the Convention seem less to reflect a power struggle than a hasty and ill-considered process.

The *Mandate* was the point of departure for the process of distributing delegates to geographical areas and groups within the SPLM/A. The *Mandate* specified the number of delegates (between 300 and 600), and groups from which the delegates were to be drawn: various parts of the SPLM/A organisation, with the exception of representatives of the affiliated associations (youth, women, teachers, church groups, etc.) and of the civilian population from counties and refugee camps. It is interesting that the latter groups were included at this early stage, while other aspects of the preparations, such as the drafting of the *Agenda*, gave the impression of the National Convention as a party congress. The fact that the "Movement" part of the SPLM/A was close to non-existent at the local level is the probable reason for early inclusion of the civilian population in the delegations. There were no local SPLM structures inside the controlled areas that could be asked to elect civilian representatives to a party congress. Without representatives of the local population the only "ordinary" Southern Sudanese at the Convention would have been lower ranks of the army.

The manner in which the Convention Organization Committee approached the issue of representation is illustrated by the lack of discussion of the nature and size of constituencies from among the local population. The Committee presented tidy categories of delegates despite the fact the COC's access to demographical data must have been rather limited and that even armed units within the SPLM/A lacked consistent structures. The COC even ran into difficulties when attempting to identify representatives from the army: the Committee was not even sure how many Independent Area Commands (IACs) there were, and they had to consult John Garang in order to establish the correct number. That senior leaders of the SPLM/A who were members of the COC were unable to account for the basic structure of the rebel army indicates the state of the Movement's structures and general organisation at the time. This may be the main reason that the size of delegations could not be specified further or differentiated.

The lack of information was even more acute when it came to defining the civilian delegations. The Committee ended by proposing a total of 571 delegates, which was safely below the limit of 600 set in the *Mandate*. Mario Muor presented a distribution key for delegations suggesting a total of 250 county representatives. Concerning the size of delegations, the COC was unwilling to differentiate between constituencies, with the exception of Aweil which got a double quota based on an assumption of a large population. The chiefs, women, peasants and "intellectuals" each got two representatives from the 29 districts.[64] The main reason for this solution was that the COC lacked both the resources for, and an interest in, obtaining the demographical data necessary to tailor the size of delegations to the size of the population.

Uneven representation was exacerbated by the fact that the civilian population from areas of the Southern Sudan outside the reach of the SPLM/A were given the same quotas as the areas it controlled. The infighting since the split in 1991 had created strong animosity towards the SPLM/A in the areas controlled by the Nasir faction, and as long as forces hostile to the Movement occupied these areas, little could be done to change civilians' attitude. Apparently the quotas were deliberately impracticable. Even during the third COC meeting in August, Mario Muor asked how these quotas could be filled.[65] Yousif Kuwa answered that the population in these areas would "be represented by their elder statesmen or officers from those districts that are either members of SPLM/SPLA or sympathisers."[66] The final outcome was that these localities were represented mainly by SPLM/A fighters originally from Nasir faction areas. The significant number of Southern Sudanese living in refugee camps and in exile was a complicating factor, and these groups were given special quotas. The closest the COC came to discussing fundamental aspects of representation at the NC was when Pagan Amum asked the Committee to pay atten-

---

[64] *Minutes* (2), p. 8. Whereas the discussion over who were eligible for the 20 seats as "Sudanese Elderly Statesmen" was long and detailed, definitions of the four categories of ordinary civilians were not debated at all.

[65] *Minutes* (3), p. 5.

[66] *Ibid.* (3), p. 5.

tion to the fact that certain counties might have a mixed ethnic population, and that both ordinary "peasants" as well as chiefs should be elected as delegates.[67]

Table 4.1. The COC's proposal for the composition of delegations to the NC[68]

Types of Delegation	Number of Delegates
30 District delegations based on colonial borders	250
SPLA specialised units	12
22 Independent Area Command delegations	132
General Field Staff Command Council	80
Paramilitary organised forces	8
SPLM/A chapters abroad	24
SPLM supporters and sympathisers in Govt-held towns	6
Displaced and refugees	44
Popular and syndicated organisations excluding Bishops	15
Total[69]	571

When comparing the COC's proposal for delegations (Table 4.1) with the instructions given in the *Mandate*, it is evident that the categories are almost identical, except that "special categories" and "chairman nominated" delegations are not mentioned in the former.

Elijah Malok informed the COC on 24 August that their suggestions had been accepted by John Garang.[70] But, when Garang issued the list of delegates to the rest of the Movement on 30 August, the composition of delegates was quite different, as can be seen in Table 4.2.

The headings of the categories were slightly altered, but the most significant change was in the number of delegates within each category, which was increased unevenly: in particular the delegates by position (from 80 to 154), chapters abroad (from 24 to 46), popular and syndicated organisations (from 44 to 70). The result was that the Movement and leadership had their representation increased, while the percentage of civilian delegates from the districts inside the Sudan decreased from about 44 per cent to 31 per cent. However, changes in the chapters abroad delegations and associated organisations resulted in a broadening of the basis from which delegates were drawn, and conforms with the alterations made to the agenda. These changes would have implications for the National Convention's legitimacy if they had been implemented. They were not. Instead, the list of those who actually attended the NC (Table

---

[67] *Ibid.* (2), p. 6.

[68] A detailed list of the proposed delegations is presented in the *Minutes* (2), pp. 14–17.

[69] In the third meeting two representatives from two different refugee camps were added, bringing the total number to 575, *ibid.* (3), p. 14.

[70] *Ibid.* (4), p. 1.

4.3) differs from the two pre-defined lists, but curiously it is the first one, proposed by the COC, which is closer to the actual attendance at the NC.

Table 4.2. Delegations to the NC as announced by Garang on 30 August

Types of Delegation	Number of Delegates
31 Combined District delegations based on old administrative boundaries[71]	258
22 Independent Area Command delegations and specialised units/paramilitary	176
Delegates by position[72]	154
SPLM/A chapters abroad	46
Token [*sic*] from occupied areas[73]	12
Displaced and refugees	50
Popular and syndicated[74]	70
Chairman-nominated delegates	59
Total	825

Table 4.3. Delegates Registered in the NC Proceedings

Types of Delegations	Number of Delegates
Combined County/IAC delegations (25)	397
Displaced and Refugees	28
SPLM/A Chapters abroad delegates	13
Paramilitary	3
Sudanese Indigenous NGOs	1
Church	3
Nominated Delegates	11
Ad-Hoc Committee	22
Convention organising Committee	20
General Field Staff Command Council	18
Total	516

The *Proceedings* include an appendix with the delegates who actually attended.[75] According to this, only 516 out of 825 invited delegates attended, or

---

[71] Including the delegations "Nuba Mountains/Southern Kordofan" and "Southern Blue Nile/Ingessa Hills".

[72] Members of GFSCC, Bishops in liberated areas, 23 *ad hoc* committees with two members each and the COC members.

[73] "Occupied areas" meant areas controlled by government forces.

[74] Only 15 of these were allocated to such organisations inside the liberated areas, the rest were for popular and syndicated organisations abroad, which came in addition to the quotas allocated to SPLM/A chapters abroad.

[75] *Proceedings*, 'Delegates to the National Convention', pp. i–ix.

even fewer than the 571 proposed in the original COC list. Moreover, the delegates are categorised in yet another way.[76]

When comparing the list of delegates in the *Proceedings* (Table 4.3) with the prior lists of delegations (Table 4.2), who was absent? The merging and splitting up of different types of delegations precludes a straightforward comparison, but it is still possible to comment on the effects of the alterations. Of 397 delegates listed in the combined county-IAC delegations, 144 are listed with civilian titles, while 253 have military ranks.[77] This means that representation of civilians is less than 60 per cent of the original quota, and that military personnel exceeded their quota by almost 100 delegates. Part of the explanation for this is that the quotas allocated to civilians (women, chiefs, workers and intellectuals) in areas controlled by other factions were not filled, but the main reason is that the military part of the Movement was given priority.[78] It is, also, conceivable that some persons listed with military titles were meant to represent civilian constituencies.[79] But because the list of delegates does not specify which constituencies the delegates represented, it is difficult to establish how many delegates with military ranks represented civilians.

The other important category missing is the Sudanese Diaspora, which was allotted a quota of approximately 100 delegates (SPLM Chapters abroad and most of the syndicated and popular quotas). Since these "Chapters abroad" were weak and the SPLM/A did not have sufficient resources to transport delegates from other countries, it is not surprising that only thirteen attended. These quotas may have been mere tokens of recognition, so that individuals in exile would feel included. Mario Muor mentioned this when discussing quotas for refugee camps: "[He] supported the suggestion of Cdr Kuol Manyang for the representation of the refugees [*sic*] camps in Ethiopia [so that]even if the delegates find it difficult [to come] then they will feel well considered."[80]

Another group that apparently was not able to fill its quota was the SPLM/A leadership. The General Field Staff Command Council – which was

---

[76] Lesch, *The Sudan*, p. 201, claims that there were "thousands" of delegates at the NC, which is an exaggeration.

[77] This figure is based on the number of delegates from the 25 combined IAC/district quotas with civilian titles. It is possible that some of those with military ranks were elected as local representatives, but this is difficult to establish, and these delegates would still have military affiliations.

[78] Even six out of the 28 representatives from refugee camps were listed with military ranks, 'Delegates to the National Convention', *Proceedings*, p. ii.

[79] At the NC, Salva Kiir is minuted as saying: "he did not see the need for soldiers who were representing civil constituencies coming to the meeting in military uniform rather than in civilian attire. He thought soldiers representing military constituencies should be the only ones to appear in military uniform at the Convention", *Proceedings*, p. 112.

[80] *Minutes* (3), p. 3.

allotted "about 80 members" in Garang's July message[81] – ended up with only 18 delegates at the NC.[82] Of the delegates to be nominated by the SPLM/A Chairman, only eleven out of a quota of fifty-nine appeared. Without knowing who were members of the GFSCC it is difficult to ascertain why so few were listed in this delegation. Certainly, some were included in others, such as the COC delegation and the *ad hoc* committee delegation. However, when comparing the list of persons attending the Convention with the list of members elected to the National Liberation Council (NLC) – which was replacing the GFSCC – it is evident that several NLC members-to-be were absent from the Convention. The explanation for this surprising absence of senior leaders is unknown.

The overall impression made by the attendance list is the randomness of delegations. The size of the geographical delegations varies from fifty-eight (Nuba Mountains) to six (Nasir). There is no consistency in the order in which delegates are presented, but the military are generally listed at the top by rank. The number of military delegates seems to have accorded approximately with the Convention Organization Committee's plan from August 1993, while the number of civilians and the requirements for their background were not adhered to at all. To what extent inadequate civilian representation can be blamed on the novelty of the NC and the limited physical and organisational infrastructure of the Southern Sudan, is difficult to say.

The most striking aspect of the changes between the pre-Convention list of delegates and the attendance list in the *Proceedings* is the inattention to process and the unwillingness to address problems of representation from the civil population vis-à-vis parts of the SPLM/A. To be sure, proportional representation was not the sole criterion for composition of the National Convention; quotas never intended to be filled were apparently a way of recognising distant segments of the Movement and sympathising groups. How to achieve proportional representation was hardly discussed at all. But one should not take for granted that all Convention Organization Committee members believed that the civilians were to attend the National Convention for the purpose of contributing to the political development of the Movement. The reasons for including the civilian population stated in the *Minutes* are: "We would like to convince our civilian population that we are persecuting [*sic*] this war on their behalf and to let the world know that we are genuine when we talk about democracy as one of the main themes of holding the national convention."[83] The

---

[81] *Mandate*, p. 5. The exact size of the General Field and Staff Command Council (GFSCC) remains unknown. At one point Garang stated that it was "about 80", while in the press release of 21 February 1993 the GFSCC was said to consist of 61 members, *Press Release, op. cit.* (Ch. 3), p. 5.

[82] 'Delegates to the National Convention', *Proceedings,* pp. viii–ix.

[83] *Minutes* (2), pp. 4–5.

SPLM/A should "allow adequate representation of the civilian population as it is often said that a guerrilla is like a fish in the water."[84] In short, supported by a Maoist dictum, the stated grounds for having the population in SPLM/A controlled areas represented at the National Convention were to convince them of the justness of the SPLM/A cause and to impress foreign guests.

It should also be emphasised that preparations for the Convention were made in the name of a SPLM/A party congress and not a constitutional assembly. A party congress requires only delegates from within the organisation. A quite different composition is required in order to represent the people of a given territory. As long as the election of the majority of delegates was to be based on their membership of the SPLM/A, then an assembly based on neither the pre-defined delegation lists nor the people who actual met, would in any meaningful way represent the people of the Southern Sudan, southern Kordofan and South Blue Nile.

The Selection of Delegates and Their Mandate

The procedure for selecting delegates relates to the NC's legitimacy,[85] and the different types of delegations suggest that delegate-selection procedures varied.[86] A significant percentage of the delegates were directly appointed by the SPLM/A Chairman. Even more became delegates through the positions to which they had been appointed by him. Therefore, regardless of theoretical systems for allocating members, the largest single group at the National Convention were people with personal ties to John Garang.[87] Appointment by

---

[84] Ibid. (2), p. 5. The Maoist quotation reads in its original: "Many people think it impossible for guerrillas to exist for long in the enemy's rear. Such a belief reveals lack of comprehension of the relationship that should exist between the people and the troops. The former may be likened to water while the latter to the fish who inhabit it. How may it be said that these two cannot exist together? It is only undisciplined troops who make the people their enemies and who, like the fish out of its native element cannot live", Mao Zedong, On Guerrilla Warfare, http://www. marxists. org/ reference/archive/mao/works/1937/guerrilla-warfare/index.htm, Ch. 5.

[85] This is why it is mentioned here at all, despite the extremely limited material available on the subject.

[86] These conclusions are based on comments made during COC meetings in Nairobi and from lists of delegates, which are then compared to the little information available on administration in SPLM/A controlled areas. Extensive interviews with "ordinary" delegates would be the most fruitful way of extending knowledge on this topic.

[87] It is difficult to estimate the exact number of these groups. In addition to the delegation that was explicitly to be appointed by Garang, several others delegates were indirectly appointed by him. There is no evidence suggesting that Garang did not appoint the GFSCC, as appointment by the SPLM/A Chairman was the standard procedure for selecting the SPLM/A officials. Similarly, the ad hoc committees and the COC, which each had substantial delegations, were probably selected by Garang personally. This means that seventy delegates were appointed by him. Moreover, considering the fact that Garang personally approved all promotions within the army, one may argue than more than 50 per cent of the delegates were, in principle, loyal to him personally.

Garang did not necessarily mean total domination by him. As already mentioned, Mario Muor was one among several senior members of the SPLM/A who did not hesitate to voice independent opinions.

In the *Proceedings*, the majority of those in attendance are listed as members of geographically defined delegations, and these delegations contained most of the representatives of the civilian population – the so-called "people of the New Sudan". How were *these* delegates selected? Did local elections take place, or did local authorities appoint them? At the second Convention Organization Committee meeting in Nairobi, Lawrence Lual asked if it would not be better to "set a criteria [*sic*] which shall be used by the field Commanders to choose the representatives in the districts."[88] There are other statements from these meetings that leave the impression that a significant portion of the delegates from among the civilian population would be "chosen", without stating who would make this selection or how.[89] On the basis of the attitudes described above, and of what is known about how areas under the SPLM/A's control were run at that time,[90] it can be assumed that the IAC or the CMA, with or without the consultation of local chiefs, appointed most of the representatives. There were probably different degrees of participation in these processes, mainly depending on individual commanders' interpretation of Garang's messages.

Another hint about how delegations were selected is in the titles of the delegates listed. As mentioned, these reveal a considerable variation in the composition of delegations, and one might assume that the more civilians there were in a delegation, the more democratic the appointment procedure. As noted, contested areas and areas under the Nasir faction's control were mainly represented by persons with military ranks. The Nuba Mountains and Ingessena Hills were also mainly represented by military. An exception was the Messiriya delegation, which consisted mainly of chiefs.[91] It may be that the rudimentary civilian political structures in the Nuba Mountains[92] meant that election procedures in these areas may have been more democratic than elsewhere. The delegations with strong civilian representation came from areas with a strong SPLM/A presence,[93] most of which were experiencing only limited violence at

---

[88] *Minutes* (2), p. 7. It seems that this comment was directed to Malok, who had stated that "it is better for the meeting to consider the criteria for choosing the representatives from each district for the convention", p. 7. Apparently Lual believed that Malok had suggested that the COC would select delegates directly, and he thought it would be more practical if local commanders made the selection. The idea that the local population would vote themselves was not explicitly discussed.

[89] According to the *Minutes* several COC members used the word "choose" when describing the process of identifying civilian delegates, (2), pp. 5–8.

[90] See pp. 62–72.

[91] Four military and eleven chiefs.

[92] See pp. 66–67.

[93] Bor/Kongor, Torit East/West, Yei/Kajo-Keji, Yambio/Tombura, Maridi/Mundri, Kapoeta,

the time. For these areas, it is possible that some commanders, instead of personally selecting them, asked various groups (women, chiefs, and soldiers) to appoint a certain number from among themselves.

* * *

The Convention Organization Committee's theoretical approach to the planning of the NC can be illustrated through a brief discussion of its modelling of the delegation structure. It seems that the COC took as its point of departure a simplified "class structure" wherein the local community was made up of four categories: chiefs, women, peasants and intellectuals. Whether these categories were derived from a general theory or ideology, or categories the COC decided were needed at the NC, or represented the COC's notions of the demographical composition of an average Southern Sudanese village, cannot be said for sure. The last alternative is the least probable since all COC members were Southern Sudanese with extensive first-hand knowledge of the situation on the ground. Impressions from the *Proceedings* suggest that except for the women delegates, it does not seem that members felt any particular solidarity across local boundaries. In addition to infrastructural barriers, there were language problems; it is probable that most delegates considered themselves representatives of their localities rather than of any theoretical "class".

THE NATIONAL CONVENTION

Was the National Convention organised according to plan? Did the Convention signify in 1994 what it does now? Did it represent a renewal of the SPLM/A? These questions might be answered in part through a brief reconstruction of events at the Convention; the process of re-electing the leaders of the SPLM/A; the significance of the National Convention and *NC Resolutions* with special attention to the political and institutional reforms outlined in the *NC Resolutions*; and the process through which the establishment of an independent judiciary was sought. At the end of the chapter we will demonstrate how the National Convention also entailed a redefinition of the content of "New Sudan", and we will ask the question whether the Convention was transcendental or only new labels for old practices.

The Workings of the National Convention

The *Proceedings* are the main source of information on how the National Convention was conducted, and most of its agenda can be discerned from them. The Convention started on Saturday, 2 April. The first items on the agenda

---

Juba/OJS, Wau/Raga, Tonj, Rumbek, Gogrial, Abiei.

were greetings and prayers (both Christian and Islamic). Then Yousif Kuwa made an opening speech, after which John Garang officially opened the NC with his speech. The *Proceedings* do not say what took place on 3 April. On Monday 4 April Bishop Paride gave a short speech. The rest of that day and the next were spent on the presentation of position papers from all parts of the SPLM/A and associated organisations. On 6 April John Garang's opening speech was discussed, and delegates were split into various committees, discussing aspects of the Convention Organization Committee's amended *Agenda*. The following NC committees were established, each with a chairman and secretary:[94] Political Affairs; Finance and Relief; Public Services; Military Affairs; Legal Affairs; and, Social Affairs.[95] It seems that deliberations within these committees continued until 8 April,[96] while nothing was scheduled for 9 April. On 10 April, representatives of the committees and parts of the NC secretariat held a long meeting and prepared draft resolutions, which was the starting point for the plenum discussion of the following days. The first committees presented their reports and proposed resolutions on 11 April, followed by a discussion, which continued the next day. This was the last official day of the Convention, and most of it was dedicated to passing resolutions, elections and speeches. In the wake of the NC, there was apparently a National Liberation Council meeting,[97] where the chairman reportedly appointed a National Executive Committee.

Information about the "ordinary" delegates'[98] experiences and opinions is difficult to find in the *Proceedings*. There seem to have been few debates and none was particularly long. It is difficult to establish whether the *Proceedings* provide accurate accounts of debates; debates may have been longer but the secretariat might not have had the capacity to record what was said.[99] Interviews

---

[94] On how the leaders and secretaries were selected, the *Proceedings* state only: "The Chairman [*sic*] and secretaries to the six Committees were appointed and their names announced", p. 113.

[95] *Ibid.*, pp. 114–16.

[96] The *Proceedings* mention specifically that Thursday 7 April was dedicated to discussion in committees, p. 114. The report from the finance committee is dated 8 April, so this must have been the last day of discussion in the committees, p. 139.

[97] *A Major Watershed: SPLM/SPLA First National Convention Resolutions, Appointments and Protocol*, declares that the appointed NEC was approved by the NLC (Chukudum, New Sudan: Sudan People's Liberation Movement (SPLM) Secretariat of Information and Culture, 1994?, pp. 33 and 36. The list of appointments was signed by John Garang and dated 3 June, p. 38. The establishment and performance of the post-NC structures will be discussed further in Chapter 5, pp. 138–66.

[98] Here "ordinary" delegate means anyone without a senior position within the SPLM/A or associate organisations.

[99] The fact that the *Proceedings* recorded several "odd" comments suggests that debates are reported quite accurately. In other cases a long debate is reported without the debate itself, i.e. pp. 112, 128 and 132. Sometimes the secretariat did not understand the language in which the comments were made.

with participants who attended the Convention provided information of only limited interest in this respect. Unfortunately, there were few external observers, and they were present only for short periods. Moreover, significant periods of the NC were allocated to discussions in groups, and there are few clues as to who participated in which groups – let alone as to what was being said. Therefore, more research is needed to establish how the National Convention was conducted and to what extent "ordinary" delegates influenced decisions made.

The floor was opened for discussion on 6 April, and this was the first opportunity for delegates to comment on political issues. In practice few had the chance to speak before the debate was cut off in accordance with a suggestion from the head of the GFSCC delegation, Mark Nyipuch,[100] who described the preceding comments as irrelevant.[101] He was partly correct. Some of the comments related to local issues, instead of to Garang's speech. But, it had already been four days since that speech had been delivered, and many delegates probably did not speak English and might have missed much of the content. Even the exact purpose of the debate is unclear. Garang's speech was long and touched upon most important policy issues. It should therefore have come as no surprise to the Convention leadership that all the comments did not strictly relate to points in Garang's speech.

According to the *Proceedings*, Nyipuch's suggestion sparked off an extensive debate, which ended with a vote of 486 in favour of ending the debate, 46 against, and 1 abstention.[102] This cutting off of the debate and Kuwa's repeated admonitions that delegates were wasting too much time on irrelevant issues, might have affected ordinary delegates' willingness to speak in subsequent discussions. The fact is, however, that surprisingly few delegates contributed to the debates, and the rest of the deliberations were dominated by the leading personalities of the Movement. But apparently ordinary delegates were offered an alternate channel to voice grievances and opinions, since several sessions were reportedly organised for delegations to meet separately with John Garang.[103] The descriptions of these sessions read like royal audiences rather than democratic exchanges. That having been said, it must be conceded that for the SPLM/A leadership to discuss and decide on important policy issues in front of a large number of representatives from the local population and the Movement's ordinary members (i.e. the lower ranks in the SPLM/A), was itself a radical change.

---

[100] *Proceedings*, pp. 111–12.

[101] *Ibid.*, p. 112.

[102] This voting indicates 531 participants at the NC, while only 516 are on the attendance list. Moreover, at the beginning the *Proceedings* state that there were 550 delegates to the Convention, 'Introduction and Background', p. iii..

[103] *Ibid.*, 'Introduction and Background', p. vii. Except for the meeting with GFSCC, the content of these meetings is not revealed in the documentation.

Voting and Elections

The elections at the National Convention were considered important at the time they took place, and were later touted as proof of the SPLM/A's and its leadership's legitimacy as representatives of the people of the Southern Sudan. In theory, delegates could communicate their opinions through their votes for the election of leaders and of members of the National Liberation Council, and through voting on the *NC Resolutions*. These elections should not however be taken at face value, for they were far from free and fair. The following passage from the *NC Proceedings* captures the image the SPLM/A wanted the elections to project:

> The proposed resolutions were passed with little amendments. Then the election of the Chairman and his deputy took place. Cdr Dr John Garang was elected unopposed. He chose his running mate as Cdr Salva Kiir Mayardit, he was also elected deputy Chairman of the NLC/NEC. Then immediately, the ground broke loose. Drums were beaten, whistles and horns were blown, all the dancing teams simply turn [*sic*] the Convention into a dancing party. Cheers went up from all sides of the floor. There were cries such as long live the New Sudan, long live the SPLM/SPLA, long live Dr John. There was a tumultuous applause from all over the hall as the dancing teams surged forward to the podium. People were speaking through their cultures and expressing their happiness at the election of Cdr Dr John Garang into the highest office of the SPLM. It took thirty minutes to calm the situation.[104]

The SPLM/A leadership was eager to vindicate its claim of fighting the war on behalf of the population,[105] while, at the same time, it had no intention of loosening control of the Movement. These aims proved to be contradictory when it came to the elections: there had to be competition for offices if the Convention was to prove its preference for the sitting leadership, but then the leadership might have lost. There cannot have been any doubt in the minds of delegates who would be elected as the chairman and deputy chairman of the SPLM/A. There was only one candidate for each office. Ensuring continued control turned out to be more important than proving genuine popular support. Arguably, it was too early in the process of liberalisation to expect an open election with the possibility of real alternatives, and the fact that the leadership felt the need to prove its legitimacy at all might in itself be seen as a step in the right direction.

In his acceptance speech at the end of the NC, John Garang stated:

> I would like to talk briefly about the National Liberation Council. It is composed as you have seen of various nationalities, backgrounds and regions. I was doing some arithmetic and I came up with some percentages. Seventy-five per cent (132) of the National Liberation Council is freely elected. The appointees are forty-eight; thirty-two by the armed

---

[104] *Proceedings*, 'Introduction and background', p. viii.

[105] Cf. quotes from COC meeting on pp. 103–104.

forces and ten by myself. So let nobody accuse us of dictatorship. These were free elections which were held today.[106]

The *Proceedings* do not mention the formal procedure for voting at the NC, which makes it difficult to evaluate Garang's claim. Prunier states that the final elections were by acclamation, and that there was only one candidate for each of the seats.

Similar to the election of delegates to the National Convention, the process of electing members of the National Liberation Council varied. Garang, Kiir and Kuwa were *ex officio* members through their positions as Chairman and Deputy Chairman of the Movement and Chairman of the NC, respectively. And, as mentioned in Garang's speech, some were appointed, but his numbers do not correspond with those in the *Proceedings*. Thirty-six were appointed by the army, not thirty-two as Garang claimed, and twelve were appointed by Garang, not ten. The political affairs committee in collaboration with the election committee "devised ways of electing the nineteen representatives from 'affiliated and syndicated organizations'."[107] The task of the election commission was to "receive, vet and announce the results of the elections." Even if candidates for the National Liberation Council were later approved by acclamation at the NC, this was only in a limited sense a free election. Candidates representing geographical constituencies were selected during the Convention by NC delegates from the same areas.[108] The total number of representatives designated "territorial" was 112, which was 62 per cent of the NLC's 181 members, not the 75 per cent announced by Garang. Since he did not mention how the 75 per cent related to his claim of free elections, it is difficult to say whether a 13 per cent reduction makes a difference.

The *Proceedings* mention two instances of contested candidacies for positions on the NLC, and in both cases this was "investigated", and one candidate was declared the winner.[109] Who investigated and how were not recorded. In one, the refugee representative for Equatoria region, Kosti Manibe was one of the candidates. Manibe was already then a senior SPLM/A cadre and member of the COC, and it is noteworthy that he should claim a seat as representative of the grassroots, in particular when the seat was contested. Nonetheless, after the investigation Manibe was declared the rightful candidate. The account of this nomination suggests that there were limited options for other candidates to contest the seats of pre-determined candidates. But it may also be that refugee representatives thought that a person with influence such as Manibe would represent them better than a lesser personage.

---

[106] Proceedings, p. 202.

[107] 'Introduction and background', *Proceedings*, p. vi.

[108] *Ibid.*

[109] 'Introduction and background', *Proceedings*, p. vi.

The best-documented election during the National Convention is that of the Chairman for the Convention, which might be representative of the elections and voting procedures in general.[110] The Election Commission, headed by Ambrose Riiny, was in charge of this election. On the first day, it asked the NC assembly for candidates and Samson Kwaje – head of the Kenya Chapter delegation and one of the SPLM/A's senior cadres – nominated Kuwa for the Chairmanship. According to the *Proceedings*, this suggestion received applause from "the whole hall."[111] Kwaje's motion was seconded by the aforementioned head of the GFSCC delegation, Mark Nyipuch. Considering that Kuwa had been the head of the Convention Organization Committee, and was a senior officer within the SPLA, his was not a controversial nomination, and since it had the official backing of the SPLM/A leadership, it is not surprising that no other candidate was suggested. Subsequently the "Election Commission declared Crd. Yousif Kowa [*sic*] Makki as the National Chairman of the first SPLM/SPLA National Convention."[112] Some delegates might have interpreted this first election as a guide to how "elections" and voting at the Convention should be conducted. What is clearer – even though the election procedures were declared to be democratic – is that seats were not meant to be contested. In any case, even if elections had been less *pro forma*, the unconventional manner in which delegations were composed would have rendered any procedure questionable that was claimed to be electing members to the supreme body of the "New Sudan" for five years to come.[113]

Symbol of Change, Political Reform and State Formation

The National Convention has in the years since it took place been seen as a positive turning point in the SPLM/A's history, whereas the 1991 split has been viewed as *the* setback. In general, the NC has become the symbol of a new start, when old errors were admitted and new practices adopted. This was supposed to include political reforms with an emphasis on establishment of civil government structures; democratisation through elections and accountability; and the declaration of the "New Sudan".

---

[110] The somewhat briefer accounts of the election of John Garang as chairman of the SPLM/A and the election/appointment of Salva Kiir as the deputy have a strong resemblance to the election of Kuwa, *ibid*, pp. 197–99.

[111] *Ibid.*, p. 5.

[112] Ibid.

[113] The election of the NLC was presented as a remedy to Garang's practice of single-handedly appointing senior leaders of the Movement, "There were no representative political structures therefore Dr. John was simply appointing members of the Political Military High Command (PMHC) to very high offices of the SPLM/SPLA. Such appointees were neither popular nor representatives of the people. They were simply a creation and imposition of Dr. John on the people", 'Introduction and background', *Proceedings*, p. v.

Breaking with the Past: The National Convention as a Symbol of Change

Written as well as oral comments by sympathisers and members of the Movement emphasise the difference between the pre-NC SPLM/A and the post-NC SPLM/A. In his opening speech to the National Convention, Yousif Kuwa described the period before the NC as 'childhood' and what was to come as 'manhood' characterised by "responsibility, seriousness and accountability."[114] There is implicit criticism of the past as a period when the Movement was irresponsible and unaccountable. Kuwa emphasised the importance of self-reliance and the separation of the military and civil authorities. Bishop Paride's short opening speech on 4 April also emphasised the need for reforms. He warned SPLM/SPLA commanders and officers not to imitate Idi Amin by becoming "involved in trade and power struggle."[115] They should stop forcibly taking girls as wives. He positioned the church as spiritual mother of the SPLM/A, distancing himself from the SPLM/A rhetoric of the New Sudan Council of Churches as the SPLM/A's "spiritual wing".[116] And finally he asked:

> In this first SPLM/A National Convention leaders of civilians have come from all over the Sudan to bring the cry of their people to the SPLM/A Leadership. If the SPLM/A Leadership will not listen to their cry and follow the example of Jesus as in John: 13, 1–20, should these people who are both Christians, animists and Moslems call SPLM/A their Liberators?[117]

In John 13:16 Jesus washes the feet of his disciples saying "I tell you the truth, no servant is greater than his master, nor is a messenger greater than the one who sent him." Paride wanted a change, and his call for respect for the civilian population could hardly have been stronger.

Later SPLM/A documents also emphasise the element of transformation:

> From the onset of the liberation struggle in 1983 until the First National Convention in 1994, the efforts of the Movement were directed mainly to the prosecution of the armed struggle, and therefore out of necessity the military aspect was paramount and more emphasized than all other aspects of the Movement. The imperatives of the liberation struggle led the Movement in 1994 to adopt more radical resolutions that called for the building of SPLM structures and promotion of participatory democracy, the respect of values and ideals of tolerance, human rights, the rule of law, accountability, transparency, and so forth. [118]

---

[114] Proceedings, p. 3.

[115] *Ibid.*, p. 29.

[116] African Rights, 'Great Expectations', p. 29.

[117] *Proceedings*, p. 29.

[118] SPLM, *Peace through Development: Perspectives and Prospects in the Sudan*, the Sudan People's Liberation Movement, February 2000, p. 12.

One result of emphasis on the "military aspect" had been the inadequate and often downright abusive treatment of civilians by military commanders. Civilian delegates to the National Convention had grievances, and a minimal sign of willingness to change behaviour would imply admission of past errors. The *Agenda* specified grievances, but these were smoothed out into general formulations in the *NC Resolutions*. This is particularly noticeable in the treatment of questions concerning the armed forces' code of conduct. In section eleven of the *Agenda*, concerning "Code of Conduct: Public Accountability and Elimination of Corruption and Misuse of Power",[119] it is stated that there should be two codes of conduct, one for the military and another for civilians. This probably represented an attempt to address the general problem of lawlessness and, more specifically, the trouble caused by local commanders' taking the law into their own hands.[120] Subsequently, however, it becomes apparent that it was the protection of civilians against the army in general, and officers in particular, that was sought. Point 11.2 of the *Agenda* proclaims in two different ways the individual's right to life.[121] It also defines *public property* as separate from other types of property. Point 3 reiterates that "[there] shall be strict distinction between personal, private and public property."[122] This double guarantee amply demonstrates a need to change the current practice. And if that were not enough, the next paragraph reads: "In order to safeguard public and private property there shall be no authority, military or civil, that shall be involved in any illegal commandeering or confiscation." The *Agenda* continues to suggest measures to avoid abuse, and states that punishments should be effected "without distinction whatsoever", meaning that no one was supposed to be above the law. Bridewealth as a major source of corruption is mentioned,[123] probably because people had been charging undue fees, and SPLM/A officers had stolen cattle in order to pay bridewealth.[124] The *Agenda*'s treatment of this topic ends with a message obviously aimed at senior officers: "Marriage is always a private

---

[119] *Agenda*, pp. 17–19.

[120] Human Rights Watch, 'Civilian Devastation: Abuses by All Parties in the War in Southern Sudan', 1993, pp. 239–52, provides the most thorough independent report on the administration of justice in SPLM/A controlled areas in the period before 1994. Here numerous abuses of human rights and irregularities in the administration of justice are listed, which are partly blamed on the inadequate legal system of the SPLM/A. The aforementioned personal account of one of the SPLM/A magistrates also describes the pre-1994 situation, but in a more positive manner, Kuol, *Administration of Justice*.

[121] *Agenda*, p. 18.

[122] *Ibid.*

[123] *Ibid.*, p. 19.

[124] Polygamy is common in the Southern Sudan. This causes a constant need for bridewealth, which is mainly paid in cattle or money (often obtained through selling cattle).

affair and all individuals *irrespective of their ranks* [emphasis added] must deal with marriages on [a] strictly private and individual basis."[125]

The concern with putting an end to abuses of civilians and the illegal appropriation of private property was also evident in some position papers presented by delegation leaders at the NC. Their ways of expressing this concern ranged widely. One stated: "There will be no reason for the people to go to the government held towns, if self-sufficiency and stability is created for them in the SPLA held areas."[126] Another read: "Raping of women and confiscating personal belongings from civilians are likely to contribute to the people being attracted to the government 'peace villages'."[127] But in the draft resolutions and in the final *NC Resolutions* the edge had vanished, and the whole section of the *Agenda* had been reduced to this: "13.1.2 Full respect for the civil rights of the individual shall be strictly observed and protected by law in the New Sudan."[128]

It can be argued that more specificity was not possible in the *NC Resolutions*, since they were very brief. It seems, however, that a need for adherence to general principles did not always prevail. For instance, point 13.1.4 in the *NC Resolutions* states: "The use of divisive terms (like Nyagat and other derogatory words) within the rank and file of the Movement shall be discouraged."[129] Reluctance to admit mistakes is also apparent in John Garang's lengthy opening speech, which referred to errors in the past without specifying them. Therefore one may conclude that in this important area, the *NC Resolutions* failed to address the specific grievances that had been suggested during the planning sessions and at the NC itself. The fact that the SPLM/A leadership was unwilling to admit specific errors and flawed practices undermines the notions of National Convention as a symbol of change.

Nevertheless, change and reform were important issues at the NC. The focus on change can be seen as an attempt at winning back the confidence and support of civilians for the purpose of securing voluntary support for the Movement and dissuading people from fleeing from SPLM/A-governed areas. The cut-off of supplies from Ethiopia after 1991 meant that the SPLM/A had to rely to a much larger degree on what could be obtained from within the Southern Sudan. This explains the emphasis on "self-reliance" at the NC. The

---

[125] *Agenda*, p. 19.

[126] Delegation from government held areas presented by Manoah Aligo, *Proceedings*, p. 43.

[127] SPLM Chapter London (UK) and Ireland, Mr. Henry Wani Rondyang, *ibid.*, p. 100; "Peace Villages" were a hundred camps in Southern Kordofan where thousands of displaced persons from the Nuba Mountains and further south were kept virtually as prisoners, Burr and Collins, *Requiem for Sudan,* p. 310.

[128] *Proceedings*, p. 186.

[129] *Ibid.*, p. 186.

SPLM/A leadership hoped that giving the civilian population opportunities for surplus production would benefit the Movement as well.[130]

The SPLM/A's reinvigorated interest in the well being of the local population was also a result of the need to improve the Movement's image for foreigners and expatriates, of whom the most important were exiled Sudanese intellectuals and representatives of Western governments and foreign NGOs. These groups had strong views on human rights and the protection of civilians against abuses in wartime. The National Convention gave the SPLM/A a chance to declare a new start. It was a manifestation of the leadership's decision to change, and made it possible to declare the pre-1994 period to be history – the erroneous past – which should be buried so that the South could move forwards. In this context it was not necessary to specify these wrongs, but only to promise good behaviour in the future.

Political Reforms?

We have seen that political and institutional reforms within the SPLM/A had been a topic – at least at the level of rhetoric – since the split in 1991,[131] and that even before the National Convention, PMHC meetings had announced far-reaching changes. It is the NC, however, through the *NC Resolutions*, that receives credit for radically altering the SPLM/A. The most important reform was establishment of a civil government structure through election of a national political body, the National Liberation Council (NLC), together with the separation of military and civil administration and the organisation of a formal judicial system. In addition, the *NC Resolutions* present what could have become a foundation for the development of policies in several important fields such as the economy, health and education. For several years these resolutions had only limited consequences for the Movement's practice. They became important symbols of the reformed SPLM/A, however, and the very extent and detail of the policy statements of these resolutions were innovations in themselves. These new policies were drafted during the Convention Organization Committee meetings in Nimule and amended during the Convention.

Numbers 2–6 of the *NC Resolutions* presented a whole new political structure for the SPLM/A. At the top of the structure, the National Convention was supposed to convene every five years. The NLC was described as the "legisla-

---

[130] The policy of more self-reliance was also aimed at the guerrilla army directly. For instance, Resolution 14 refers to "self-sufficiency" for the civil population, and instructs "the SPLA" to produce most of its "food requirements, and ... engage in cottage industries to produce most of their soft military requirements, such as uniforms, tyre sandals (Mutwakali), pouches, belts, etc." *Ibid.*, p. 187. The detailed list of products contrasts with the general formulations regarding the respect for civilians and their property, as discussed in the paragraphs above.

[131] See pp. 54–58.

tive and central political organ of the New Sudan",[132] and was to meet annually. The SPLM/A Chairman headed a National Executive Council,[133] which officially was responsible for "executing the policies and programmes of the Movement" and for "the administration of the New Sudan".[134] These institutions were supposed to be replicated at the lower government levels (region, county, payam and village).[135] Why was this reform decided upon in the first place?

While establishment of civil administration had already been decided upon at the Torit PMHC meeting in 1991, the suggestion of a civilian council as the SPLM/A's supreme body was new and originated from the *Agenda*. With the exception of the size of the NLC, the suggestion from the COC was more or less the same as the final outcome, and there was little discussion during the NC concerning these reforms. The lack of controversy can be explained in one of two ways. Either there was general acceptance of the new concept and the idea of voting for the leadership was seen as a positive change; or the reforms were generally seen as theoretical and adopted mainly for propaganda purposes, and it was taken for granted that the real power structure would remain unchanged. The latter hypothesis is the most plausible as this was close to describing the outcome of the reform rhetoric. It is possible, however, to imagine that some reformers hoped that the *NC Resolutions* and the proclaimed changes would have an effect – in the long run – if not immediately.

Independence of the Judiciary and New Laws

Compared to the existing state of affairs, the legal reforms adopted at the National Convention were, if not radical, at least extensive. Some fourteen laws or collections of laws were to be drafted – everything from "The New Sudan Penal Code" to "The New Sudan Traffic Act".[136] Also, a three-level system of "modern" courts supervising a three-level system of "traditional" chief's courts was established, which represents formalisation and integration of the chief's courts into the "national" judicial system. Douglas Johnson emphasises how this reformed system recognised the authority of traditional structures.[137] But at the same time, these reforms also meant that the SPLM/A claimed the right to overrule the court decisions of traditional leaders. Through Resolution 9.2.3, the SPLM/A County courts were given the responsibility of supervising the

---

[132] *Proceedings*, p. 180.

[133] *Ibid.*, p. 181.

[134] *Ibid.*

[135] *Ibid.*, p. 183.

[136] *Ibid.*, p. 185.

[137] Johnson, 'The Sudan People's Liberation Army', p. 69.

"Chiefs' Courts in the County".[138] Thus, the price the chiefs had to pay for recognition and integration was subordination, which was a return to their pre-civil war status. This meant that the subsequent debate on independence of the judiciary was even more important: if the judiciary was not to be independent and justice was instead to be administered by SPLM/A leaders, this resolution involved a substantial extension of the SPLM/A's formal power over the civilian population.

Whereas the process of establishing the National Liberation Council went quite smoothly, discussions on judicial reform during the National Convention were more confrontational, and some of the underlying tensions within the Movement were briefly exposed. The core of the conflict was whether the NC should declare the establishment of an independent judiciary. Apparently, the debate started during preparation of the *Agenda* at Nimule. One passage reads: "The present situation in the Movement does not warrant complete independence of the Judiciary."[139] The reason mentioned is that a lack of qualified judges and lawyers would make it impossible to fill the necessary positions. Subsequent discussion in the *ad hoc* committee for Justice and Legal Affairs resulted in the opposite conclusion, and so the debate at the Convention had the suggestion of the establishment of an independent judiciary as its point of departure. [140]

During this debate, the leadership of the SPLM/A and delegates representing the military part of the Movement opposed the proposal. They used two sets of arguments: that there were not sufficient manpower and resources to establish a functioning judiciary, and that an independent judiciary was unfeasible during wartime. Salva Kiir said, "The New Sudan is not yet available. Let us make laws which are suitable for a Movement not a government."[141] Representatives from the legal professions disagreed referring to the need to protect civilians and stating that there had been instances of local commanders instructing judges to pass specific judgements.[142] They also argued that it was an important principle of judicial theory that the judiciary had to be independent of the executive if the people were to be secured fair trials.[143] Furthermore, the leader of the Legal Affairs Committee, Ambrose Riiny, maintained that they, in their discussion, had assumed "some semblance of a state and designed laws consistent with that presumption."[144] Here the question of the Convention's

---

[138] *Proceedings*, p. 184.

[139] *Agenda*, p. 21.

[140] *Proceedings*, p. 134.

[141] *Ibid.*, pp. 137–38.

[142] *Ibid.*, p. 137.

[143] *Ibid.*, pp. 137–38.

[144] *Ibid.*, p. 138.

status came up for the first time during the Convention. Pagan Amum, then leader of the Political Affairs Committee, replied, "This Convention is a Convention of the Movement. It is not a State Convention."[145]

Finally, John Garang got to the core of the controversy. He argued that the military delegates feared that an independent judiciary would be outside their control and become a base of opposition. Garang seemed to share this fear, and suggested that "independence" be replaced with "supremacy of the law: over everyone".[146] It is difficult to establish the exact meaning of this phrase, but the purpose was evidently to avoid the establishment of an independent judicial institution in SPLM/A controlled areas. Despite Garang's opposition, the formulation remained unchanged, and establishment of an independent judiciary was announced through the *NC Resolutions*.[147] The effect of this decision is evaluated in Chapter 5.[148] Here it can be concluded that this was a victory for the reformers who wanted to open up civil society and regulate the power of the SPLM/A.

Regarding Amum's statement it is worth noticing that the question of the NC's status was brought into the discussion. This demonstrates once again the general confusion over the issue. However, a question that was not brought up was whether the NC even had a mandate to set up an independent judiciary. But if Salva Kiir argued for postponing the establishment of such an institution, he did not question the NC's mandate to do so.

The New Sudan

> I, John Garang de Mabior, do hereby solemnly swear, in the name of the fatherland, the New Sudan, and of all our people and in the name of Almighty God, that I shall faithfully uphold the aspirations of our people and the aims and principles of the SPLM/SPLA, and to execute without fear or favour, to the best of my ability the duties of the office of the Chairman of the National Liberation and the Executive Councils, so help me God.[149]

After elections, the members of the NLC, the deputy chairman and the NC chairman all had to swear slightly modified versions of the oath quoted above. The phrasing of these oaths illustrates the confusion about the exact purpose of the National Convention. Was it for the Movement or the "New Sudan" government? For that matter, what *was* the "New Sudan"?

---

[145] *Ibid.*

[146] *Ibid.*, p. 139.

[147] *Ibid.*, p. 184.

[148] See pp. 154–55.

[149] *Proceedings*, p. 198.

The concept of a "New Sudan" dates to the SPLM/A manifesto of 1983.[150] During the 1980s, "New Sudan" meant unequivocally the government that was to replace the current one in Khartoum, following the anticipated victory of the SPLM/A. This was the case, for example, in the radio speech made by John Garang after the NIF coup in 1989:

> I greet you in the name of the glorious Sudanese Revolution; in the name of New Sudan; a United Democratic Sudan of peace, justice, equality and progress, a New Sudan with a new personality, a new identity, a prosperous, confident, proud and Great New Sudan.[151]

But after the 1991 split, "New Sudan" disappeared from SPLM/A rhetoric until it resurfaced in the documents of the National Convention. To explain why the term "New Sudan" was suddenly put back into circulation, and why it occurred when it did, it is necessary to recapitulate how the issue of the National Convention's status was handled during the planning process.

Already in the 30 July 1993 *Mandate*, there is ambiguity concerning what kind of convention the COC was to prepare – for the SPLM/A only or for the Southern Sudan as a whole. The *Mandate* states: "The Convention shall be held under the SPLM/SPLA, and shall be designated as the First SPLM/SPLA National Convention."[152] But it also states that the NC must be composed "so that our whole people is effectively represented in the shaping of our destiny at this crucial point."[153] Point 6d of the *Mandate* stipulates that "civilian representatives" shall be elected from the "various Counties".[154] If the NC was to be a party congress, better wording would have been some variation of the following: "representatives from local SPLM chapters inside the liberated areas." The actual formulation in the *Mandate* may therefore indicate a desire to set up a meeting for the entire population of the Southern Sudan, not only the SPLM/A. Yet, the document gives the overall impression of preparation for a party meeting, rather than a popular assembly. For example, the nature of the topics to be discussed – in the report by the chairman, revision of the manifesto and developing policies on different topics – supports this interpretation.

What did members of the Convention Organization Committee believe they were preparing? The question of the National Convention's status sur-

---

[150] 'Statement to the Sudanese People on the Current Situation in the Sudan, by Dr. John Garang de Mabior, Chairman and Commander-in Chief, SPLM/SPLA', 10 August 1989, quotes the 1983 manifesto: "This imminent, latent and impending disintegration and fragmentation of the Sudan is what the SPLA/M aims to stop by developing and implementing a consistent democratic solution to both the nationality and religious questions within the context of a United New Sudan", p. 23.

[151] *Ibid.*, p. 1.

[152] *Mandate*, p. 4.

[153] *Ibid.*, p. 6.

[154] *Ibid.*, p. 5.

faced in August during the COC's deliberations in Nairobi. The Committee discussed Muor's suggestion to add the passing of a constitution at the NC to the agenda. Then, one of the least-known members of the COC, Zamba Michael, asked if a constitution would be "sovereign or binding".[155] Pagan Amum, then leader of the COC's finance committee, understood the question to mean whether a constitution would be for the SPLM/A or for the Sudan, and answered that "the decisions of the convention were going to be binding on the SPLM/SPLA and not on the whole of Sudan."[156] This statement is almost identical to the answer he would give during NC discussion on establishment of an independent judiciary in the Southern Sudan. It is also interesting that he refers to the "whole of Sudan" instead of "the (whole of) Southern Sudan".[157] Whether other COC members concurred with Amum cannot be discerned from the *Minutes*, since his statement ended that discussion. Nevertheless, judging from its decisions, it appears that at this stage of the planning the COC prepared a party congress.

The *Agenda* prepared by the COC during October and November 1993, demonstrates how the NC to an increasing degree appeared to be a meeting intended to proclaim a new state. The *Agenda* does not address this issue directly, except for one passage concerned with popular participation in the "SPLM/SPLA liberated areas", which reads:

> The correct political line of the Movement towards civilians is that all SPLA soldiers and citizens in the liberated areas together with the supporters of the Movement inside Government occupied towns (or abroad) are all considered Freedom Fighters. The fallacy that in order to become a full-fledged SPLM/SPLA member one must undergo military training has already been corrected by the Torit Resolutions, and the COC recommends that the Convention reinforce this position.[158]

Here, the COC tried to define the whole of the population of the Southern Sudan as "freedom fighters" and hence as members of the SPLM/A, which in consequence would to some extent erase the difference between a party congress and a constitutional assembly. This concept was, however, abandoned in the draft resolutions presented at the NC, and the final resolution reads: "The civil population in the liberated areas shall be popularly organized so that they fully participate in the struggle."[159] Other formulations concerning the status of the SPLM/A vis-à-vis the civil population in the draft resolutions and final *NC*

---

[155] *Minutes* (3), p. 8.

[156] *Ibid.* (3), p. 8.

[157] His later appointment as secretary general of the National Democratic Alliance might be another indication.

[158] *Agenda*, p. 24.

[159] *Proceedings*, p. 187.

Resolutions give indications of the Convention's being a *de facto* constitutional assembly.

The oath sworn by Yousif Kuwa when assuming the position of NC Chairman appears to be the first text in which the term "New Sudan" was used in connection with the Convention. But it was Garang's opening speech that started discussion of the phrase. In the speech, the "New Sudan" is used as a metaphor of the SPLM/A's objectives at the time:

> The SPLM/SPLA has advanced the concept of the New Sudan as a socio-political muta-tion, a qualitative leap out of the Old Sudan, or else an interim political arrangement leading to a referendum on self-determination at the end of the interim period, and it is this principle that guides us in all peace talks.[160]

Thus, the "New Sudan" would be a product of the SPLM/A's military victory or successful peace negotiations; it was not available at that time. The difference from the pre-1991 period was that two future scenarios had emerged: a united Sudanese state genuinely different from the "Old Sudan", or an independent Southern Sudanese state. This change again demonstrates how the political pressure created by the 1991 split compelled the SPLM/A to modify its united Sudan policy. At this point, the substance of the "New Sudan" was comprehensible enough; confusion and ambiguity sprang up at the end of the Convention when yet another definition was launched.

The preamble of the draft resolutions states, "We the people of the New Sudan do hereby pass the following resolutions."[161] Since this formulation was not in the COC's *Agenda*, it must have been added during the NC. But apparently "the New Sudan" was considered too vague, and in the wording of *NC Resolutions* was as follows:

> We, the people of the New Sudan, represented by this Convention, proclaim the birth of the New Sudan, which for the time being, shall consist of Bahr el Ghazal, Equatoria, Southern Blue Nile, Southern Kordofan and Upper Nile Regions; and, accordingly, pass the rest of the resolutions as follows.[162]

Similar wording appeared in Garang's acceptance speech at the end of the NC. Garang said that the NC represented the people of "New Sudan", and that "this Convention represents the will of the people of the five regions."[163] Here the term "New Sudan" not only signified a future change of government, but was also the current SPLM/A government.

What caused these changes in the meaning of the term "New Sudan"? In answering this question three points might be considered. Firstly, in the

---

[160] *Ibid.*, pp. 21–22.
[161] *Ibid.*, p. 168.
[162] *Ibid.*, p. 180.
[163] *Ibid.*, pp. 201–202.

period following the 1991 split, the "New Sudan", as part of a dual negotiating strategy, defined a distance between the Movement's policy and the openly secessionist agenda of the Nasir faction, while at the same time representing the SPLM/A as advocates of moderate self-determination. Secondly, as the scope of the National Convention changed and it became clearer that it was not going to be presented as a party congress, but rather as a popular assembly, it became necessary to define the people to be represented at the NC. By referring to the 'New Sudan' instead of 'the Southern Sudan', the SPLM/A leadership could reassure members and sympathisers outside the Southern Sudan defined by the 1956 colonial borders, in particular the representatives from Southern Kordofan and Southern Blue Nile, that they would not be left out. This might soften the scepticism of these groups towards the SPLM/A new self-determination policy. Finally, the "New Sudan" was much more flexible than the "Southern Sudan", since the former was SPLM/A's invention that could be modified when necessary. The confusion surrounding the term "New Sudan" was caused by the desire to invest a term with an overly flexible range of meanings.

ASSESSMENT

What then was the National Convention? We have demonstrated that the answer to this question changed over the course of the planning process, and that – in the end – the National Convention served several purposes. It marked a political renewal by announcing an elaborate political programme and the intention of equipping the SPLM/A and areas under the Movement's control with civil structures. It sought to confirm the SPLM/A leadership's claim to represent the people of the Southern Sudan. And finally, through re-definition of the term "New Sudan", it drew the SPLM/A closer to an official embrace of a secessionist agenda. The positive judgements of scholars referred to are deserved: there is no doubt that the National Convention displayed Southerners' support of the SPLM/A, marked the beginning of a new era of democracy and reforms. By the same token, it was an efficient way of dismissing old sins as "the past", and asking for a vote of confidence.

These positive aspects notwithstanding, issues concerning the preparations and the National Convention itself do not conform with the official versions. Confusion marked the planning process and even obscured the origins of the plans for the Convention. The SPLM/A leadership wanted to project the NC as an event planned over several years, and as presenting well-crafted and up-to-date policies. This was different from what actually took place; the concept of the Convention was changed along the way through the different agendas presented. The issue of who would represent the "people of the New Sudan" at the

NC also evolved during the planning, and who actually attended as delegates appears to have been quite arbitrary and decided by the local setting.

The course of the National Convention itself resembles the pattern of the planning process. The intended purpose of the points on the programme is uncertain. The political reforms were to some degree reiterations of policies already adopted by PMHC meetings in 1991 and 1992, while other reforms were innovations – in particular the new configuration of central government structures (the National Liberation Council and the National Executive Council), and also the establishment of an independent judiciary. The elections and the proclamation of the "New Sudan" were – from a formalistic point of view – flawed, but they still represented positive signals to delegates and observers and boosted confidence in the Movement and its leadership.

Therefore, investigation of the National Convention's success eventually reduces to the question of which is more significant, the change of policy and stating of good intentions, or the inability to immediately convert rhetoric into practice? Formalists may dismiss the National Convention based on its flawed procedures, while pragmatists would probably ignore this and point to the fact that an important change took place. Yet, even pragmatists may admit that if symbolic events such as the National Convention are to be imbued with any historical significance, changes at the rhetorical level have to be accompanied by real actions and proof of commitment. Thus the answer to the question of the importance of the National Convention lies ultimately in its aftermath, in the extent to which actual changes can be attributed to the event.

CHAPTER 5

After the National Convention: Challenges and Obstacles

> Isn't it strange, surprising and pathetic? Are we not slow as a tortoise[?] This might underline that we are not serious about affecting [sic] and executing the institutions and civil structures that the National Convention created. But why create them when they are not going to function and deliver the goods to our great people? Is it not better for us to be doing something else, something more useful?
>
> *James Wani Igga*, SPLM Secretary General and Secretary for Finance and Economic Planning[1]

Supporters claim that after the National Convention the SPLM/A was radically transformed, from a militaristic, ineffective and exclusive rebel army to a democratic, streamlined, popular movement. But as Wani Igga's statement indicated, by 1996 it had become evident that such changes would not happen overnight. Moreover, considering the efforts put into defining the function and power of central SPLM/A organs, it might be surprising that the most significant changes in fact occurred at the somewhat neglected local levels. By the end of the decade, considerable strengthening of the local civil administration and attempts at empowering popular political structures could be observed in the more tranquil areas controlled by the SPLM/A. This change was not matched at the central and regional levels, where the most significant change was the adoption of liberal rhetoric.

The New Setting

In the period 1995–2000, the SPLM/A and its sympathisers had reasons for renewed optimism. Between late 1995 and the spring of 1997, the SPLM/A, in co-operation with armed groups within the National Democratic Alliance (NDA), managed through sweeping offensives to take back most of the territory had been lost after the 1991 split, as well as parts of eastern Sudan. The area under government control in Equatoria and the Bahr el-Ghazal was re-

[1] *Keynote Address*, presented to the *Conference on Civil Society and the Organization of Civil Authority in the New Sudan*, Sudan People's Liberation Movement (SPLM), 29 April 1996, p. 7.

duced to Juba and a few garrison towns.[2] In 1998, after the SPLM/A failed to capture Wau and Torit, the offensive lost momentum and the frontlines stabilised.[3] In Upper Nile the situation continued to be confused, but towards the end of the decade many Nuer commanders and soldiers returned to the SPLM/A.

This development was a consequence of both changes within the Sudan and regional and international processes. First, the NIF regime's radical Islamist agenda had increased the Sudan's international isolation and led to the estrangement of the government from neighbouring East African countries. By 1993, the United States and European countries had concluded that Hassan al-Turabi and President Bashir were leading a government actively supporting international terrorism, and consequently the Sudan was branded a "rogue state".[4] The SPLM/A could exploit Bashir's repeated calls for *jihad* to portray the war as religious, and thus win sympathy and support in the US and Western Europe. Similarly, slave raids conducted by government-supported militias caused outrage. The Western countries however were unwilling to directly support the opposition in toppling the regime.[5]

Neighbouring countries were apparently not restrained in the same way. The friendship between the Sudan and the new governments in Eritrea and Ethiopia evaporated as soon as the latter two discovered NIF sponsorship of the armed opposition groups within their own countries.[6] By 1996, both were ready to give military assistance to the SPLM/A and the NDA, and to facilitate political alliances against the NIF regime. Sudanese-Ugandan relations also turned sour after Khartoum's forces reached the Ugandan border in 1994 and

---

[2] I.e. Raga, Aweil, Wau, Gogrial, Torit and Kapoeta. GoS also controlled outposts along the railway to Wau.

[3] The halt was also connected to the border war between Ethiopia and Eritrea, which to the warring parties made the fate of the SPLM/A and the Southern Sudan rather insignificant in comparison. In addition it became important for both countries to ensure a certain degree of co-operation from the government in Khartoum. By the end of the decade, Uganda had made moves to improve relations with Khartoum with the aim of crushing the Khartoum-supported Lord's Resistance Army, which caused havoc in northern Uganda.

[4] In 1993 the Sudan was put on the US list of countries supporting terrorism. By 1995 it was clear that wanted terrorists like "Carlos" and Osama bin Laden had been given refuge by the NIF government. In the same year, an assassination attempt on the President of Egypt, Hosni Mubarak, was blamed on the Islamic regime and the assassins were harboured in the Sudan. The USA imposed economic sanctions on the Sudan in 1997 and bombed a pharmaceutical plant in Khartoum North in 1998, Holt and Daly, *A History of the Sudan*, pp. 192–93; Edgar O'Ballance, *Sudan: Civil War and Terrorism, 1956–99*, 1977, pp. 179–80, 183–86, 189–90.

[5] Yet, it has been alleged that the US government gave military equipment to Eritrea, Ethiopia and Uganda, which was destined for the SPLM/A, O'Ballance, *Sudan: Civil War and Terrorism*, p. 190; 'Outfitting Guerrillas?', *Sudan Up-date*, Vol. 7 (23), Dec. 1996.

[6] 'Testimony of Roger Winter Director U.S. Committee for Refugees on Terrorism and Sudan before the African Affairs Subcommittee Senate Foreign Relations Committee', 15 May 1997, pp. 6–7.

started to provide arms to the Lord's Resistance Army, which was attacking the SPLM/A as well as causing havoc in Equatoria and Northern Uganda. The NIF government consequently faced international isolation, and hostility from most of the neighbouring countries, while the SPLM/A and NDA obtained powerful allies. The new political balance had ramifications on developments at the fronts, where support from abroad caused a remarkable resurrection of the SPLM/A's exhausted military machine.

Secondly, as we have seen,[7] what had begun as the Nasir faction in 1991, and in 1993 had become the SPLA United, began to disintegrate. Some parts of the faction continued to portray themselves as competing liberation movements,[8] while others became local warlords without pretensions other than banditry, plundering the local population and looting relief deliveries.[9] Most of these groups ended up allied with the NIF regime, and both Lam Akol and Riek Machar signed "peace agreements"[10] and obtained positions in the government of Khartoum.[11]

Indeed Riek Machar arranged his own "national" convention in 1995, called the "Founding convention of the South Sudan Independence Movement/Army (SSIM/A)". This was clearly a copy of the 1994 SPLM/A National Convention, with the goal of creating unity within Machar's movement and changing its name and supposed scope. At the meeting, the new name was duly adopted, and a national liberation council and national executive council were elected. However, according to Peter A. Nyaba, the head of the preparation committee, the convention was a failure.[12] The SSIM/A started to fall apart during the meeting, which concluded with little consequence.

Just as some southern factions allied with the government in Khartoum, the SPLM/A, through the NDA framework, linked up with the Northern opposition parties, which agreed to active involvement in fighting the civil war. In 1995, a conference in Asmara formalised SPLM/A co-operation with, among others, the *Umma* party and Democratic Unionist Party.[13] For the first time in

---

[7] See pp. 37–38.

[8] These were mainly Lam Akol's and Riek Machar's factions.

[9] Kerubino Bol's "SPLA – Bahr el Ghazal" is the best example here, but William Nyuon's group might also be placed within this category.

[10] These were not comprehensive peace agreements intended to stop the fighting in the Southern Sudan. Rather, they formalised an already existing alliance between Khartoum and the Southern factions opposing the SPLM/A. These factions were supposed to continue fighting the Movement.

[11] The initiative was named "Peace from within". The argument used when promoting it was that it granted the South self-determination, but few expected this to be more than an empty promise.

[12] Nyaba, *The Politics of Libration*, pp. 143–46, provides a biased, but nonetheless informative, account of the convention.

[13] Kevane and Stiansen, *Kordofan Invaded*, 'Introduction', pp. 3–7; Peter N. Kok, *Governance and Conflict in the Sudan, 1985–1995: Analysis, Evaluation and Documentation*, 1996, pp. 216–68.

history these northern parties recognised Southerners' right to self-determination with full secession as an option, and it was agreed to create a secular state when the NIF regime was ousted. With support and encouragement from neighbouring countries, even the old enemies Sadiq al-Mahdi and John Garang were persuaded to collaborate.[14] This political polarisation – whereby the SPLM/A's rivals in the South joined with the NIF regime while northern opposition parties allied themselves with the SPLM/A – also had consequences for the developments in the different theatres of war. New fronts were opened in the east with support from Eritrea. In 1997, in the Southern Blue Nile region a massive offensive was launched by the SPLM/A with considerable assistance from the Ethiopian army.[15] The troops almost reached the Damazin dam, which provides electricity and water to several northern cities, including Khartoum. The fighting involved regular battles with fixed positions, rather than guerrilla hit-and-run strikes. The war had come to the North,[16] which not only had a symbolic effect, but also meant that the government in Khartoum had to spread its army to several fronts.

With regard to territory, it is fair to say that the SPLM/A had the upper hand by the year 2000, but a recurring factor – oil – threatened once again to tilt the balance between the two warring parties. In addition to holding their defensive positions in the garrison towns, the Khartoum regime tried to secure areas with known oil reserves around the town of Bentiu in what was called Unity Province. In 1997, China National Petroleum Corp. won a contract for construction of a pipeline from the oil fields to Port Sudan. This was completed in 1999. From then onwards, a significant amount of oil was produced and exported by foreign oil companies, while government forces and allied militias provided security. The areas south and east of Bentiu held by the Nasir faction and *Anyanya 2* militias served as buffers against SPLM/A sabotage teams.[17] By 2000, oil production had become a significant source of foreign revenue for the government in Khartoum,[18] and allowed a considerable in-

---

[14] In particular Eritrea was keen on facilitating the NDA, and in early 1996 even handed over the keys to the Sudanese embassy in Asmara to the NDA chairman, Mohamed Osman El-Mirghani. *Sudan News & Views*, 18 February 1996, p. 2.

[15] John Young, 'Sudan's South Blue Nile Territory and the Struggle Against Marginalization', in P. Kingston and I.S. Spears (eds), *States Within States: Incipient Political Entities in the Post-Cold War Era*, 2004.

[16] The SPLM/A also captured Kurmuk in 1987 and again in 1989, with aid from Ethiopia. Back then these reverses caused outrage in Khartoum, but government forces managed to re-capture the town after a few weeks, *ibid.*, pp. 3–5.

[17] Hutchinson, 'A Curse from God?', pp. 314, 323. The *Anyanya 2* commander, Pulino Matiep, is included in this group, even if he was not a part of the split in 1991.

[18] In his paper 'GOS Revenue, Oil and the Cost of the Civil War', 2002, Stiansen sought to estimate Khartoum's revenue from oil productions. He concludes that in 2000 the revenue derived from oil production was the government's most important source of income, p. 8. Considering that Sudanese oil production has increased since 2000, it is reasonable to assume that

crease in military expenditure.[19] Consequently, from 2000 onwards the government in Khartoum's strategy was to acquire more expensive military equipment in preparation for a major offensive. Meanwhile, continuation and expansion of the oil production was their main military objective.

By 1995, it became evident that Operation Lifeline Sudan (OLS) was not a temporary emergency operation, but would continue until the war ended or donors stopped funding it. Political and military developments had important consequences for OLS and the foreign NGOs' activities in the Southern Sudan. Insecurity, and the various guerrilla factions' and warlords' preying upon the NGOs' resources, required measures to protect relief operations. The UNHCR negotiated *Ground Rules*[20] wherein signatory factions committed themselves to the safety of relief operations. The SPLM/A offensives created food crises in the areas where the fighting took place, but they also secured other areas where internally displaced people could return or seek refuge, and where long-term projects could be implemented – despite the threat of air raids. The SPLM/A's 1998 attempt to capture Wau caused tension between the SPLM/A and the foreign NGOs, as drought and heavy fighting in the Bahr el-Ghazal triggered a famine, the worst in the Southern Sudan since 1991–92, and many died as a consequence.[21] Attempts to assist victims proved to be highly inadequate. The NGOs blamed both the SPLM/A and the government in Khartoum for the catastrophe. The warring parties were accused of stealing food supplies and hindering access for the relief agencies, while the SPLM/A maintained that Operation Lifeline Sudan and the NGOs were not doing enough for famine-stricken civilians.

A decade of activities under the OLS umbrella in the South ended with a serious dispute over the SPLM/A and its Sudan Relief and Rehabilitation Association's right to administer the foreign NGOs' activities in SPLM/A

Stiansen's conclusion is valid for subsequent years as well.

[19] An IMF report criticises a planned 35 per cent increase in military expenditure from 1999 to 2000, *Sudan: Staff Report for the 2000 Article IV Consultation and Fourth Review of the First Annual Programme under the Medium-Term Staff-Monitored Program*, Washington DC: IMF, May 2000. There has been proved to be a considerable increase in the import of expensive military hardware, the Chinese state oil company is one of the major shareholders in the Sudanese oil consortium, Greater Nile Petroleum Operating Company. China is one of Khartoum's main suppliers of small arms and small arms production facilities.

[20] See pp. 51–53.

[21] Perhaps as many as 100,000 people died because of the famine, Luka Biong Deng, 'Famine in the Sudan: Causes, Preparedness and Response: A Political, Social and Economic Analysis of the 1998 Bahr el-Ghazal Famine', 1999, p. 66. Another account of the famine can be found in Jemera Rone, *Famine in Sudan 1998: The Human Rights Causes*, 1999. OLS and the SPLM/A – SRRA conducted a joint inquiry into the causes of the famine, but this report has not been available, OLS/SPLM/SRRA, 'Joint Targeting and Vulnerability Task Force Final Report', 1998, mentioned in Bradbury, Leader and Mackintosh, 'The "Agreement on Ground Rules" in South Sudan', 2000, p. 58 (the page number refers to the online version, where pagination does not correspond with the report's 'Contents').

controlled areas. The Movement had for several years tried to extend its authority over these activities. This effort was intensified in 1999 when the SRRA secretary general, Elijah Malok, presented a *Memorandum of Understanding* intended to give the SPLM/A the same authority as the government in Khartoum had in dealing with the aid agencies operating in their territory. Observers interpreted this as an attempt to assert its sovereignty over their territory. In March 2000, after a period of negotiation, SRRA decided the agencies had to agree to its terms if they wanted to continue operating in the SPLM/A areas. Those with funding from the European Union terminated their operations. However, in general, the humanitarian situation improved in the 1994–2000 period and millions of dollars were spent annually on humanitarian relief and, to a far lesser extent, development activities.

The military advances – by excluding the government forces and rival factions from large areas of the South – gave the SPLM/A the opportunity to prove that the *NC Resolutions* were meant to have consequences beyond mere rhetoric. The continued presence of Operation Lifeline Sudan and foreign NGOs was an important factor in implementing the reforms. The WAR could be fought with Kalashnikovs, but a future peace had to be won in a different manner: the extent to which the reforms adopted at the National Convention were realised would test whether the SPLM/A had matured into a real people's liberation movement. Moreover, the degree of development of the state structures and the Movement's ability to put their promises into effect could prove to be valuable at the negotiation table. It is therefore reasonable to conclude that external political factors and military development in the period 1995–2000 provided the SPLM/A leadership with the opportunity as well as strong incentives to implement the *NC Resolutions*.

A Civil Society in the Southern Sudan?

What kind of organisations and institutions in the Southern Sudan in the second half of the 1990s can be included in the term "civil society"? The confusion between the emerging civil sphere of the SPLM/A government and civil society is reflected in the issues presented at the 1996 conference on *Civil Society and the Organization of Civil Authority of the New Sudan*. A need was perceived to define differences between civil society within the Southern Sudanese context and the civil authority. Part of the reason for this was that most of the civil branch of the SPLM/A was made up of the Sudan Relief and Rehabilitation Association, which had for a while claimed to be an NGO. Another reason was that it was hoped that Operation Lifeline Sudan administration, the foreign NGOs and external donors would finance both the SPLM administration (the "Civil Authority") as well as local NGOs (the "Civil Society"). Therefore, there was a requirement to demarcate the borders between spheres of responsibility, and to justify the existence of both types of institutions.

Sudanese Indigenous NGOs

The first Sudanese Indigenous NGOs (SINGOs), were the closest thing to civil society organisations in the Southern Sudan. These organisations were externally financed and focused their activities on providing services to the local population and carrying out activities for the foreign NGOs. The model activities of civil society organisations – to build organisations and networks expressing the opinions and needs of groups or certain geographical areas to the state – have not been the SINGOs' main ambition. There seem to have been two reasons for this divergence. First, the activities carried out by SINGOs are those which external donors are willing to fund, and to a certain extent the local population puts socio-economic progress before political activities. Secondly, providing services to the local population and attracting donor money were the only activities these organisations could safely engage in without threatening the SPLM/A's monopoly on power.

Indeed, African Rights states that merely by providing services, the SINGOs can be seen as competing with the SPLM/A for local prestige,[22] a view not borne out during local research for this book. It is also difficult to estimate the impact the SINGOs have had on socio-economic development in SPLM/A controlled areas. They seem to have provided a politically acceptable alternative for educated Southerners to contribute directly to the improvement of the lives of the civil population outside the Movement's structures. Acceptance of these organisations' activities, has helped to improve the SPLM/A's external image, but it is uncertain what impact they may have had on political development. This is a theme worth exploring in future research, since the development of SINGOs is relevant to both the discussion of imposed ideologies through relief and development aid, as well as aspects of governance in areas administered by rebel movements.

Peace and Reconciliation – Churches and Civil Society

The SPLM/A actively encouraged the establishment of the New Sudan Council of Churches (NSCC) and during the 1990s, relations with the Southern Sudanese churches improved.[23] However, there remained mutual distrust and scepticism. The core of the dispute has been NSCC unwillingness to succumb

---

[22] African Rights, *Food and Power*, p. 317.
[23] See p. 142.

to SPLM/A control and the persistence of a right to pursue an independent agenda. The SPLM/A leadership interpreted this as something close to disloyalty, and saw the New Sudan Council of Churches as a competitor, not only among the Southern Sudanese, but also within the international community. They viewed the NSCC as a haven for dissidents. In an environment where neither party wanted to accuse the other openly, whether the New Sudan Council of Churches really aimed at becoming the voice of Southerners or was only trying to follow its own programme is difficult to say. In 1997, there was a reconciliation meeting between the SPLA and the churches, organised by the NSCC. At least officially, this meeting appears to have brought the parties together and given the churches recognition to continue the role they had been playing in the intramural reconciliation process.

The "people-to-people" peace process on a popular level has consisted of several meetings between representatives of civilians caught up in the factional fighting during the 1990s. This has been characterised as a grassroots approach since the formal reconciliation process mainly consists of large meetings where the senior leaders of the factions have played only a minor role. There have been meetings between Nuer and Dinka, between different sub-tribes of the Nuer, as well as of various parties in Equatoria. This process has made manifest a considerable weariness among the civilian population caused by the factional fighting among Southerners; to end that fighting has been a prerequisite for security and the establishment of civilian structures. The meetings made it difficult for faction leaders to justify continuation of this fighting, and the "people-to-people" peace process contributed considerably to the peace agreement between John Garang and Riek Machar in early 2001.

Yet, the SPLM/A has had problems settling local disputes and effectively policing areas under its control, and these problems have not been solved through the "people-to-people" process. By allowing the process to take place, however, the SPLM/A demonstrated the political change that has taken place within the Movement. The increased reliance on the support of the local population and the foreign NGOs ever since the demise of the Mengistu regime in Ethiopia is also an important factor.

Operation Lifeline Sudan and the Foreign NGOs

Some scholars have characterised the political system in the Southern Sudan as dominated by foreigners and their priorities, nicknaming it "NGO-istan".[24]

---

[24] Volker Riehl, *Who is Ruling in South Sudan? The Role of NGOs in Rebuilding Socio-Political Order,* 2001. A similar perspective is in most of the NGO literature on this topic. In addition to the African Rights series, also in Bradbury, Leader and Mackintosh, 'The Agreement on Ground Rules', and in Iain Levine, 'Promoting Humanitarian Principles: The Southern Sudan Experience', 1997.

The tendency to demand that expatriate personnel be exempted from local law has been seen as a symbol of the foreign NGOs' power as well as of double standards. The focus of this debate has been the *Ground Rules* of 1995. As a consequence of high insecurity and increased aid operations, Operation Lifeline Sudan and the NGOs wanted improved protection from harassment and looting by the different armed fractions, including the SPLM/A.[25] The *Ground Rules* of 1992 were a set of principles, which were not observed by either side. In 1995 a new policy was adopted, the principles were extended, and these were printed in a small booklet.[26] The *Ground Rules* changed from an ultimatum to "the basis for a programme of education and consensus-building".[27] OLS arranged several workshops with the aim of explaining the rules to SPLM/A officials and officers. In order to make them more acceptable, emphasis was put on the similarity between these rules and traditional systems of justice.[28] The effectiveness of this approach as well as the entire *Ground Rules* policy has been questioned.[29]

The power wielded by these organisations may, however, have been overestimated. They have two points of leverage over the SPLM/A and the other factions: the threat of withdrawing and the ability to influence international opinion. They have been unwilling to use either. The NGOs themselves work within a competitive environment in which bad publicity for the SPLM/A can easily backfire on the agencies, in the sense that they can be viewed suspiciously for co-operating with guerrillas. As a result, donors might become more reluctant to fund projects in the Southern Sudan. Most the funding has been earmarked for emergency health aid and distribution of food and relief items. The administration of relief projects is extremely costly, and their benefits are not in proportion to the resources consumed in getting the aid to beneficiaries. Moreover, the threat of withdrawing is not particularly effective as there is little benefit in these projects for the SPLM/A beyond what can be "taxed" after food is distributed. Little money has been available for "soft" projects such as community development and support to local government structures,[30] which

---

[25] Unless specifically mentioned otherwise, the information regarding the *Ground Rules* is drawn from African Rights, *Food and Power*, pp. 326–31.

[26] The *Ground Rules* can be found in Appendix 2 in Bradbury, Leader and Mackintosh, 'The Agreement on Ground Rules'.

[27] African Rights, *Food and Power*, p. 327.

[28] African Rights puts it this way: "some observers have wondered how culturally appropriate it was for relatively young Europeans and North Americans to give lectures to Sudanese bishops and elders about humanitarian principles", *ibid.*, p. 328.

[29] Bradbury, Leader and Mackintosh, 'The Agreement on Ground Rules'.

[30] The most important programme in this regard has been the Sudan Transition and Rehabilitation (STAR) programme funded by USAID, but it has distributed most of its funds to foreign NGOS, SINGOs and local enterprises. Little has been available for strengthening the SPLM/A governmental structure, A.T. Salinas, and B.C. D'Silva, 'Evolution of a Transitional Strategy and

would have had much greater potential as economic leverage against the SPLM/A. However, even if such funds had been available and used actively in attempts to influence political development within SPLM/A controlled areas, it is far from certain that such measures would have had the desired effects.

Summary: Civil Society

The increased significance of Southern Sudanese organisations which are not affiliated with the SPLM/A is arguably an indication of the Movement's relaxation of control. What made this change possible was the SPLM/A's ability to capture larger areas and make them relatively safe. The competition for political supremacy was more or less over by 1995 and it was possible for the SPLM/A leadership to relax political control. The process of re-establishing trust could begin. However, the importance of the funds made available for locally based organisations such as the SINGOs should not be underestimated, and it is unlikely that any of these would have been established without external funding. Likewise, the churches and the New Sudan Council of Churches, without the good will and funding of international organisations, would not have managed to grow rapidly, and would probably not therefore have been perceived as threatening by the SPLM/A. Yet, despite increased diversification within the domain of locally funded organisations, it does not appear that the political influence of ordinary Southerners has increased significantly, regardless of the extent to which they have seen increased influence as a priority.

Structural Constraints

In a comprehensive analysis of the implementation of reforms within the SPLM/A and the areas under the Movement's control, structural limitations imposed by the civil war, e.g. lack of security and inadequate infrastructure and resources, should be discussed separately in order to be fully appreciated. These structural constraints have been presented by the SPLM/A leadership as the main reasons for slowness in the realization of the *NC Resolutions*.

Security

Maintenance of security is perhaps the most important requisite for creating an environment favourable for comprehensive governmental structures and social services. In SPLM/A controlled areas, this variable was influenced by several

---

Lessons Learned: USAID Funded Activities in the West Bank of Southern Sudan, 1993 to 1999', 1999.

factors. Most important was the distance from territory held by the government or competing factions. Others were the SPLM/A's ability to avoid splits and fighting within the Movement, to control tribal and clan fighting, to prevent cattle rustling, and to limit problems of desertion (precipitated by both the pursuers and the pursued harassing the local population).[31] The level of security dictates priorities for the local leadership: if the level of insecurity is high, measures to address it will be given priority over other tasks, including, justifiable halts in political reform and liberalisation processes. Food production and civilian movement will also be impeded by insecurity; in the worst case the local population will migrate to safer areas, within or outside SPLA control, leaving local authorities with no one to govern. Proximity to the front often leads to a high concentration of SPLA soldiers in an area, who often themselves pose a threat to security and increase pressure on available food resources. This also leads to conflicts over authority, as army commanders claim overall responsibility because of the immediate threat from the enemy. Important in this connection is the level of trust between SPLA commanders and the local population.

With regard to local security, there are three typical situations in the Southern Sudan. First, the Khartoum government occupies fortified garrison towns, and the SPLA controls the surrounding countryside. In these cases there is a high degree of insecurity because of the many SPLA soldiers in the area, and because government patrols or militia can harass the soldiers as well as the civil population. Secondly, in areas where a high level of insecurity is caused by the SPLA's inability to control local resistance and unrest. The situation in these areas can be just as difficult as in those close to towns held by government forces. Parts of Eastern Equatoria have been the most typical example.[32] A third category involves larger areas that are firmly under the control of the SPLM/A. It is mainly in these areas that the SPLM/A can develop civil administration with goals beyond supplying nearby troops, as it did to some degree in parts of Upper Nile and Bahr el-Ghazal in the period 1989–91. These achievements were nullified soon after the attempted coup in August 1991, when the Nasir faction took control over most of the Upper Nile and GoS strengthened its position in Bahr el-Gahzal. We have seen[33] that the Nuba Mountains have been an exception in this regard: despite constant fighting and international isolation, there has reportedly been an elaborate civil administration since 1992–93.

---

[31] Herbert Herzog, 'Report: Mission on Governance to Western Equatoria, Southern Sudan 27/07-22/08 1998', 1998.

[32] Johnson, *The Root Causes, passim*.

[33] See pp. 66–67, 89–90.

The setbacks for the SPLM/A in the period 1991–94 meant that by the time of the NC in 1994, there were few areas with a level of security sufficient for more than rudimentary local administration. The southern corner of Western Equatoria with Yambio at its centre, was the only town of significance held by the SPLM/A, and was therefore the main area where such activities could take place in the 1994–97 period. This area was significantly expanded by the SPLA offensives in 1995–97, when most of the Lakes area and Western Equatoria came under SPLM/A control. There was a similar development in SPLM/A controlled parts of the Southern Blue Nile region.[34] The Movement remained in control during the rest of the period under review, and in these areas created a stable political climate for the establishment of local political and administrative structures.

In short, the continuing high level of insecurity in most SPLM/A controlled areas in the period 1992–96 represented a serious hindrance to the establishment of more than basic local structures and severely limited opportunities for popular participation in decision-making processes.

Resources

The SPLM/A's inability to exploit the South's resources is well known,[35] and must be reckoned as an underlying factor in its slow implementation of reforms. The term "resource", however, can be further refined to include two main categories, human and material.

The SPLM/A has had two bases of human resources to draw upon: members of the movement predominantly assigned to military tasks, and other educated Southern Sudanese, mainly living abroad. Recruitment from the latter group has been limited because the SPLM/A leadership was sceptical of people outside the Movement, and, in any case, these people were often less than willing to commit themselves to a wage-less and uncomfortable life that included growing their own food. Training administrators has mainly been regarded as the responsibility of the foreign NGOs, but since few NGOs have had the funds or the interest for such projects, few have been trained.[36] However, the Sudan Relief and Rehabilitation Association arranged some courses during the period 1995–2000,[37] and candidates for training might have been drawn from outside the Movement. The SPLM/A has nevertheless chosen to rely

---

[34] Young, 'Sudan's South Blue Nile'.

[35] The Southern Sudan is rich in natural resources, and – especially in the southern parts – has optimal conditions for agriculture.

[36] The mainly German funded Institute for the Promotion of the Civil Society is the only organization strictly geared towards this type of activity.

[37] Herzog, 'Report: Mission on Governance', p. 23.

mainly on personnel already within the organisation, and our findings suggest that the SPLM/A leadership has not to any significant degree been willing to divert human resources from military tasks to civil assignments. The central secretariats and the regional administration have therefore remained more or less unmanned.

The SPLM/A's limited material resource base during this period was devoted to the "war effort". Little can be said about liquid funds.[38] The SPLM/A's budgets and accounts have not been accessible to the present author,[39] but it can be assumed that liquid funds were in very short supply, and in general were not available for development of civil government structures. The SPLM/A's income was limited because of its scanty taxation base and inability to institutionalise tax extraction. Consequently, it aimed at obtaining financial gifts from friendly countries and international donors for the establishment and maintenance of civil structures. It is mainly USAID that has been willing to contribute to the development of the society within the SPLM/A controlled areas and this money was generally aimed at SINGOs and local enterprises.[40] The result was that there was no money available to pay salaries, and to build and maintain government infrastructure. Slowing down of reforms caused by lack of liquid funds could to some extent have been reduced by contributions of infrastructure, office and communication equipment, vehicles, etc. But in this case too the army was given priority over civilian use.[41]

In most areas of the Southern Sudan there was a chronic shortage of food during the period 1995–2000. To give food to civil administrators instead of to the army could therefore have had direct consequences for the number of soldiers the Movement could mobilise and feed.[42] Even though the SPLM/A several times launched programmes for self-reliance, some have argued that relief aid[43] and food "mobilising" from the local population remained the main sources of food for SPLM/A military operations.[44]

---

[38] 'Liquid funds' in this context are understood as funds readily available and without restriction on how they should be spent. Examples are tax revenue, gifts to the Movement from sympathetic governments and income from mining and logging.

[39] In fact, it is improbable that most of the Movement's activities are budgeted, or the expenditures accounted for, at all.

[40] Salinas and D'Silva, 'Evolution of a Transitional Strategy'.

[41] Some regional governors had access to vehicles it seems, but they were also military leaders.

[42] It is necessary to take logistics into account: food surplus in southern Equatoria cannot feed army units in northern Bahr el-Ghazal as long as there is no means of transporting the food to where it is needed, and in such cases the surplus can just as well be used as salary for civil administrators.

[43] Johnson mentions that the SPLA normally taxed 20 per cent of relief food from the civilian population, *The Root Causes*, p. 152.

[44] Rone, *Famine in Sudan 1998*, pp. 118–20.

To develop local and central administrations in SPLM/A areas required a considerable amount of resources, which had to be acquired from somewhere. Either the Movement had to compromise spending on the army and the fighting of the war, or external agencies had to step in. Foreign agencies could, however, not do anything as long as their own donors were unwilling to support civil administration projects inimical to principles of neutrality. The result was that civil administration had to rely on internal SPLM/A resources and, consequently, was allocated only the amount of resources seen necessary to sustain the war effort.

Logistics and Communication

One of the basic attributes of a working civil administration is its ability to move information, people and goods within and between administrative units. Owing to a combination of climatic constraints and weak government finances, the establishment and maintenance of effective systems of communication and transport have been an exacting challenge in most of sub-Saharan Africa. This challenge was extraordinarily severe in the areas controlled by the SPLM/A in the 1990s. The rudimentary infrastructure established during colonial times, which was repaired and enhanced during the period of the Addis Ababa Agreement, had by the time of the split in 1991 been more or less destroyed.[45] During the rainy season, much of the Southern Sudan is rendered roadless, and only customised vehicles are of any use. In the 1990s, a number of basic airstrips remained usable, and some new ones were cleared. Air services were normally administered by OLS or the foreign NGOs, however, who would often do little to help the SPLM/A administration, even if some aid organisations were more willing than others to accommodate its needs. It is therefore reasonable to assume that the SPLM/A's civil administration mainly relied on movement on foot or by bicycle. To date, there has never been a comprehensive telephone system in the South, the closest being a rudimentary telegraph network established during the colonial period. There is no regular post service, and the main means of passing information has been through radio or by messenger. The result is that distance is still a much more important restriction on administration in the Southern Sudan than in most other places.

---

[45] Duffield et al., *SEOC Review*, give a detailed account of the logistical challenges met by the SEOC when trying to transport food over land and by air to locations in rebel-held areas of the Southern Sudan in the period 1991–94. This review and Karim et al., *OLS Review*, pp. 38–70, also provide several local case studies. SPLM/A's military victories in the late 1990s increased security but the road conditions were not significantly improved until 2003.

Summary: Structural Constraints

The structural difficulties of establishing and maintaining a government structure in SPLM/A controlled areas become more important as the area an administrative or political unit tries to cover increases in size. Put differently, it is easy to govern a village when its borders can be reached within a couple of minutes' walking, and where messages can be handed over personally. At the payam level, this is still fairly easy: messages and news can reach the whole area in less than a day. At the county level the structure is already stretched, and for an extensive administration, the county commissioner must rely on competent payam administrators.

It is at the county level that overall security becomes crucial for the efficiency of administration. If the general security level is low and the administrative centre is under the control of hostile forces, it is even more difficult to transport goods and communicate. This is because roads are designed to provide easy access from the centre to surrounding areas, which means that SPLM/A vehicles in many cases must take long detours circumventing garrison towns. This challenge increases with the size of the administrative echelon, thus difficulties caused by enemy held areas and towns within an administrative unit have been even more severe at the regional and central levels. There, the general logistical and communication problems have constrained efficient governance. The limited success of SPLM/A administrative reforms might be explained partly through structural constraints. Important as they are, however, they do not fully explain the lack of progress. Political factors must also be taken into account when the implementation of these reforms is assessed.

IMPLEMENTATION OF RESOLUTIONS

Although the National Convention itself has received positive attention from scholars, the implementation of its Resolutions has not been applauded. African Rights writes:

> By the time of the April 1996 Conference on Civil Society, Southerners were complaining that the Convention had been a charade, and that there was little point in organising a second Convention (or indeed another conference addressing similar issues) until the resolutions of the First Convention had actually been implemented.[46]

African Rights points out, however, that there has been a radical change in the Movement's rhetoric, with an increased emphasis on the importance of civil society and democracy.[47] Peter A. Nyaba's 1997 book on his experiences in both the SPLM/A and Nasir faction, similarly describes great hopes for the

---

[46] African Rights, *Food and Power*, p. 309.
[47] *Ibid.*, p. 311.

future of the Southern Sudan under the SPLM/A's reformed leadership structure, but by the end of 1999, in the second edition of the book, he has added several pages describing his disillusionment with political developments: "What is the SPLM and where is it?"[48] Nyaba's point was that he could not find the liberation *movement*, but only a liberation *army*. The pre-1994 militarism had continued even long after the National Convention.

How was the planned transformation outlined in formal documents, and what attempts were made to implement it at the various administrative levels? Hitherto, implementation of the *NC Resolutions* and the subsequent amendments and elaborations have received only limited scholarly attention. Comments on political developments after the NC have mainly revolved around the various meetings and conferences arranged by the SPLM/A. These activities have been important, and, to a certain extent, they are the SPLM/A's most significant achievement regarding governmental reform in the period up to 2000. In assessing the implementation of political and administrative reforms outlined in the *NC Resolutions*, however, it is unsatisfactory merely to investigate meetings. Although speeches and reports from these meetings can serve as benchmarks and illustrations of the process, a more comprehensive approach is required for a proper evaluation of political changes in the SPLM/A and the Southern Sudan as a whole in the second half of the 1990s.

SPLM/A Reforms, 1994–2000

The following chronology focuses on meetings and important documents, and presents an overview of the implementation of the reforms outlined in the *NC Resolutions* and on this process's internal logic. It takes the first meeting of the National Liberation Council (NLC) immediately after the NC as its point of departure. The introduction of the Leadership Council at the last NLC meeting in December 1999 represents a radical break with the reforms envisioned in the *NC Resolutions*, so the year 2000 is a suitable endpoint to the period studied here.

1994–95: The NC Resolutions, 'A Major Watershed' and Two Conferences

A civil government structure at the central level was initiated at the National Convention with the announcement of the birth of the "New Sudan" and of the primacy of the SPLM over the SPLA; the election of the National Liberation Council (NLC); and election of the SPLM/A Chairman. The first steps in

---

[48] Nyaba, *The Politics of Liberation*, p. 198.

carrying out the *NC Resolutions* were taken during the first meeting of the newly elected NLC, which took place immediately after the NC.[49] During this meeting two important amendments to the *NC Resolutions* were drafted and enacted.[50] These consisted of a list of persons appointed to the central secretariats and the office of regional governor, and a protocol explaining the ranking of positions within the civil and military hierarchies. These additions, together with the *NC Resolutions*, were presented in the publication *A Major Watershed*,[51] which was the only official publication from the Convention.

In 1995 two conferences with bearings on the implementation of the *NC Resolutions* were organised. In September[52] the SRRA initiated a "Conference on Humanitarian Assistance to the New Sudan". This was an opportunity for Operation Lifeline Sudan, foreign NGOs and the SPLM/A commanders to discuss hindrances to the implementation of humanitarian assistance programmes and the role of these programmes within the "New Sudan". The draft report from the conference has been characterised as surprisingly frank and open about the problem of lawlessness and the diversion of relief aid, and has been interpreted as an indication of a new openness within the Movement.[53] The second conference was the "SPLA Senior Officers Conference", which was held in the period 21 September – 21 October 1995. Reportedly, more than 800 officers participated.[54] Its main purpose was to facilitate implementation of the *NC Resolutions,* and to stop corruption and harassment of civilians by military personnel.[55] The conference was divided into two parts. [56] In the first, the NGO representatives and other foreigners "shared with the SPLM/SPLA the problems and difficulties faced in the humanitarian work in New Sudan."[57] In the second part, internal issues were discussed, including the separation of civil and military structures.

---

[49] Interview with Martin Okerruk, General Secretary NEC 26/3- 2002.

[50] The protocol was signed by John Garang on 6 June 1994 and the list of appointments is signed 3 June 1994, after the NLC meeting, *A Major Watershed*, pp. 38 and 46.

[51] *A Major Watershed*, pp. 39–46.

[52] September is indicated in the project papers, while the *Sudan Democratic Gazette* reported in June 1996 that the conference took place in November, p. 4. African Rights, *Food and Power*, p. 309, does not mention any specific date in its account.

[53] African Rights, *ibid.*

[54] Conference Organizing Committee, *Concept Paper: Conference on Civil Society and the Organization of Civil Authority of the New Sudan*, [no date], p. 8. The *Sudan Democratic Gazette* claims that it was more than a thousand, June 1996, p. 3. However, since the *Concept Paper* was prepared by the Movement itself and the organising committee would have no interest in underreporting the number of participants, 800 appears closer to the fact.

[55] Rohn, Adwok Nyaba and Maker Benjamin, 'Report on the Study of Local Structures', p. 7.

[56] *Concept Paper*, pp. 8–9.

[57] *Ibid.*, p. 8.

The SPLA Senior Officers Conference can be seen as a part of the process of implementing reforms owing to the involvement of a high number of military personnel, whereas previously only senior commanders had met during PMHC meetings.[58] The co-operation of senior commanders stationed in SPLM/A controlled areas was crucial for the effectiveness of the reforms. Those areas were rather isolated and the local SPLA commander had almost absolute authority. Moreover, by 1995 the new system for the local levels had not been outlined in detail; the *NC Resolutions* stated that the civil and military administrations should be separate, but it provided only a sketchy outline of new civil structures.[59] More research is required, however, to evaluate the achievements of these conferences, and to what degree they contributed to actual improvement in relations between the SPLA and civilian leaders as well as the foreign NGOs.[60]

The 1996 "Conference on Civil Society and the Organization of Civil Authority"

Perhaps the most important of the conferences organised in the wake of the National Convention was the "Conference on Civil Society and the Organization of Civil Authority" which was held in New Cush on 30 April – 4 May 1996. As in the case of the Convention, the purpose of convening the conference has been debated. The programme for the conference announced that "the primary objective of the Conference [was] to deliberate thoroughly and pass resolutions and recommendations that will help strengthen civil society and encourage the establishment of effective and accountable civil authority in the New Sudan."[61] Recommendations of the conference were meant to be adopted by the Movement. John Garang said in his opening speech to the conference that the NEC/NLC would meet later to "discuss the recommendations of the

---

[58] *Sudan Democratic Gazette* writes: "The importance of the conference lay in convincing the military leadership of the movement of the need to pursue the creation of a working civil society in the liberated areas", June 1996, p. 3.

[59] *NC Resolutions*, pp. 188–89.

[60] *Sudan Democratic Gazette* claims that there was a connection between this conference and the subsequent successful military offensive in October, but this is difficult to prove, June 1996 (73), p. 3.

[61] Sudan People's Liberation Movement (SPLM), 'Programme: Conference on Civil Society and the Organization of Civil Authority of the New Sudan', 29 April to May 1996, p. 2; Rohn, Adwok Nyaba and Maker Benjamin, 'Report on the Study of Local Structures', p. 8, give a similar description of the conference, stating that the objective of adapting the resolutions at the conference was to outline the role of civil society in SPLM/A controlled areas; to facilitate the growth of civil society; the establishment of local government structures; and to secure the rule of law through the establishment of a judiciary and para-legal training. The report is, however, slightly critical as it indicates that there was a lack of awareness as to how the conference recommendations would affect local autonomy.

conference, enact them into law, and to adopt the necessary measures for their implementation."[62] It seems, however, that neither the National Executive Council nor the National Liberation Council met until early 1997, almost a year after the conference, and it is unclear whether the recommendations were adopted as promised.[63] African Rights states that the real purpose of the conference was to enthuse foreigners: "Overall it resembled more a piece of theatre than [a] legislative process."[64] Nevertheless, when referring to the conference as a "legislative process" African Rights indicates that they expected the conference to issue laws and policies. But how could such a conference legitimately be a legislative forum? This question will be discussed further in the following.

1997–2000: Draft Constitution and More Meetings

The most important event of 1997 – in terms of improving the relationship between the SPLM/A and the civilian population and the international community – was the meeting between the SPLM/A leadership and Southern Sudanese church leaders at Kejiko on 21–24 July. The meeting was reportedly characterised by open dialogue and the addressing of delicate issues. Its report was fittingly called "Come Let Us Reason Together". This meeting did not have any direct consequence for the implementation of the SPLM/A reforms, but it was important for the "people-to-people" peace process. Both the SPLM/A and the NSCC were instrumental in this work, and it was necessary for them to coordinate efforts and find a platform for future co-operation.

The second official National Executive Council and National Liberation Council meeting was arranged at Bamurye in Kajo Keji County on 9–15 January 1997. It has not been possible to obtain any documentation from this meeting. It is likely that the resolutions from the 1996 "Conference on Civil Society and the Organization of Civil Authority", including the Civil Authority of New Sudan structure, were officially adopted by the Movement in the course of the NLC meeting.[65] As will be discussed in the following pages, another outcome was establishment of a Constitutional Committee, which drafted a constitution for the SPLM. In December 1998 at the third NLC

---

[62] Conference Organization Committee, *Report and Recommendations: Conference on Civil Society and the Organization of Civil Authority,* Himan-New Cush, 30 April – 4 May 1996, p. 5.

[63] Cf. note 62.

[64] African Rights, *Food and Power,* p. 311.

[65] There are two reasons to believe that this is what happened. John Garang indicated that the resolutions would be adopted. The resolutions from the 1998 NLC meeting mention that the 1997 NLC meeting had adopted at least 52 resolutions (p. 11), while the 1998 NLC meeting and the National Convention adopted fewer. This difference might be explained by assuming that the 1997 NLC meeting adopted the 45 resolutions from the 1996 Civil Society Conference, and some others were added during the NLC meeting. But clearly, more information is required before this hypothesis can be confirmed.

meeting, at Chukudum, a draft constitution for the SPLM/A was presented but rejected by the assembly. The fourth, and last meeting, was held in late 1999, at Guruk in Rumbek, when the NEC was dissolved and replaced by a much smaller Leadership Council.

Four other conferences were organised in this period: the "SPLM Women's Conference" held at New Cush, on 21–25 August 1998; "Rehabilitation and Restructuring of Legal Institutions and Law Enforcement Agencies", 14–20 April 1999; "Conference on Rights and Strengthening Resilience and Sustainable Livelihoods in Bahr el-Ghazal", May 1999; and "Workshop on Economic Good Governance", Yambio, 28 October – 3 November 1999. Of these meetings, it is the last that has had the strongest impact on implementation of the political reforms, and it spurred the drafting and publication of *Peace Through Development*, a booklet.[66] This – in addition to outlining the SPLM/A's economic policy – provides the most comprehensive outline of the Movement's strategy for achieving peace and at the same time announces the movement's policy towards most sectors of society. The women's conference was of little consequence beyond a symbolic recognition of women's role in the Movement, and was a result of the SPLM/A's need to constantly demonstrate gender awareness.[67]

* * *

The period 1994–96 was one of initial enthusiasm and concentrated efforts towards assimilating the new official policy into the Movement. It seems, however, that the civil society conference in 1996 marks a change of attitude. Subsequent conferences were less consequential and there appears to be a tendency to produce policy papers rather than action. Did these changes at the surface level have consequences for developments within the SPLM/A and the areas under the Movement's control? The last NLC meeting and the inauguration of the SPLM Leadership Council represent the end of the implementation of the *NC Resolutions'* central leadership structure. At the same time reforms at the local level finally started to pick up momentum.

A Constitution for the "New Sudan"?

We have seen that the *NC Resolutions* as a whole might be seen as a skeletal constitution for the "New Sudan". They could not be permanently altered except through another national convention. But, they were not detailed enough to serve as a blueprint for the implementation of reform. The need for

---

[66] The booklet was issued in 2000, it explains that it "is one of the main outputs of the economic governance workshop held in Yambio, New Sudan, during the last quarter of 1999", p. i.

[67] Endre Stiansen, 'Expectations of Development', 2002.

further elaboration of the reforms and institutions outlined in the *NC Resolutions* was the official reason for several revisions of the structures in the period 1994–2000, although there appear to have been other motives as well. Since there was no agreed procedure for how alterations could be made, and as these were not pursued in a consistent manner, the result was that by the end of the period the constitutional status of the "New Sudan" was, at best, unclear, and sometimes ambiguous.

Immediately after the National Convention a protocol, which specified the chain of command within the new structure, was presented in *A Major Watershed*. How the chain of command was arranged would have significant impact on the structure's functionality and the relative distribution of power between civil and military positions. The introduction of the protocol after the National Convention was beyond the scope of the National Executive Council and the National Liberation Council, and this might be the reason that the SPLM/A leadership tried to validate protocol arrangements by associating them with the Convention.[68] There is no trace of any deliberation or voting over a protocol arrangement in the *Proceedings* from the National Convention.

It will be recalled that the drafting of the SPLM/A Constitution was postponed during preparations for the National Convention. At the Convention, the Constitutional and Legal Affairs Committee, headed by Ambrose Riiny, was mandated to continue after the Convention, and one of the tasks assigned to it was discussion of "the concept of SPLM constitution",[69] while, simultaneously, the Political Affairs Committee would revise the SPLM/A Manifesto.[70] For the next two years little attention was apparently given to these issues, but in 1996 the "Conference on Civil Society and the Organization of Civil Authority" revivified the process by recommending establishment of a "Constitutional Committee", which would "prepare a draft constitution of the New Sudan."[71] In 1997 James Wani Igga was appointed to lead the committee.[72]

There was a significant difference between the mandate of this committee and that from the National Convention, in the sense that the old committee

---

[68] The origin of the 'Protocol' is not explicitly stated but it opens with the phrase "the system adopted by the National Convention of the Sudan People's Liberation Movement…", while it ends with John Garang's signature, dated 6 June 1994.

[69] 'Introduction and Background', *Proceedings,* p. xv.

[70] *Ibid.,* p. xiii.

[71] Recommendation 19 reads: "(The Conference further recommends that NEC/NLC takes appropriate actions to:) Establish a judicial review committee and possibly a Constitutional Committee to review laws and prepare a draft constitution of the New Sudan", Conference Organization Committee, *Report and Recommendations,* p. 18.

[72] Nyaba, *The Politics of Libration,* p. 199; John Luk confirmed in an interview that he and Wani Igga were members of this committee, Nairobi, 22.03.2002. It is quite probable that a committee had been established for this purpose, as was the SPLM's preferred approach. Moreover, it is not surprising that Wani Igga was given this task since by then he had managed to obtain a high position within the movement and was clearly interested in political reform.

was only to discuss the *concept* of a constitution while the new committee was given the task of *drafting* one. Moreover, the James Wani committee seems to have decided to combine preparation of a constitution with revision of the 1983 Manifesto, since the items originally expected to be included in the revised Manifesto were instead included in the document *Vision, Programme and Constitution for the Sudan People's Liberation Movement (SPLM)*.[73] It is probable that the committee used the political structure of the Ugandan National Resistance Army as a model for its work.[74] There are also significant differences between the system described in the 'NC Resolutions',[75] and the one outlined in the *Draft Constitution*. The latter outlines structures and functions in a much more elaborate and specific manner than the *NC Resolutions*. The main difference, however, is in the size of all parts of the governmental structure. For example, future national conventions – which the *Draft Constitution* suggests should be called "National Congresses" – were supposed to have "at least 3,000 [delegates]",[76] and the NLC was to be 350 members, almost a doubling of its size.[77] Considering that not all of the 825 delegates invited to the first National Convention were able to come and the difficulties in arranging NLC meetings had been one of the official reasons given for their meeting infrequently,[78] to suggest such huge meetings while the war continued appears somewhat counter-intuitive.

The suggested procedure for how the *Draft Constitution* would be adopted gives the impression that the Constitution Committee wanted to replace the *NC Resolutions* with the *Draft Constitution* as the fundamental law of the "New Sudan" as well as of the SPLM. The *Draft Constitution* states, "Any Provisions and Resolutions of the 1994 National Convention that are not incorporated into this Constitution shall be considered as part of this Constitution unless

---

[73] The content of the *Draft Constitution* will be discussed below.

[74] Nyaba, *The Politics of Libration,* p. 199.

[75] Reproduced in *A Major Watershed*.

[76] The relative distribution of delegates among the different categories is, however, more or less similar, *Draft Constitution*, p. 30. The *NC Resolutions* states nothing about the size of future national conventions.

[77] Another difference is in the organisation of the NEC. The *Draft Constitution* suggests that the NEC should be replaced by the National Political and Executive Committee (NAPEC) together with an SPLM Political Secretariat, pp. 36–37. A closer look at the NAPEC reveals that it is larger than the NEC, consisting of approximately 40 members.

[78] There may be several reasons for the legislators' suggestions. There was a desire to define principles for how SPLM/A controlled areas should be governed, regardless of the realism in the proposal, in order to give direction to the reforms. To propose large assemblies might have been seen as a way of signalling the SPLM/A's good intentions and democratic inclination towards external sources of funding, in particular Western countries, the multilateral organisations and foreign NGOs. Thirdly, the plans in the draft constitution could also be used as a point of departure for future peace negotiations, as well as for preparing the establishment of governmental structures in peacetime.

otherwise amended or repealed by some legal or procedural action."[79] There is still an important difference between the suggested procedure for adopting the *Draft Constitution*, and requirements for amending it after its adoption, even though the Constitution Committee must have been well aware that the *Draft Constitution* represented a restructuring of the whole SPLM/A government system.[80] The text in the *Draft Constitution* made it possible to enact it right away with the SPLM/A Chairman's approval. It is possible that the Committee wanted to give the impression that the changes suggested were unimportant and so could be adopted without the approval of a national congress or convention. This mode of reasoning would have been consistent with the procedure for the prior presentation of the protocol and subsequent reorganisation of the National Executive Council into the Leadership Council.

The process for adopting the *Draft Constitution* did not follow its pre-set trajectory. In March 1998 John Garang approved the draft by a provisional order,[81] and in late December 1998 the *Draft Constitution* was presented for approval at the third NEC meeting and the National Liberation Council meeting. Then the NEC, which was *not* mentioned at all in the procedure described in the *Draft Constitution*, proposed that the document not be adopted by the NLC but was rather to be reviewed and presented to the next national convention, or congress, scheduled to take place in the spring of 1999. This suggestion was endorsed by the subsequent NLC meeting.[82] Furthermore, the NEC, and subsequently the NLC, asked Garang to appoint a new committee to review the draft prior to the next convention. The available sources suggest no explanation of why the National Executive Council suddenly was involved in the adoption process, and this question might be pursued in future research. Even more complications arose when a second national convention or congress did not convene in 1999, five years after the first National Convention. Instead, a fourth National Liberation Council meeting was held at Guruk in Rumbek County in late 1999. Accounts of the meeting mention no discussion or the adoption of a constitution.[83]

---

[79] *Draft Constitution*, p. 79.

[80] Concerning the adoption the *Draft Constitution* says, "The Constitution shall come into force by a Provisional Order of the Chairman and shall subsequently be passed by simple majority of the NLC present.", p. 79. While an amendment after the adoption required "three quarters (3/4) majority decision of the members of the National Congress [National Convention]", which is clearly a much higher threshold than the former.

[81] Herzog, 'Report: Mission on Governance', p. 9. Nyaba claims that the draft was radically altered and presented as "The SPLM Vision 1997" (*The Politics of Libration*, p. 199), but the present author has found no document with this title, and it has therefore been impossible to confirm this.

[82] In the *Report and Resolutions of the National Liberation Council (NLC),* one may once again notice the way the NEC appears to have made the actual decision, which was subsequently, passively accepted by the NLC, p. 6.

[83] John Luk and Nyaba support the impression that the discussion of a constitution ended at the

It is difficult to establish exactly why the *Draft Constitution* was shelved, but apparently there was a desire within the SPLM/A leadership to move away from elaborate structures based on abstract ideals and towards more practicable goals. One resolution of the 1998 NLC meetings entailed an indirect criticism of the Constitution Committee when a new committee was going to be established with the purpose to

> review, evaluate and recommend the restructuring of the SPLM political, legislative, executive and judicial structures aiming at streamlining and making them responsive to the objective realities, organizational challenges and practical requirements of the current phase of the liberation struggle.[84]

This committee probably finished its work during 1999 and proposed the introduction of the new Leadership Council at the 1999 NLC meeting. The 1998 NLC meeting can therefore be seen as a turning point when a new policy was adopted, called "realistic" by its supporters and a "regression" by the SPLM/A's critics.

Even if the *Draft Constitution* was not formally enacted, it continues to be referred to as part of the Movement's legal basis. *Peace Through Development* states that the ideals of the National Convention[85] have been "enshrined in the draft '*SPLM Visions, Programme and Constitution*'."[86] The *Draft Constitution* introduced the concept of the SPLM as the central body connecting two separate structures: the SPLA or military wing, and the civil government, which now started to be called the Civil Authority of the New Sudan. This is how the structures are presented in *Peace Through Development* the last official publication concerning the organisation of the SPLM/A and the "New Sudan" in the period investigated here. Therefore, on the one hand the process of adopting a constitution has been delayed, while on the other hand, some changes to the *NC Resolutions* proposed in the *Draft Constitution* have already been enacted. This inconsistency has ramifications for the legitimacy of the "New Sudan" government structure.

The result of the alterations to the *NC Resolutions* was confusion concerning the *formal* status of both the "New Sudan" and the people living within SPLM/A controlled areas. The *NC Resolutions* strongly emphasised its mandate from "the people". Initially the National Liberation Council as representatives of the people, was set above the SPLM/A-New Sudan structure, while the NEC and the General Military Council were subordinate. In the aftermath of the Convention, the formal power of the Movement's organs vis-à-vis the NLC

1998 NLC meeting and did not come up again during the 1999 meeting.

[84] *Report and Resolutions*, p. 6.

[85] I.e. "participatory democracy, the respect of values and ideals of tolerance, human rights, the rule of law, accountability, transparency, and so forth", p. 12.

[86] *Ibid.*

has increased. The impression gained from the *Proceedings* and the *NC Resolutions* – that the Movement and the "New Sudan" were seen as two aspects of the same thing – has been confirmed in later documents, including the *Draft Constitution* and *Peace Through Development*. One consultant points out that the implication of the *Draft Constitution* is that the whole population of the territory defined as "New Sudan" is regulated by a civil authority which has its legal base in the constitution of a movement.[87] Put differently, an organisation takes on responsibilities that in most other cases are the prerogative of a state.

By 2000 the official line of the SPLM/A leadership was that the Convention as well as the *Draft Constitution* and even the Civil Authority of New Sudan were results of the Movement's political activities, and it was necessary to be a SPLM/A member in order to participate in the Civil Authority of New Sudan.[88] The "New Sudan" had become a state within a party. This meant that the "individual inhabitant of the territory will thus have his everyday life regulated by a SPLM Civil Authority irrespective if he/she is a SPLM member or not."[89] In *Peace Through Development* the Movement presents some clarification: the *Draft Constitution* is not for the "New Sudan", it is for the SPLM/A. After the civil war is over, a constitution for the "New Sudan" would be drafted. Meanwhile, the SPLM/A constitution will function as the constitution of the "New Sudan".[90]

At the 1999 National Liberation Council meeting, a new structure for the central government was presented. The National Executive Council was replaced by the Leadership Council, which included seven commissions. Each commission consisted of several secretariats.[91] The official reason for this alteration was, without further elaboration, "to ensure better mobilization of internal resources". Except for the reduction in size, how the new Leadership Council structure was supposed to be more efficient than the NEC was not explicitly stated, and as long as this remains the only visible innovation, the change certainly appears regressive in terms of democratic reform.[92]

---

[87] Herzog, 'Report: Mission on Governance', p. 15.

[88] Membership can be obtained either through becoming a soldier or registering as a member and paying an annual membership fee, *Draft Constitution,* pp. 25–26.

[89] Herzog, 'Report: Mission on Governance', p. 14.

[90] *Peace Through Development*, p. 17. By early 2003, the SPLM/A had still not adopted a temporary constitution for the "New Sudan", and it is unlikely that there will be any clarification on this issue until after peace negotiations are finalised or collapse.

[91] 'Major Shake Up of SPLM/A Structures: Move to Ensure Self-reliance', *SPLM/SPLA Update*, 1, January 2000, pp. 1–3; 'Briefing and Comments on IGAD Talks and NLC Meeting in Rumbek', *South Sudan Post*, Issue 6, Vol. 2, pp. 17–20.

[92] In a press conference following the 1999 NLC meeting Elijah Malok made a statement seeming to confirm the preference for efficiency over democracy: "Mr. Elijah Malok told the audience that the new structural organization of the SPLM is a positive move towards better performance of the SPLM organs. He said the SPLM is not yet a government and therefore its structures are war structures.", p. 19.

SPLM/A critics have claimed that "the formation of the Leadership Council and the appointments therein reflect a re-militarization of the Movement, a return to the bad old days of the Movement which produced the split within the ranks in 1991."[93] The Leadership Council is supposed to be "the highest political organ of the Movement."[94] If this implies that this Council is above the NLC as well, this supports the interpretation of a regression to the pre-1994 PMHC structure. But this is not explicitly stated in documents from the meeting. As of October 2004, the NLC had still not convened since 1999, which means that – at least in effect – the NLC has been abolished, and the process of formalising the *Draft Constitution* been tacitly postponed for an indefinite period. In connection with the recent peace negotiations the SPLM/A delegation consulted an advisory council consisting of SPLM/A cadres at different levels of the Movement's local government structures, and this indicates that although the NLC is virtually defunct, important issues are brought up in a larger forum that may be functionally equivalent to the NLC.[95]

Moreover, whether the NLC was involved in appointment of the Leadership Council in 1999 is not mentioned in the available documentation. Instead, documents refer to the Chairman's authority – not the NLC's – when explaining the new structure. It appears therefore that the Leadership Council is subordinate to the Chairman. The implication of all this is that the formal basis of the structure outlined in the *NC Resolutions* has been radically altered. At different instances, new outlines and organisational structures have been introduced. Seen from a strictly formal point of view, this practice undermines decisions made at the NC, and hence the legitimacy of the whole government structure. However, others would – and the SPLM/A does – argue that new structures must be adjusted to actual conditions in the South, and that alterations have to be expected for structures to function. The special conditions of a wartime government are indeed a factor that must be taken into account, but it might have been more sensible to state the experimental nature of the project right from the start.

Major Political and Administrative Reforms at the Central and Regional Levels

The sketchy *NC Resolutions* required further specification and elaboration of the SPLM/A administrative structure, which resulted in a process by which the content of reforms was developed in tandem with their implementation. Vari-

---

[93] Nyaba, *The Politics of Libration*, pp. 212–23.

[94] 'Major Shake Up', p. 1.

[95] A brief account of the political developments in the period 2000–04 occurs in the latter part of Chapter 6.

ous meetings and conferences became vehicles for legitimising alterations made to previous resolutions. Despite several conferences and the publication of policy papers, by the year 2000 it had become evident that actual changes in the way the SPLM/A was run had been limited.

What hindered implementation of the *NC Resolutions*? One observer answers this question in the same way as the SPLM/A leadership by referring to factors such as "the lack of resources, the reluctance of some SPLA officers to give up power, and continuing logistical difficulties on the ground."[96] These problems were real, but insufficient to explain the lack of results. Additional questions must be answered: Whose resources were not forthcoming; how did some SPLA officers come to be in a position where they could refuse to give up power; exactly which logistical difficulties hindered the handing over of power to the liberation councils at the different governmental levels; why enact reforms that within the existing conditions could not be implemented; were these the only reasons why the reforms did not proceed as planned in the period up to 2000?

The SPLM/A Chairman and the National Liberation Council

As mentioned earlier, prior to the National Convention in 1994 there were no formal checks on John Garang's powers as Chairman and Commander-in-Chief of the SPLM/A. His *actual* room for political manoeuvring is difficult to estimate, but apparently he had the last word in most policy issues and in matters concerning administration of the Movement and areas under its control. Local autonomy was a result of inadequate logistics and communication rather than of policy.[97] The *Proceedings* of the Convention explicitly state that election of a National Liberation Council was meant to remedy this situation.[98] An analysis of the new structure's formal outline of the distribution of powers at the central level shows what the SPLM/A and the Convention Organizing Committee suggested as a solution to this problem. Analysis of relevant documents issued in the period 1994–2000, most importantly the *NC Resolutions* and the *Draft Constitution*, demonstrates that compared to the stated intention, formal checks on the Chairman's power were surprisingly limited. The fact that the NLC was even weaker in reality enhances the impression that there was unwillingness or inability to limit the Chairman.

It was in particular the power to appoint and dismiss almost all other officials and officers within the Movement, the army and the Civil Authority of

---

[96] Lesch, *The Sudan*, pp. 201–202.
[97] Johnson, *The Root Causes*, p. 92.
[98] See Ch. 4, Section 2.

New Sudan, that made this position hugely powerful.[99] It was also nearly impossible to remove the Chairman. According to the *Draft Constitution*, the chairman can be dismissed only by a 3/4 vote of an extraordinary national convention, called for by 3/4 at least of the National Liberation Council members. These requirements ensured that Garang was virtually irremovable.[100] Therefore even at the formal level the promised restraints on the Chairman's power were inadequate.

The most significant formal changes wrought by the National Convention were the very establishment of a formal structure, and the requirement that the chairman's decisions were made subject to approval by a different body. These changes would have had an impact if they had been implemented. But the limited degree of re-distribution of formal powers following the Convention demonstrates a certain unwillingness to give the reform rhetoric real consequences for the organisation of the SPLM/A and the Southern Sudan.

The National Liberation Council can be seen as a smaller version of the National Convention in the sense that – similar to Convention delegates – NLC members were supposed to represent either geographical areas or parts of the SPLM/A organisation.[101] According to the *NC Resolutions*, the SPLM/A Chairman had the right to appoint both the head of the NLC and the whole National Executive Council (NEC). Moreover, the NEC was supposed to meet frequently, and consisted of, in addition to the Chairman and Deputy Chairman, secretaries with responsibilities for different sectors of the "New Sudan" government administration, later called the Civil Authority of the "New Sudan". Between National Executive Council meetings, the chairman was delegated the power to issue provisional orders that were to be revised at the next NEC meeting and at a subsequent National Liberation Council meeting.[102]

A Major Watershed explains the relationship between the NLC and the NEC in the following way:

> [The] National Liberation Council (NLC) and National Executive Council (NEC) constitute the Central and Executive Committees of the SPLM, as a Liberation Movement, as well as a political Movement and at the same time they form the organs of [the]

---

[99] The Chairman is obviously the leader of the SPLM/A, and he appoints the whole cabinet and leaders of the lower government echelons (Regional Governors and County Commissioners). He is also the SPLA Commander-in-Chief and appoints his General Staff and approves every promotion.

[100] Provided that all the 3,000+ delegates attended, which is rather unlikely when, for example, workers are given a quota of 115 in an area where there is no industry, and certainly not as many workers as the number of representatives; several hundred delegates were already appointed by the Chairman and cannot be reckoned to vote against him; and the vote would probably rely on the army which was personally loyal to Garang.

[101] The NLC is described in *Draft Constitution*, pp. 34–36; cf. *A Major Watershed*, pp. 1–3.

[102] It does not say when such orders can be used, but common sense would dictate that this was when decisions could not wait till the next NEC or NLC meeting.

Administration of the emerging New Sudan. In all these three instances, the NLC represents the Legislative body [*sic*] while the NEC represents the Executive Body.[103]

The SPLM/A leadership wanted to emphasise that they had not established a state or a state structure. Yet, this quotation suggests that the National Liberation Council was intended as a kind of parliament for the "New Sudan", with the NEC as its executive. This ambiguity can be explained as a vestige of the SPLM/A leadership's united Sudan policy, since a separation of government structures and party structures would give the "New Sudan" more resemblance to an independent state. Another relevant factor might be the desire to maintain direct control over "liberated" areas, as more autonomous structures would require a formal division of power and clearly defined decision-making processes.

The passage quoted above also indicates that there was confusion over the new structures as simultaneously central organs of the SPLM/A and the government of the "New Sudan". Establishment of the Civil Authority of the "New Sudan" was a way to distinguish between the Movement and the government structure, but it altered relations between the two bodies. The pre-eminence of the SPLM over the SPLA became even clearer with the introduction of the Leadership Council. But whether the Leadership Council took over the position of the NEC within the SPLM/A – Civil Authority of New Sudan structure is unclear. Relations between the NLC and the Leadership Council are not accounted for in descriptions of the new structures, another testimony to reluctance to distinguish between the Movement and the "New Sudan". But the structures for managing military affairs were not affected by the introduction of the Leadership Council, as these tasks continued to be delegated to a General Military Council appointed by the Chairman after the National Convention.[104] This brief description of the changing formal status of the Chairman, National Liberation Council and the National Executive Council and the relations between these institutions in period after the National Convention indicates that procedures for designing reforms as well as the way they were formally adopted were faulty, and in themselves obstacles to implementation.

Despite flaws at the formal level, if the political and administrative reforms outlined by *NC Resolutions* and other documents had been fully implemented it would have represented a fundamental change in how both the Movement and its territories were run. This was not the case. The National Liberation Council (NLC) did not have the opportunity to exercise the limited formal

---

[103] *A Major Watershed*, p. 40.

[104] 'NCR 8.2.0', *A Major Watershed*, pp. 9–10. As part of the Asmara Declaration a Joint Military Committee was established in order to co-ordinate military operations within the NDA. That John Garang was made head of the JMC does not appear to have had any consequential influence on the SPLM/A's military planning.

power vested in it. The NLC was supposed to be the legislative body of the movement, and to secure the ordinary members, and the general population, an opportunity, through their representatives, to influence the Movement's decisions. A minimum criterion for this to happen would be that the NLC met regularly. Organising the first NEC and NLC meetings immediately after the NC was a good start. But two and half years would pass before the next official NLC meeting. Some parts of the NEC may have held unofficial meetings, but these have not been documented.[105] The third NLC meeting was in December 1998, while the fourth and last for this period was in late 1999. The fact NLC meetings were held at all, indicates some will to implement the government structure enacted by the National Convention.

That the NLC met four times in the period 1994–2000 does not necessarily mean that the council functioned as intended, i.e. as the legislative assembly of the "New Sudan". In order for it to work properly, members needed to have the opportunity to reach informed and independent decisions on issues under consideration. In 1999 Peter A. Nyaba claims that the "institutions and structures of governance created by the First National Convention like the National Liberation Council (NLC) and the National Executive Council … have yet to become functional and effective":[106] not all members of the NEC had the opportunity even to attend its meetings, and they were not given documents in advance so that they could prepare properly. Such problems were probably even more pronounced for the NLC, since it was a much larger assembly, and most of its members were even less centrally placed within the SPLM/A, an assumption supported by close study of the *Report and Resolution* document from the 1998 National Liberation Council meeting.[107] Both General Military Council and NEC meetings were arranged immediately prior to the NLC meeting, and these adopted several resolutions that were apparently adopted by the NLC without comment or amendment; the resolutions that "derived from the actual NLC plenary session"[108] appear to have been relatively unimpor-

---

[105] In a speech at the Civil Society and Civil Authority Conference in 1996 Timothy Tot Chol stated that the NEC had "met only 4 or 5 times since it was formed in 1994", 'Civil Authority in the New Sudan: Organization, Functions and Problems', p. 4. The *Report and Resolutions* from the 1998 NLC meeting refer to "the third ordinary NEC meeting", which was held immediately before this NLC meeting, pp. 1 and 6. Since there had already been 4–5 meetings by 1996, one might assume that there were several NEC meetings in addition to the "ordinary" ones.

[106] Nyaba, *The Politics of Libration*, p. 198.

[107] It has been possible to obtain adequate documentation only from the 1998 NLC meeting, while information from the 1994 and 1999 meetings is available through secondary sources. The only information acquired about the 1997 meeting is that it took place.

[108] *Reports and Resolutions*, p.11.

tant.[109] This document leaves the impression of the NLC as a body for formal approval and not for important debates.

To what extent may the contingencies of war and the limited resources of the Movement be blamed for the shortcomings of the NLC? The NLC was supposed to be the Movement's and the "New Sudan's" highest political body between conventions. A deviation from the meeting schedule ought to have been accepted only if the Movement's existence was at stake. An ordinary democratic government would require its legislative body representing the people to meet at the established intervals – otherwise the government would be considered illegitimate. This means that, according to its own policy, to convene NLC meetings should have been the Movement's political top priority. As mentioned in the chronological overview, the SPLM/A organised several large conferences in the period 1995–2000, and even if these were for the most part externally financed, they still drew attention and manpower with organisational skills away from the arrangement of NLC meetings.

Some would argue that logistically National Liberation Council meetings were impossible to accomplish at the required times. But in 1994 the SPLM/A was considerably weaker than in the 1995–2000 period, and more than twice as many delegates attended the National Convention than the NLC. It is therefore fair to claim that had it had the political will to convene the NLC according to its schedule, the SPLM/A leadership would probably have managed to do it.

The Judiciary and the Regional Level

After the decision at the NC to establish an independent judiciary,[110] the issue was shelved for several years. The 1996 "Conference on Civil Society and the Organization of Civil Authority" found the "judicial and legal systems deficient" and identified several practical measures that should be taken.[111] It appears, however, that nothing was done until 1998. What triggered the decision to resurrect the plans for a judiciary is unclear. Whatever the reason might have been, the 1998 NEC meeting decided that a chief justice was to be appointed and that a Court of Appeal should be established, a decision that was endorsed some days later by the NLC.[112] The chief justice was to head the

---

[109] These resolutions were formulated in general terms and did not commit the Chairman, the JMC or the NEC to any specific goals. The issues were: support to the NDA; comment on the recent attempted assassination, which was blamed on Kerubino Bol; appeal to raise funds for the SPLM/A members arrested in connection with the assassination; more money for the "security organs"; extending the life of the NLC from May 1999 to December 1999; a National Anthem; and empowerment of women, *ibid.*, pp. 11–12.

[110] See Ch. 4, pp. 126–28.

[111] *Agenda*, pp. 22–23.

[112] *Report and Resolutions*, p. 7.

administration of the "New Sudan" court system and be president of the Court of Appeals. The extent of its independence from the "executive" is not explicitly mentioned, but it is worth noting that "the head of state"[113] would appoint the chief justice and that this appointment was to be approved by the "parliament"[114]. In the spring of 1999, at the conference "Rehabilitation and Restructuring of Legal Institutions and Law Enforcement Agencies", the appointment of the first chief justice was announced.[115] The available documentation is not sufficient for evaluating whether attempts at establishing a new court structure strengthened the legal protection of civilians in the SPLM/A areas or not.[116]

At the regional level a regional liberation council and some sort of regional executive were supposed to have been established. Little progress was made in this regard during the period 1994–2000. The regional governors were military leaders and seem to have been more concerned with the army than with politics and administration. But more research would be needed to establish exactly why this government level was developed only to a very limited degree, while significant progress was made at lower levels.

* * *

A point of criticism of the pre-1994 system was the militaristic fashion in which the Movement and the people were governed. One of the alleged achievements of the NC reforms was the decision to separate civilian affairs from the military, and weaken the predominance of the latter over the former. Most importantly, leaders at the central, regional and county levels, i.e. the Chairman, the regional governors and the county commissioners, head the civil administration while also being supreme military commanders at their levels. This makes it difficult to assess the relative strength of the civil and military branches.

One test case occurred during the process of defining this structure. This involved the ranking of NEC secretaries vis-à-vis regional governors. In an ordinary centralised state structure, the regional level would be subordinate to the central in the sense that central ministries would be empowered to instruct the regional level. In the case of the new SPLM/A structure adopted by the National Convention, the secretariats' right to instruct the regional level would not only be a minimum criterion for implementation of "national" policies,

---

[113] I.e. John Garang

[114] I.e. the NLC.

[115] The conference was in itself a symbol of increased interest in judicial issues. This may have been caused by one or several of the following reasons: clarification of difficult issues; official blessing from Garang; insight brought by external participants; or the promise of external funding.

[116] E.g. the explicit statement of the independence of the judiciary in the *NC Resolutions* is not reiterated in later documents such as the *Draft Constitution* and *Peace Through Development*.

but it would also symbolise the shift to the new policy whereby the NEC as part of the civil government structure would instruct high-level military leaders. The protocol printed in *A Major Watershed* demonstrates that the SPLM/A was *not* willing to take this step. The regional governors were placed in the hierarchy above the heads of the central secretariats.[117] The reason for this may be sought at the personal level and in the Movement's history. Some of the highest-ranking members of the SPLM/A were regional governors, and were generally regarded as "natural" leaders of their regions, in particular Yousuf Mekki in the Nuba Mountains, Malik Agar in Southern Blue Nile and Samuel Abu John in Equatoria.[118] It would have been very difficult for them to accept subordination to lesser personalities given posts as secretaries at the central level.

Parallel to political reforms at the central level, attempts were made to establish the new administrative structure and define its role within Southern Sudanese society. Secretaries with responsibility for various sectors were appointed to the NEC immediately after the NC. Most secretaries started developing policy, and they tried to recruit and train a core staff as well as establish links with the regional and county levels. The SPLM/A leadership was unwilling to provide qualified manpower and funding for this modest start. If previous attempts at financing the administration of the SRRA can be used as a measure, the new structure would base its activities on subsidies from OLS and the foreign NGOs and donors. Some would even argue that the whole purpose of announcing the establishment of the civil administration was to attract more international funding for the Movement.[119] Such funding was not forthcoming during the first years, and as a result the NEC secretaries became unimportant.

A closer look at the list of persons appointed to the various positions within the government reveals that they were recruited from among leaders of the SPLM/A. This increased the confusion over the difference between the new structure and the SPLM/A itself, while ensuring that even limited power was not given to more people than was strictly necessary. Notably, many members of the civil government had also been members of the Convention Organizing Committee (COC), including four out of five regional governors. Whether they were appointed to these positions because they were important members of the SPLM/A, or because they belonged to the reformist section of the Movement cannot be said for sure.

---

[117] *A Major Watershed*, p. 41.

[118] *Ibid.*, p. 36. Samuel Abu John is a person with special seniority. He is from the Zande people and was an officer in the *Anyanya 1* guerrilla army during the last part of the first civil war, as well as a senior politician during the period of the Addis Ababa peace agreement. Interview by Atem Yak Atem in *Horn of Africa Vision*, Vol. 1 (5), 1998, pp. 29–31.

[119] E.g., African Rights, *Food and Power*, pp. 311–12,

Statements made by some of these secretaries indicate that they felt marginalised. Since the *Concept Paper* from the 1996 "Conference on Civil Society and the Organization of Civil Authority" states a desire to "set up policies for the establishment of effective, efficient and accountable structures of civil administration",[120] it is clear that the work within these sectors had not got very far by 1996. Appointees worked on policy papers and elaborated on the sketchy outline of structures in the *NC Resolutions*. Several summed up their experiences at the 1996 "Conference on Civil Society and the Organization of Civil Authority". They were surprisingly critical and openly stated their disappointment with general developments. Lawrence Lual, the secretary of education, said: "I am now standing before you as the whole ministry (...). I am the Alpha and Omega for Education. This state of affairs is terribly embarrassing for me and the movement for that matter."[121] The regional administration fared no better. Regional Governor Kuol Manyang Juuk of Upper Nile Region reported, "as a governor my office has no research team, planners or reference books at the time I am making this speech. I have bodyguards and signalists, that is all."[122] Similar frustrations were reflected in the speeches by other representatives for the central and regional civil authorities.[123]

More research has to be conducted in order to detail the development of the central administration, but the establishment of a central finance secretariat indicates that the implementation of reforms foundered on lack of resources and the SPLM/A leadership's unwillingness to empower the new structures. Prior to the NC there was no formal system for handling the Movement's finances, with the possible exception of the SRRA, which had to account for its spending to external donors. This omission was supposed to be amended by establishment of a secretariat of finance. James Wani Igga was appointed to head this secretariat. In a speech at the Civil Society conference in 1996 he complained that he had presented a detailed policy paper to the National Executive Committee in August 1995, but that nothing had happened.[124] He had no power to levy taxes and demand fees. There was no revenue:

---

[120] P. 10.

[121] Lawrence Lual Lual, 'Statement on the State of Education Services in the Liberated Areas of the Sudan Today', presented to the Conference on Civil Society and the Organization of Civil Authority in the New Sudan, Sudan People's Liberation Movement (SPLM), 1996, p. 2. Lual defected to the Khartoum side less than a year later.

[122] Speech presented to the Conference on Civil Society and the Organization of Civil Authority in the New Sudan, Sudan People's Liberation Movement (SPLM), 1996, p. 1.

[123] In particular the following speeches: James Wani, 'Keynote Address'; Secretary for Public Administration and Local Government, Daniel Awet Akot, 'Experiences and Problems Encountered in the Organization of Civil Authorities at National Level'; Deputy Governor Equatoria Region, John Okwaki, 'Position Paper of Equatoria Region[:] Civil Authority Structure[:] its Establishment and Problems'; Secretary of Commerce and Supply, El Tahir Bior Abdallah Ajak, 'Speech'.

[124] *Keynote Address*, p. 6.

since the creation of the Secretariat of finance no region nor any of our NEC institutions ever deposited or remitted any penny. Oh dear! Yet it is two years already.[125]

Not only the external critics, but also reformists within the SPLM/A such as Wani had become impatient.[126]

In 1998 a new secretary of finance and economic planning, Arthur Akuien Chol, explained that in the previous year the NEC had decided that 70 per cent of the tax collected at the county level should be remitted to the central level, "but so far little has reached us". He continued, "I do not know whether the authorities in the counties collect and use the money or not. Maybe they are spending the money on war effort in their locality."[127] Thus by mid-1998 there was still no official system for tax extraction, or even routine communication between one of the most crucial secretariats and its lower echelons. Considering the importance of finances for a working government it is easy to extrapolate from this secretariat to the others. The education and health secretariats were in a better position than the others, however, since they had more ready access to external funding, but for this they also had to compete with the Sudan Relief and Rehabilitation Association, the New Sudan Council of Churches, SINGOs and local administrations.

Is it possible to consider the Civil Authority of New Sudan as a coherent centralised administrative structure at all? The regional level blocked communication between the central and local levels and as a result each county and central secretariat can be likened to an isolated administrative island. Can this state of affairs be attributed to lack of political will or were the structures impractical? Apparently, the answer is a bit of both, but compared to the political aspect – where unwillingness to hand over executive and legislative powers was an important factor – lack of resources, communication and educated personnel is the more crucial aspect. If the UN and other donors had provided the necessary training and funding, the SPLM/A leadership would have allowed establishment of more elaborate civil administration structures. While the Leadership Council represented a setback for democratic reforms, it does appear that the central secretariats improved their capacity.

The Local Level

In the period after the National Convention, attempts were made to expand and reform the system of local government in SPLM/A controlled areas. As was the case at the national level, civil administration was supposed to be separated from the military, and the population was to be involved in decision-making

---

[125] *Ibid.*, pp. 6–7.

[126] Towards the end, the *Keynote Address* turns into a lament over the general lack of progress.

[127] *Horn of Africa Vision*, 5/98, p. 19.

through local congresses and political bodies at three different levels (county, payam or village/boma). Although empirical material on this topic is meagre, it is still possible to conclude that the degree to which these reforms were implemented varies considerably. The general tendency has been of a reform process slow to pick up speed, but unlike the stagnation at the central and regional levels, there was positive development through a continuous drive towards realising and improving structures. The fact that local levels of the SPLM/A government structure were not strictly defined might have encouraged local adaptations and a more pragmatic approach, which again made implementation more feasible and the system more viable.

Formal Outline

Neither regional nor local government levels were designed to check the power of the central level, since the SPLM/A Chairman appointed the regional governor and the county commissioner. These positions were vested with powers at their level corresponding to those of the chairman at the central level. The structures were less elaborate than those at the central level, and consequently better adjusted to the situation at hand. These incorporated the old system of chiefs' courts, which were given judicial authority at the lower levels.[128]

The *NC Resolutions* draw up the general outline of the lower political and administrative levels: "The System of Congresses, Liberation Councils and Executive Councils shall be replicated at the Regional, County, Payam and Village levels."[129] The outline was not thorough and required clarification in order to be implemented in a uniform manner. The *Report and Recommendations* booklet from the "Conference on Civil Society and the Organization of Civil Authority" suggested that, "to resolve the issue of unclear definition of roles and functions involving various levels of Civil Authority the Conference recommended that the existence of Regions, Counties and Payams be legalised by law."[130] This recommendation indicates that attempts at establishing civil structures at the local levels had failed at least partly because of lack of formal definitions of these levels. Apparently the 1998 *Draft Constitution* tries to meet this recommendation by providing a detailed outline of the different organs and their functions. Although the *Draft Constitution* was not formally adopted by the SPLM/A, it seems that it has been used as a point of reference for structuring local political and administrative institutions.

As it is the principal administrative layer, the county level may serve as an example of the legal outline of the local government structure. A closer look at

---

[128] See pp. 72–73.
[129] *A Major Watershed*, pp. 7–8; an outline of the administration is provided as well, pp. 20–22.
[130] *Ibid.*, pp. 15–16.

the structures at county level drawn up in the *NC Resolutions* and *Draft Constitution*,[131] reveals that the County Congress was intended to be the supreme political body in each county, and consist of at least 1800 delegates. The delegates would be drawn from different payams, a number of associations (e.g. youth and women), the administration, chiefs, and delegates appointed by the SPLM County Chairman, who was also the County Commissioner. The congress was expected to meet twice a year, and its most important activities were to elect the County Liberation Council and to review decisions made by the Commissioner and his administration. The County Liberation Council was supposed to be composed of at least 51 members, and was to meet every three months and its decisions were to be reviewed by the County Congress. A County secretariat would take care of the day-to-day administration and arrange meetings of the County Congress and County Liberation Council. The *Draft Constitution* presents an almost identical structure for the boma and payam level, with only the size of the different fora and the frequency of meetings differing. To follow these requirements in the wartime context was clearly unrealistic, and the Constitution Committee must have been aware of this. To implement this system in every SPLM/A controlled county was as unattainable as the plans for the central and regional levels, consequently it appears that the Committee wanted to promote an ideal instead of effective solutions.

Implementation of the Reforms

Neither the available source material nor the scope of this book allows a comprehensive analysis of the implementation of political and administrative reforms at the local levels. Nevertheless, a brief survey of some local areas in the South indicates considerable local variances and that outcomes often depend on the level of security guaranteed by the SPLA and on access to competent administrators. There have, however, been some common challenges experienced where the new system replaced the old Sudan Relief and Rehabilitation Association (SRRA) and Civil/Military Administration (CMA) structures.

The first few years after the National Convention were a transitional period during which the newly established civil government structures had to compete for authority with the two already established organisational structures of the SPLA and the SRRA.[132] Prior to the National Convention, the local SPLA commander had the responsibility for security and providing supplies – food mainly – for the soldiers under his command. He had a Civil/Military Administrator who was the main link between the SPLA and the local population, often represented by chiefs. The SRRA monitored food production and as-

---

[131] *A Major Watershed*, pp. 20–22; *Draft Constitution*, Ch. 7–9.
[132] SRRA see pp. 73–75.

sessed the need for relief, as well as co-ordinating activities of the foreign NGOs. In some areas it functioned as a local administration. The new SPLM structure had to be wedged in between these two systems, taking over the responsibility of internal security, policing and food mobilisation from the SPLA; and from the SRRA, overall responsibility for provision of services and governing the local population. With administrative structures even at the village level, the new system also interfered with chiefs' authority.

The need to clarify fields of authority might partly explain why large numbers of SPLA officers and SRRA personnel participated in the previously mentioned conferences in 1995. The issues of protocol and chain of command were replicated at the County level, where local SPLA commanders refused to acknowledge the authority of civilian administrators. Complications occurred when the Commissioner, as the senior official, might be a civilian or have a lower rank in the army than that of the local SPLA commander. Active "reschooling" of the military commanders was required in order to address this problem.[133]

A general characteristic has been the establishment of new bomas, payams and counties. Both Rumbek and Yirol have been divided, and two new counties established. Bor County has been divided into North and South. In Rumbek and Yei, bomas have been divided. It appears that SPLM/A officials were not behind these divisions, but that they were created at the demand of the local population, who wanted to administer themselves and to negotiate directly with foreign NGOs for establishment of projects in their areas.

Yei River County in Western Equatoria illustrates this process. Western Equatoria has had the best conditions for establishing local structures. The area has been relatively secure since 1997, and after the first attacks on Yei in the late 1980s the SPLM/A has had a policy of trying to win the confidence of the local population through encouraging civil institutions.[134] This means that here one might expect the results of the reforms to be considerable.

Yei – Western Equatoria

Yei was among the major town centres "liberated" by the SPLA during the 1997 spring offensive. Yei is divided into five payams: Lanya, Morobo, Otogo, Tore and Yei town. A census was taken in 1983, and the county's population was 340,599.[135] The county administration was until 1997

---

[133] This was part of the purpose of the Senior Officers Conference mentioned above, pp. 140–41.

[134] Johnson, *The Root Causes*, pp. 85–87.

[135] 217,319 for Yei Rural Council, 96,063 for Kajo Kaji Rural Council and 27,214 for Yei Town Council, Johnson, communication with the author, 1 September 2004.

located in Otogo payam[136] in the southeast, since the town itself was still under government control. Yei is strategically placed close to the Democratic Republic of Congo and Uganda borders on the road to Juba. The capture of this town, together with Maridi, 120 km to the northwest, and Mundri, 130 km to the north, opened the southern parts of Bahr el-Ghazal for dry-season land transport. Consequently, Yei became a centre for relief and military operations and the SPLM/A moved parts of its administration from Nairobi to Yei.[137] For some years the town was regarded as the unofficial capital of the "New Sudan".[138] Yei was also to be a showcase for the new local administration system, the first county to be provided with a civilian administration.[139]

In 1995 the first significant effect of the *NC Resolutions* was experienced in Yei when Clement Ajo was appointed the first County Commissioner. According to Rohn, Adwok Nyaba and Maker Benjamin, "Report on the Study of Local Structures in Maridi, Mundri and Yei Counties" (1997), Ajo issued legislation and regulations for the county and payams, partly for the purpose of fighting corruption, which he thought could cause serious problems for the administration if not checked,[140] but also because the county administration's main task was to mobilise food and increase local support for the SPLM/A. Travelling on local roads was dangerous because of land mines,[141] and bicycles were the main means of transportation. When the SPLM/A recaptured Yei town in early 1997, there was no liberation council established at any of the local levels, and only a rudimentary county administration. However, the county administration offices could at least be moved from Otogo to the town. Yei, as an administrative centre, posed additional challenges to the County Commissioner's authority since the main regional administration of the SRRA was situated there, as well as the Commander of SPLA Sector II (Central and Western Equatoria). In addition, the regional governor had an office in Yei, and, as already mentioned, several of the national secretariats together with the SPLM leadership had moved there by 1998. It was difficult for the Commissioner of Yei to exercise his authority vis-à-vis the SPLM/A's senior civilian

---

[136] At that time the payam was called Ombasi, Interview with Justin Madi Samuel, head of administration in Otogo payam, 18.02.2002.

[137] By mid-1998 the following secretaries were established in Yei: legal affairs, local administration, interior, general health, as well as the SPLM HQ, Herzog, 'Report: Mission on Governance', p. 24; also, parts of the finance administration were moved, Atem Yak Atem, 'Rebuilding a Financial Base: An Interview with Arthur Akuiem Chol', *Horn of Africa Vision*, Vol. 1 (5), June 1998, p. 21.

[138] A title becoming increasingly nominal as the UNHCR moved its headquarters to Rumbek, and the SPLM and SRRA administrations followed suit.

[139] Herzog, 'Report: Mission on Governance', p. 23.

[140] Rohn, Adwok Nyaba and Maker Benjamin, 'Report on the Study of Local Structures', pp. 23–24.

[141] This was still a problem in 1998, Herzog, 'Report: Mission on Governance', p. 30.

and military commanders, and interference was one likely obstacle to the management of local administration.[142]

In 1998, however, there was a drive within SPLM/A controlled areas towards the election and establishment of liberation councils at the county, payam and boma levels. It is uncertain whether this urge was a consequence of the then expanded area under SPLM/A control, or of the drafting of a constitution at the central level of the SPLM.[143] In Yei a new turn in the implementation of reforms was apparently caused by a one-month course in civil society leadership skills in late 1997. The trainees were sent back to the payam and boma levels to set up civil authority structures.[144] Herzog reports how, as explained to him, the first boma elections in Otogo took place in the period 15–19 June 1998. The meeting was organised by one of the trainees, and 5,670 out of 8,000 inhabitants attended. Three persons nominated themselves for election as chairman of the boma liberation council, while the organiser appointed five more candidates. Participants voted by lining up behind their preferred candidate. The one receiving the most votes became chairman and the rest became secretaries and assistant secretaries. In addition the organiser appointed three ordinary members of the council.[145]

At the time Herzog conducted his investigation in July–August 1998, all the payams of Yei had held their congresses; the county congress took place on 20–24 July. He was informed of a similar high frequency of meetings in the other counties of Western Equatoria. According to Herzog, the boma administration consisted of a Boma Administrator heading a Boma Committee Executive. The administrator was often the local chief who also led the home guard and chief's court. The County Commissioner appointed the other members of the boma executive.[146] The Boma Liberation Council was supposed to meet every month to review the work of the executive.[147] There is no data available on how these institutions worked, but there are indications that the liberation councils at the lower level had little influence on political decisions, if they convened at all.

---

[142] This problem might have been exacerbated by the fact that Yei was the point of customs clearance for goods moving into the SPLM/A area. This activity generated a certain amount of revenue that might have been difficult for the Commissioner to avoid sharing with seniors.

[143] Herzog focuses on the process of establishing a constitution. But this was a process mainly taking place in Nairobi and, as mentioned, the plans were already shelved by 1998, 'Report: Mission on Governance', p. 9,

[144] *Ibid.*, p. 12.

[145] *Ibid.*, p. 17. It is difficult to say if this procedure was followed in the whole county. Herzog refers to a similar event from Karika boma in Mundri County. In Maridi all seven bomas held their congresses in the period 12–26 August 1998.

[146] *Ibid.*, p. 21.

[147] *Ibid.*, p. 22.

Lakes Region: Rumbek – Yirol

In the southeastern part of Bahr el-Ghazal called Lakes region lie the two counties of Rumbek and Yirol, named after their administrative centres. The counties are located within one of the SPLM/A core areas, and a large share of the Army's foot soldiers have been recruited from the region. Lack of resources and manpower, insecurity and distance to international borders have prevented the development of elaborate local political and administrative structures. This area was hit hard by the factional fighting during the first half of the 1990s, which facilitated the government in Khartoum's recapture of the towns in the 1992–93 offensives. As at Yei, the government's occupation was limited to the towns' immediate environs, and the surrounding area was under SPLM/A control. During the Uganda-supported offensive in spring 1997, the SPLM/A easily ousted the tiny isolated garrisons in both towns, and the counties of Rumbek and Yirol have been under absolute SPLM/A control since then. This has not ended insecurity, however, as the towns have been subject to frequent aerial bombardments and to sub-tribal and inter-clan fighting. The latter problem has been seen as a result of inadequate policing and security arrangements, and interpreted as an indication of the SPLM/A administration's inadequacy. The two counties have also remained relatively close to the main front in the north, and the struggle for control over the oil fields. Insecurity, enemy harassment, SPLM/A food "mobilisation", and drought have caused food deficits during most rainy seasons since the war started in 1983, sustaining a continuous demand for food aid. This has resulted in continuous relief activities, but not much long-term development.[148] The main activities of the local administrations, beyond collecting food for the SPLM/A and trying to maintain security, have been to facilitate the work of the foreign NGOs.

In Yirol, the first County Commissioner established liberation councils at the payam level, but these did not function. It was not until 2001 that this work was taken up again by one of his successors. There were problems with land and grazing rights when people who had fled the area returned and found their land occupied by others. The efficiency of the County administration appears to a large degree to have depended upon the personality of the commissioner, a situation reminiscent of colonial times.[149] In Rumbek, much the same development seems to have taken place, but with some interesting differences. In the late 1990s, as the SPLM/A consolidated its hold over the areas

---

[148] Norwegian People's Aid has had a long-standing agriculture and veterinary project in the western part of Yirol county, where, among other things, co-operatives and ox-plough schemes have been introduced. The SINGO BYDA has in later years also established long-term projects close to Yirol town. Since the influx of UN agencies and foreign NGOs to Rumbek town in 2000, the number of long-term projects has also increased in this area.

[149] Collins, *Shadows in the Grass*.

captured during the 1996–97 offensive, the UNHCR decided to move its Southern Sudan headquarters from Yei to Rumbek. Consequently, most of the other foreign NGOs and the SRRA followed suit, making Rumbek the hub of relief activities and leaving Yei as a backwater. The regional governor moved his office from Tonj to Rumbek as well. This concentration of offices re-created the problems of Yei, with overlapping authority and interference from above. The general impression from Yirol and Rumbek is that the local civil administration was less developed than at Yei, but that there were clear similarities between the systems. Except for the SINGOs and the chiefs, there seemed to be no popular organisation or participation in the decision-making processes.[150]

Southern Blue Nile

For areas such as the Southern Blue Nile region the history of political reforms is different. This area has been at the front of the NIF government's aggressive Islamisation programme, but it was the SPLM/A's decision to take the struggle to the North that brought the region into the civil war.[151] It was not until 1997 that the SPLM/A had a breakthrough in the area. During the late 1980s the SPLM/A had managed to establish a foothold in the Ingessana Hills on the border with Ethiopia, but they were not able to hold Kurmuk, the closest town. After support from Ethiopia ended in 1991, the SPLM/A was considerably weakened, and could do little to prevent Islamisation by the NIF and active suppression of the Christian minority. Until 1997 mostly Arabs from farther north had held positions requiring education.[152] There was expansion of large mechanised farms and exploitation of natural resources, in particular gold. Combined with heavy repression, this caused resentment towards the NIF regime in the region. When the SPLM/A took over, the business elite and most educated people, even primary school teachers, left.

Many people in the Southern Blue Nile region are Muslims but do not identify themselves as Arabs, and their interpretation of Islam is regarded as unorthodox.[153] Tensions have built up between the mainly non-Muslim SPLM/A and the local population. The SPLM/A has tried to appoint local educated people who fled from Khartoum controlled areas or defected from governmental forces, instead of SPLM/A cadres from other parts of the South. Even though both administrators and local people oppose the NIF govern-

---

[150] This is not a definite conclusion and it is possible that more extensive fieldwork may reveal more subtle channels of influence.

[151] The first civil war did not reach the Southern Blue Nile. One reason for this might have been the secessionist agenda of the *Anyanya 1*.

[152] Young, 'Sudan's South Blue Nile', pp. 70–71.

[153] *Ibid.*, p. 71.

ment, there are mixed feelings concerning an independent South, and the majority do not want to be left behind as a tiny minority in a future North Sudan. Social services are limited and infrastructure has been almost totally destroyed, leaving the population worse off than when the area was under NIF control. This means that the SPLM/A is under constant threat of losing the goodwill of the local population, unless they improve the situation. In sum, the SPLM/A's most important priority seems to have been to prove that it was worthwhile for the local population that the war was brought to them.

Progress at the Local Level?

In the period up to 2000, the achievements of the Civil Authority of "New Sudan" at the local level appear to be limited. The provision of basic social services and welfare was beyond the scope of this administration, and these tasks were left to foreign NGOs. It was even expected that the NGOs would take care of the training of administrators. Formal democratic procedures existed, but these do not appear to have been well comprehended by either the local population or the people responsible for elections. Yet, if the political aspect of the reforms was not implemented as planned, the administrative aspect has fared much better, at least in the more tranquil localities. Most important at a conceptual level may be the areas where the dominance of the military was reduced. There seems to be a consensus concerning the ideal that the civil population should be administered through civilian structures within which they have the right to be heard and to complain. But in the 1994–2000 period the wartime situation was used by the army as a way to justify interference in civilian matters, as well as to give civil structures a militaristic profile.

STAGNATION AND CHANGES: AN ASSESSMENT

There has been uneven development of political structures in the Southern Sudan since the 1994 National Convention. The implementation of the reforms at the national level stagnated soon after the Convention. The National Liberation Council and the National Executive Council met, but not as often as they were intended to, and their influence on political development within the Movement was weak. NEC secretaries responsible for different sectors were appointed, but wielded no real power nor did they have access to adequate resources for executing their tasks. Structures at the regional level were weak. The office of the Regional Governor lacked administrative capacity and the governors functioned as advisors and mediators for the County Commissioners when they met problems they could not solve alone. The shaky legal foundation of the process has been a problem, exacerbated by the introduction of contradictory constitutional documents.

It is first and foremost at the local level that the reforms have had an impact, even if they were slow to gain momentum and the effect varied across SPLM/A controlled areas. The main achievement in most places was that civil structures could to some extent protect the local population from abuse of power by military personnel, and that civilians were given the opportunity to live their lives with minimal interference from the SPLM/A. Improvement of the lives of the local population had become an end in itself. With regard to the development of democratic institutions it was still hardly possible for the average villager to have a say in local politics. But at least the chief's power increased vis-à-vis the military administrators.

How can this difference between the local level and the central and regional levels be explained, and how does it relate to the structural constraints presented earlier? Put differently, in discussing the malfunctioning National Liberation Council and lack of progress in implementation of the reforms in general, the key question is to what extent the SPLM/A leadership's inertia can be blamed, versus the contingencies of war and the Southern Sudan's current predicament. Critics blame the Movement, while supporters blame the lack of resources and the need to give priority to the war. We have attempted to demonstrate how these factors are interconnected. The difference between the central and the local levels is telling. Much more in the way of resources and manpower is required for establishment of functioning central and regional government structures. Reforms at this level would also mean radical transfer of power. The expectation that USAID and other donors would provide substantial funds for development of these structures might also be added to the explanation. But this will not happen as long as the SPLM/A leadership does not display willingness to give the central secretariats and other civilian officials more political room to manoeuvre. At the local level, a broad range of external and internal factors influence the outcome, but the fact that less power and prestige were at risk seems to have given local authorities more autonomy. Our research indicates that these factors have been equally important: without the will to make radical alterations in the political configuration, improvement in the logistical and resource situation would not necessarily mean significant progress in reform and vice versa.

The most striking change during the period 1994–2000 has been the SPLM/A's adoption of new rhetoric. Regardless of political manoeuvres and revisions of previous decisions, the Movement's leadership has officially committed itself to democracy and the protection of the civilian population as one of the most important objectives of the war. Before the National Convention, political meetings were mainly confined to peace talks and discussions among the top leaders of the SPLM/A. After the Convention, official meetings involving several institutions and assemblies of large numbers of people were frequently convened. The decisions reached at these meetings might have been inconsequential, but they were important in the sense that they provided opportunities for local representatives to voice their opinions.

CHAPTER 6

Conclusion

This book has analysed changes within the Sudan People's Liberation Movement/Army in the 1990s, and in particular attempts at reforming the Movement's political and administrative structures. Investigation of the National Convention in 1994 offered a way of describing political development in the Southern Sudan within the period. Detailed examination of this one event has provided insight into the general political development and the interaction of major Southern Sudanese constituencies. But although the National Convention was a significant achievement for the SPLM/A, the meeting and its results have not matched expectations.

The SPLM/A itself has described the decision to hold a National Convention as having been made before the split of 1991. But during the formative years 1983–1991, the goal of the movement had been to gain sufficient military and political momentum to topple successive governments in Khartoum. For this purpose a military organisation was well adapted; democracy, the promotion of civil society, and human rights were not priorities. Discussion of a National Congress before the summer of 1991, if there was any, has left no written traces. The fact that the SPLM/A's official statements in 1991–92 fail to mention the idea, and even display a negative attitude towards such meetings, undermines claims that the decision to organise the National Convention was reached earlier than February 1993. By then the SPLM/A's setbacks had reduced the insurgency to a pre-1988 level; the situation grew even worse thereafter. It is clear that the Convention was intended to assist the SPLM/A in escaping the political and military quagmire of the early 1990s.

Two events in 1991 – the cut-off of supplies from Ethiopia and the factional split – had a deep impact on the SPLM/A and on its military capacity. A propaganda war with other southern factions forced the Movement to change its policies, most notably by abandoning the commitment to a unitary Sudanese state in favour of support for self-determination. This brought the SPLM/A closer to public opinion, but it flirted with the secessionist stance that would spell international isolation. The result was the declaration at the National Convention of an ambiguous "New Sudan". In any case, with several guerrilla groups claiming to fight on behalf of Southerners, it was imperative to show that the SPLM/A was their legitimate representative.

The military setbacks of 1991–93 seemed to reinforce the SPLM/A leadership's determination to reform the Movement's political strategy. Until 1991 the SPLM/A had ridden a wave of success towards Juba and Khartoum. It was easy to justify the channelling of all resources into the military effort. Much changed after 1991. When in 1992 desperate attempts to capture Juba failed, no one believed that the war would end shortly. Consequently, at least until the fortunes of war changed, some new political arrangements were needed. The prospect of prolonged war also increased the importance of resources that could be extracted from foreign aid agencies operating inside the South. Since these agencies emphasised civilians' welfare, concern for civilians became a matter of some priority to the SPLM/A. Our assessment (in Chapter 3) of local institutions in SPLM/A controlled areas found that remnants of the colonial system of indirect rule were important for day-to-day administration, and that new church organisations and the opening up to local NGOs (or SINGOs) in 1993 appear to have been spurred mainly by the need for foreign NGOs to find local partners, rather than by any political strategy of the SPLM/A. Yet, this development would not have taken place if the SPLM/A had not allowed it.

A number of questions arise from the history of the National Convention's planning process about the SPLM/A's commitment to democratic change. To what extent was the outcome of the NC pre-determined by an extensive planning process? Who controlled or influenced that process? To what extent did changes in the Convention's agenda during the planning process indicate expansion of the Convention's intended scope? And in light of the manner in which NC delegates were selected, could the SPLM/A legitimately claim that the Convention gave it a mandate from the people of the Southern Sudan?

That the SPLM/A did indeed take the planning process so seriously is itself impressive, especially given the circumstances under which it took place. But it must be said that the way the Convention was planned undermined its outcome, in several ways. Establishment of a large Convention Organizing Committee was a promising start, but it was dominated by a few senior cadres, and it had to consult John Garang on most important issues. Whether meetings at Nimule, where the first draft of the political resolutions was hammered out, were more inclusive than those in Nairobi is uncertain, but the only voice that "the people of the Southern Sudan" had in the process, even indirectly, was through SPLM/A cadres appointed by John Garang.

The agenda for the National Convention was radically altered during the course of planning. What appeared initially to be a party congress came increasingly to resemble a constitutional assembly. Members of the COC themselves became uncertain about what exactly they were organising. Various drafts indicate that the scope of the Convention was expanded until the final agenda was quite clearly that of a constitutional assembly. This development has bearings on the legitimacy of the Convention: the SPLM/A is not a state structure.

By what right did a convention of the SPLM/A purport to be an assembly of the Southern Sudanese people? The Movement did not have party structures within the occupied areas, and considerable parts of the Southern Sudan were outside the SPLM/A's military control. People with military titles and top cadres of the Movement were over-represented at the Convention, and civilian delegates were outnumbered. All of this would not have been a problem if the National Convention had acted like a party congress. But the assembly declared a new state; established a five-layered government structure; and elected John Garang leader of the "New Sudan". How then should the Convention be judged? Should its formal shortcomings be forgiven in light of the improvements the NC represented compared to what had gone on before, and to what its rival factions were doing? A pragmatic approach would be to assess how the SPLM/A leadership used its new mandate.

The SPLM/A leadership wanted to present the 1994 National Convention as the congress of a political party, for several reasons. Such a stated purpose would preclude a declaration of independence from the North; the leadership intended to establish a more elaborate and efficient government in the Southern Sudan without signalling a separatist agenda. Secondly, a party congress would not require the same degree of popular involvement as a constitutional assembly. Preparation of an agenda and election of delegates could take place with the involvement of only a few cadres and commanders. Finally, if the SPLM/A were to establish a state structure based on democratic principles, opposition voices must be heard, and electoral arrangements put in place. A mere party meeting avoided these difficult questions.

But the National Convention itself, and the resolutions it adopted, much more closely resembled the business of a government than that of a party congress. The Southern Sudan ended up with what amounted to a one-party state, with the leader of the SPLM/A as its head.[1] Structures established at the NC apply to both the state and party; the only road to political power is through the Movement; the judiciary is the only formally independent government institution in "liberated" areas, and the Convention approved of even this only after extensive discussion.[2]

After the National Convention, the SPLM/A's position improved both politically and militarily. Yet, observers have been disappointed with the results of the National Convention. At the central or "national" level, the most important outcome was the establishment of several secretariats, and the organisation of sundry meetings and conferences. At the local level there was little change

---

[1] Rohn, Adwok Nyaba and Maker Benjamin give the following comment: "Through the resolutions (and in the protocol determined by the NC), it is quite clear that the National Convention, being a movement convention, saw the movement and the state as one (NCRs 2.5.0, 3.5.1 and others)", 'Report on the Study of Local Structures', p. 25.

[2] It would take several years before this decision was implemented.

during the period 1994–96, but after the SPLM/A captured several large towns and their surrounding areas, the basis for local reforms was in place. Noticeable changes occurred in several localities, particularly within the political dimension, but reform of local structures left much to be desired.

In his acceptance speech on the last day of the National Convention, John Garang summed up the results of the meeting.[3] He emphasised the renewal that the NC represented and went on to explain what this consisted of. "New Sudan", he said, differed from the "Southern Sudan": it represented a break with the past, and it included Southern Kordofan and Southern Blue Nile. But Garang maintained the ambiguity of the term "New Sudan" by saying, "(…) let us not be misunderstood in the rest of the regions of what we call the old Sudan. We have interests there also."[4] Whether "New Sudan" would be expanded or not remained to be seen. Concerning the new laws that had been adopted, he said that their most important function was to protect civilians, lest they "suffer from liberation."[5] These statements captured the essence of the National Convention, which was establishment of a government structure and promotion of the SPLM/A as a movement now dedicated to the protection of the civil population of the Southern Sudan.

The National Convention was a significant event in the political history of the Southern Sudan, and represents a turning point in the SPLM/A's history. But its consequences have been less momentous than expected. The effect of inadequate resources, insecurity, and lack of infrastructure should not be underestimated. And the SPLM/A leadership has been unwilling to share executive and legislative power in the manner envisaged in the *NC Resolutions*, or to give priority to establishment of the civil government structure sketched out in these resolutions.

Positive developments both politically and on the battlefield during the second half of the 1990s were largely owed to the NIF regime's increasing national and international isolation, and to increased aid to the SPLM/A from neighbouring countries. To what extent the changes wrought by the National Convention influenced this development is difficult to determine. But it is important not to undervalue their impact at the level of political discourse. The SPLM/A leadership, through the opening up of civil organisations and the stated aim of establishing democratic structures, committed itself. When the war ends, most of the reasons put forth for the lack of progress of political reforms will be nullified and the SPLM/A leadership will be accountable in an entirely different way.

---

[3] Partly transcribed in the *Proceedings* until the point where the secretariat ran out of tape, pp. 201–204.

[4] *Ibid.*, p. 201.

[5] *Ibid.*

Post-Script October 2004

The period between the forming of the Leadership Council in January 2000 and announcement of the first breakthrough in peace negotiations between the Khartoum government and the SPLM/A on 20 July 2002, saw a continued growth of the SPLM/A's political and military control over the Southern Sudan and its people. Military action took place mainly along the borders between north and south, in northern Bahr el-Gahzal, Upper Nile, the Nuba Mountains and along several fronts in the Blue Nile region, but also in eastern Equatoria. Although small victories were won and towns were captured and recaptured, a decisive victory was not in sight for either side. Peter Gadet's defection to the SPLM/A was a notable event: an important militia leader in the Upper Nile, he gave the SPLM/A an opportunity to strike Khartoum where it hurt most: the oil fields.

SPLM/A dominance over southern politics was confirmed by Riek Machar's return to the fold in January 2002. By then his own movement had collapsed and his political influence all but disappeared, but Riek still embodied open opposition and competition for power. His submission meant that the wound of 1991 was almost healed, a development paralleled by the work of the New Sudan Council of Churches in facilitating reconciliation at the local level in northern Bahr el-Gazal and in Upper Nile. Apparently the SPLM/A leadership did not consider organising another – overdue – national convention in the period 2000–2002, or take any other steps that would broaden decision-making, even though they were about to enter into peace negotiations and despite adequate funding, time, manpower and security. Ignoring the commitment to organise a second convention confirmed that SPLM/A leaders had seen the 1994 National Convention mainly as a way to change the Movement's image and to rally support.

Two factors are central for the analysis of external factors in the political developments of this period. The Sudan's oil production interested other countries in improving relations with Khartoum. Embassies were reopened and aid trickled in. But the most important change resulted from the attacks on the USA on 11 September 2001. Having accommodated Osama bin Laden during the 1990s and promoted militant Islamism in the region, the Sudan could easily have been included in the "Axis of Evil" and become a target for retaliation. Al-Bashir and his government therefore tried hard to become an ally in the "war on terror." The governments of Afghanistan and Iraq became the targets for US vengeance. In the Sudan the Bush administration chose the less expensive and potentially more prestigious path of promoting peace and reform.

The Danforth Initiative posed several tests to measure the willingness to make peace between the parties. The most important was a cease-fire in the

Nuba Mountains, which was achieved on 19 January 2002. Proper peace negotiations were resumed within the IGAD framework and the breakthrough of the Machakos Protocol occurred in the summer of 2002. This came as a great surprise to most observers; there had been numerous peace initiatives and negotiations, and nothing had indicated that the Machakos round was going to be any different. In fact, parallel to the IGAD process there was a competing peace initiative led by Egypt and Libya and favoured by Khartoum.

The Machakos Protocol elicited great optimism. It established exception from application of the Sharia, provided for self-determination for the South, and laid the foundation for subsequent negotiations. Some observers hoped for peace before the end of 2002, but important issues remained to be sorted out before a final agreement, and fighting continued on most fronts. In Equatoria the SPLM/A took Torit on 1 September 2002, causing Khartoum to suspend negotiations; when a government force re-took the town, negotiations resumed. At the end of 2002 a cessation-of-hostilities agreement was signed. The remaining issues to be negotiated included the fate of the SPLA after the war was over. Should it be merged with the Sudan Armed Forces or remain a separate entity? Other issues concerned distribution of power, oil revenue, and resources in general. The fate of the "contested areas", i.e. the Southern Blue Nile, Nuba Mountains and Abyei, proved particularly difficult. Almost a year would pass before significant progress could be observed.

In September 2003 direct negotiation between Vice-President Ali Osman Taha and John Garang was presented as a last resort. In Naivasha, weeks of intense discussions finally produced a breakthrough on issues related to security arrangements after the war. The agreement called for two separate armies and one joint force, the latter to be stationed in the South, in the contested areas, and in Khartoum. All militias would join one of the two armies. Further negotiations between Garang and Taha followed, but momentum was lost. The US Secretary of State, Colin Powell, tried to pressure the parties to promise a final agreement before the end of 2003. But all efforts to speed up the process failed. Not until January 2004 was peace brought another step closer, when an agreement on wealth sharing was reached. More pressure from the USA, Britain, and Norway achieved limited results in the following three months.

Then, in May 2004, the issues of the contested areas and power sharing were finally resolved. The Nuba Mountains and the Southern Blue Nile were to have limited autonomy within the northern Sudan. Abyei would be part of both the North and the South and, after the interim period, a referendum would finally decide for one or the other. Garang would be vice-president of the Sudan, but outside the order of succession. The Machakos peace process provided unprecedentedly positive international media coverage.

During the spring of 2004 the news turned sour. One year earlier attacks on government forces and installations in Darfur by local armed groups caused the latent low-intensity conflict there to escalate. These groups later presented themselves as two opposition forces, the Sudan Liberation Movement/Army and the Justice and Equality Movement. When Khartoum responded by recruiting and arming local militia groups, which internationally and by their victims became know as *Janjawiid*,[6] the conflict turned into a humanitarian disaster. The militias mainly attacked civilians. Many people were killed and more than a million ended up as refugees.

During the summer of 2004 it became clear that a final peace in the South would depend partly on a solution in Darfur. Garang made it clear that he could not be part of a national government that suppressed a rebellion fighting for causes similar to those of the SPLM/A. At the same time it became clear that what foreign observers had believed to be a solution of non-controversial details in some of the peace protocols would entail more hard bargaining. At the time of writing it is far from certain that peace in the Southern Sudan is at hand. If a comprehensive peace agreement *is* achieved, the existing government structures of the SPLM/A will be the point of departure for a future Government of the South Sudan.

Politically, the Southern Sudan has been holding its breath since the signing of the Machakos Protocol. The SPLM/A has continued consolidating its position through co-opting local groups and prominent individuals. This process has been most visible in Upper Nile and Equatoria. Regional consultation meetings were arranged during 2003, most impressively in the Nuba Mountains, where the SPLM/A gained a "mandate from the people" to finalise a peace agreement on their behalf. During the summer of 2004, after the signing of the six protocols in Naivasha, the SPLM/A leadership toured the whole of the "New Sudan". These are signs that the SPLM/A leadership recognises a need for legitimacy, even as it appears unwilling to share power or subject itself to the will of the people or to the SPLM membership at large.

The peace process has been criticised as exclusive and secretive. Northern members of the National Democratic Alliance, militia leaders and representatives of civilian groups in the South have demanded in vain to have seats at the negotiation table. But the long and difficult negotiations that ended with the signing of the six protocols would very likely still continue if a more inclusive process had been adopted. However, a lasting peace depends on the involvement of all these groups in reaching important decisions as soon as a comprehensive peace agreement is signed. It is the responsibility of the SPLM/A leadership to ensure that civil groups as well as major ethnic groups are included in decision-making during the six and a half year transitional period, both at

---

[6] *Janjawiid* means armed men on horseback. This has been a continuation of Khartoum's strategy of fighting by proxy as has been observed in other parts of the Sudan as well, see Chapter 2 note 56.

the Southern Sudan level and nationally. Political and economic marginalisation of ethnic groups or geographical areas is a recipe for continued military
conflict and creates further opportunities for the manipulation of southern
politics from Khartoum.

* * *

Peace will bring fundamental changes to the Southern Sudan and to the political and economic framework within which the SPLM/A operates. Under the
agreements already reached, the South will receive fifty percent of the revenue
from oil production in the South, and a massive influx of aid money into the
region is expected. The demands for functioning political and administrative
structures, and for political and economic rights and freedom of the press will
probably be considerable. Khartoum might try to impose its will on the South
through economic policies and by manipulating politicians and parties, perhaps combining with northern traders and business people who will try to
exploit new opportunities. Natural resources and outsourcing contracts will
attract interest from other countries and from multi-national companies. There
will be a need for law and order at a level totally different from what has existed
hitherto. The local population will demand protection from raiding and the
violence caused by local feuds; foreigners will demand a secure environment
for their investments. The main priority of the Movement will have to shift
from the war effort to establishing a viable government that can provide immediate and sustained benefits for the people of the South.

The prospect of peace presents enormous challenges to the leadership of the
SPLM/A. The process of policy reform that took place within the Movement
during the 1990s has been important, not because of its impact on the management of the SPLM/A and the administration of the areas under the Movement's control, but because it has brought to the fore the issue of how the
Southern Sudan should be governed and what is required to achieve this. In
addition, political liberalisation has engendered increased tolerance for opposition. But the lack of substantial changes within the political and administrative
structure of the Movement, now that peace is nearer, may become a threat to
the SPLM/A's survival as a political force in a post-conflict Sudan.

The peace negotiations have strained the leadership of the SPLM/A and its
educated members. Lack of political reform and administrative changes have
meant that there is still only a small group of people who both have the trust of
the leadership (John Garang), and are capable of representing the Movement
in detailed negotiations on economic and judicial issues. And parallel to the
negotiations a huge international apparatus has been built up for the planning
of reconstruction and provision of foreign aid to the post-war Sudan, which
has also demanded attention from senior decision makers and technical personnel. The SPLM/A leadership has also had to tour the Southern Sudan and

pay numerous visits to foreign governments and support groups. It is highly likely that the slow pace of the peace negotiations and the parallel planning process has been caused in part by the Movement's lack of technical capacity and the strain on decision makers.

These problems will only intensify when a peace agreement is reached. It has already been agreed that the SPLM/A will have 28 per cent of the seats in the National Assembly and that at least 20 per cent of National Civil Service positions will be filled by Southerners. The political and administrative structures in the South will also have to be manned. The SPLM/A alone does not have the qualified manpower to fill these positions. This situation might have been different if plans for democratic institutions had been given more resources and these had been invested with real power. In particular, if the Liberation Councils at the Southern Sudan/national level and a civilian administration structure led by national ministries had been given the opportunity to develop, it is likely that the conversion to peace would have been much easier. There would have been a large number of people trained in democratic participation and civil administration. There are still several ways for the SPLM/A to tackle this challenge. One is to use all available manpower regardless of political affiliation, but even this might not be enough. It is also possible simply to leave posts vacant. The worst possible solution is to give administrative posts to persons without qualifications as a favour or reward. This must be avoided at any cost as it would result in inefficiency and abuse of power which again would undoubtedly bring disillusionment and resentment in their wake for "the people of New Sudan".

Appendix 1

COMMENTS ON IMPORTANT SOURCES

Most of the sources discussed in this dissertation are SPLM/A documents, which are rather hard to come by. At least until 1993, it appears that the Movement did not put much effort into preserving records of their decisions. This is understandable considering their limited resources, and that such records had little immediate value.[1] There are still some documents available, but these are mainly press releases, official resolutions and speeches made by John Garang. By the time of the planning for the National Convention there seems to have been a change in this policy. The preparations for the NC as well as the NC itself can be followed in some detail through different types of minutes and documents, some obviously not intended for the public. The period after the NC shows a much greater openness and a willingness to document the process of implementing the *NC Resolutions*. Several conferences were held and some of them are quite well documented.

Unfortunately, it has not been possible to get hold of minutes and resolutions from three out of four National Liberation Council meetings, nor to obtain sufficient oral accounts to amend this short-coming. In fact, it has not even been possible to establish whether such minutes exist.[2] However, as has been demonstrated in Chapter 5, it is still possible to deduce some possible facts from the one available set of resolutions as well as other sources commenting on these meetings. Below is a presentation of some of the key documents employed in the research for this book.

CHAPTERS 2 AND 3

Chapter 2 – on the general political development in the Southern Sudan in the period 1991–94 – relies partly on secondary literature, but also on newsletters from the Southern armed factions, two extensive reviews of relief operations during the period[3] as well as other indigenous NGO reports and newsletters. Chapter 3 is divided into two sections. The first section, focusing on political changes within the SPLM/A in the aftermath of the split, utilises press releases and resolutions from the meetings in the Political Military High Command.

---

[1] Quite the contrary, leaking of documents could cause more damage than word-of-mouth leaks.

[2] Nevertheless, considering the new interest in written records within the SPLM/A after the NC, and the fact that resolutions exist from one of the meetings, it is rather likely that at least the resolutions adopted at the meetings were recorded.

[3] Karim et al., *OLS Review*; Duffield et al., *SEOC Review*.

The second section which analyses the local institutions in the 1991–94 period, mainly utilises documents and reports from the international humanitarian organisations.

CHAPTER 4

Chapter Four discusses the National Convention and the preceding preparations and is the part which most heavily relies on SPLM/A documents. This chapter uses documents from the planning process prior to the NC. A Convention Organizing Committee (COC) was formed in July 1993 and their written mandate, the minutes from the five meetings held in Nairobi during August 1993 (referred to as the *Minutes*), and the semi-official announcement of the results from these meetings are central documents in this chapter. What is special about these *Minutes* is that they try to account for the debate prior to the decisions at a level of detail where each person's comment is accounted for. Yet, the *Minutes* only provide summaries of the comments and contributions to the discussions, which means that what is written is what the reporter, Joseph Garang[4], perceived the person was saying. Also, the *Minutes* are written in rather feeble English, which sometimes is close to unintelligible. This heightens the inaccuracy as it might well be that the reporter was using incorrect words or phrases.

While paying attention to these shortcomings, Chapter 4 discusses how the agenda for the National Convention was developed, and how the quotas for the delegations were decided. Chapter 4 relies almost solely on the *Minutes and Proceedings of the SPLM First National Convention (NC)* (referred to as the *Proceedings*) The *Proceedings* consist of 236 pages, appendices and introduction included, and was written by the Convention secretariat.[5]

The document is not a complete narrative of the NC; it is, instead, a patchwork of summaries of speeches; full text of speeches; summaries of comments; draft resolutions; the actual *NC Resolutions*, a list of delegates; and lists of members elected to the National Liberation Council. The various sessions of the NC are unevenly accounted for. For example, the exact timing of the elections was recorded, while certain days are not accounted for at all. As a record of debates and – most importantly – decisions, the document is unsatisfactory. Most of the speeches and position papers seem to be reiterations of written documents instead of transcripts of the actual speeches. It is difficult to establish to what degree these documents reflect what was actually said at the NC, considering that some of the speakers might not have read directly from their

---

[4] Garang is a common name in parts of the Southern Sudan, and whether this person is related to John Garang is unknown to the author.

[5] The *Proceedings* were signed by four persons: Elijah Malok, Martin Okerruk, Kosti Manibe, and Stephen Wondu, 'Introduction and Background', p. xv.

manuscripts. The parts where the *Proceedings* give short summaries of the some of speeches and comments might be closer to the facts.

Furthermore, it is unclear exactly for whom the *Proceedings* were written. One expects that the composition of an as accurate as possible record of the events and decisions of the Convention would be given priority, but instead the voting and debates are presented quite inaccurately. When reading passages like the one concerning John Garang's election quoted in Chapter 4,[6] it is tempting to believe that the *Proceedings* were written just as much as a propaganda piece, demonstrating how the organisation has improved. Moreover, the passage suggests one important purpose for the meeting, namely to demonstrate the SPLM/A leadership's legitimacy. The description of the "spontaneous" celebration of the election of John Garang and Salva Kiir gives the impression of having been staged, or at least heavily encouraged. This description is also quite different from the one given at the end of the *Proceedings*. The former tells a story of spontaneous dancing and reading of poems, while the latter describes the reaction to the elections of the SPLM/A leadership in the following way: "The August Convention went wild with joy of this [the election of John Garang]. Revolutionary songs were sung, revolutionary slogans were chanted for a considerable time to show the consent of everyone to Dr John Garang's election."[7] It might be that both the chanting and singing took place as well as the dancing, but the dissimilarity of the two accounts shows that they were written with different purposes in mind. The one with the dancing and poems emphasises the cultural diversity and how the SPLM/A harbours them, while the other is planted within the old left-wing rhetorics where uniformity and the dedication to the revolution is focused upon. Nevertheless, close scrutiny and familiarisation with source material from this period makes it possible to filter out most of the propaganda, which still leaves a rich source of information about the political process surrounding the NC. Also, the minute-takers had problems with local languages, e.g. on the discussion on the suggestions from the political committee the *Proceedings* say "Someone from Yirol: Spoke in Dinka. He was applauded by those who knew Dinka."[8]

Another interesting aspect of the document is that it is possible to follow the development of the *NC Resolutions* closely. First, the COC drafted the *Agenda* which was the point of departure for the discussion at the NC. Then, during the first days of the convention, the *ad hoc* committees gave their comments together with different parts of the SPLM/A. After that, different parts of the suggested resolutions were discussed in committees. Later, the leaders and secretaries of the committees came together and put together a draft resolution

---

[6] See Ch. 4, p. 118.

[7] P. 198.

[8] *Proceedings*, p. 145.

which was discussed at the final session of the NC. At the end, the final resolutions, the *NC Resolutions*, were adopted by the assembly. This documentation of the different stages of the drafting provides an insight into issues discussed and controversies that emerged during the NC. There are however some factors reducing the value of the document. Most of the debates are not accounted for, and often it is only the results of the debates at the different stages that are presented. In the cases where opinions *have* been recorded they tend to be shrouded in set phrases and slogans, and only delicate nuances show difference in opinions. There are exceptions, however, as has been demonstrated in Chapter 4.

Unfortunately, it has turned out to be difficult to find independent accounts of the NC, which could have counter-balanced the bias and the missing parts in the *Proceedings*. Interviews with participants, and with one of the observers, left much to be desired.[9] Some of the informants had difficulties in remembering exactly what happened; others were unwilling to give precise information, while others again gave contradicting records. It is however necessary to point out that the interviews were conducted prior to the acquisition of the most important parts of the written sources, and the information from these documents could therefore not be utilised for the purpose of formulating more precise questions or help trigger the informants in their recollection of the events. They did, however, substantiate the doubts about the exhaustiveness of the *Proceedings*.

CHAPTER 5

Chapter 5 relies on a variety of sources. Two single documents receive special attention. The first is the *Vision, Programme and Constitution of the Sudan People's Liberation Movement*. This document is referred to as the *Draft Constitution* since it has not been formally adopted by the Movement. However, it is often referred to as a part of its constitutional basis; hence, the legal status of the document is somewhat ambiguous. The fact that it is not the formal constitution of the Movement does in some sense reduce its value as a historical source, but it is still significant, in particular when studied as a product of a political process. It also provides an insight into the political priorities and power relations within the SPLM/A at this moment This becomes evident when the document is compared with the second document which receives special attention in Chapter 5, *Report and Resolutions* from the 1998 meeting of the National Liberation Council (NLC) – the meeting where the decision on not adopting the draft constitution was made. The *Report and Resolutions* is interesting be-

---

[9] Members of the COC Elijah Malok and Martin Okerruk were interviewed. The NPA Resident Representative Helge Rohn was present one of the days. Other NC delegates interviewed: Ayan Magwat, chief Makeny Kamic Apetbiu, and Adiel Maher.

cause it is the only record obtained from the NLC meetings, and it is particularly valuable because it was preceded by meetings in the two other central SPLM/A councils of that time – the National Executive Council and the Joint Military Council – whose resolutions are included in the *Report and Resolutions*.

One set of documents is related to the 1996 Conference on Civil Society and Civil Authority. It has been possible to collect a range of manuscripts for the speeches held at this conference, preparation documents as well as a booklet which was publicised in the aftermath. The booklet contains a short description of the conference and the resolutions adopted. Some of the people appointed to the new positions at the central and regional level delivered speeches on their experiences from the execution of their offices, some of them quite frank and open. As the contexts in which these speeches were held are known, studying these speeches provides a glimpse into the process of implementing the *NC Resolutions*. It has also been possible to obtain documents from several other conferences of varying significance which gives insight into various aspects of the implementation of different aspects of the *NC Resolutions*.

Chapter 5 also includes a brief analysis of changes at the local level at different locations within the Southern Sudan. Most of these locations were visited during the field trip, and – in addition to documentary sources – this analysis draws upon insights obtained during the field visit and discussions with local authorities, Sudanese Indigenous NGO staff, and International NGO personnel. This information has been contrasted and complemented with different types of reports and studies.

Bibliography

PUBLISHED AND UNPUBLISHED SUDAN PEOPLE'S LIBERATION
MOVEMENT/ARMY – SUDAN RELIEF AND REHABILITATION ASSOCIATIONAL
MATERIALS

a. 'The Constitution of Sudan Relief and Rehabilitation Association' dated 2 Sep-
    tember 1984.[1]

b. 'Statement to the Sudanese People on the Current Situation in the Sudan, by
    Dr. John Garang de Mabior Chairman and Commander-in Chief, SPLM/SPLA',
    10 August 1989.

c. The SPLM/SPLA Political High Command, *The SPLM/SPLA Torit Resolutions*,
    Torit, 12 September 1991, pp. 1–13.

d. The SPLM/SPLA Political High Command, *Bedden Falls Resolutions*, Bedden Falls,
    9 August, 1992, pp. 1–11.

e. Briefing Notes on Sudanese Conflict by John Garang de Mabior, 10 February
    1993, pp. 1–12.

f. SPLM/SPLA Press Release, Kampala, 20 February 1993, pp. 1–5.

g. 'Communication from The Chairman and C-in-C, SPLM/A to The Chief of Staff,
    SPLA to be communicated to all GFSCC members and All Units/Ref. No.: Con-
    vention/Date: 30/7/1993', pp. 1–6.

h. Minutes of the Convention Organisation Committee (COC) 1–5, Nairobi:
    1. 15 August, pp. 1–14.
    2. 17 August, pp. 1–17.
    3. 18 August, pp. 1–14.
    4. 23 August, pp. 1–3.
    5. 26 August, pp. 1–3.

i. Communication from The Chairman and C-in-C, SPLM/A, to Cdr Yusuf Kuwa
    Makke, Chairman COC [with copy to all units within the SPLM/A as well as "all
    village, payam, county and IAC councils"], Ref. No.: SPM/SPLA/Conven./Date:
    30/8/1993, pp. 1-8.

j. *Agenda for the First SPLM/SPLA National Convention and Recommendations of the
    Convention Organizing Committee (COC)*.

k. 'Minutes and Proceedings of the SPLM First National Convention (NC)', 15 April
    1994.

---

[1] See Ch. 3, note 70, for an evaluation of this source's authenticity

l.   *A Major Watershed: SPLM/SPLA First National Convention Resolutions, Appoint-ments and Protocol*, Chukudum, New Sudan: Sudan People's Liberation Movement (SPLM) Secretariat of Information and Culture, n. d. (1994?).

m.   Conference Organizing Committee, *Concept Paper: Conference on Civil Society and the Organization of Civil Authority of the New Sudan*, [no date].

n.   Sudan People's Liberation Movement, *Programme: Conference on Civil Society and the Organization of Civil Authority of the New Sudan* (29 April to 4 May 1996).

o.   Conference Organization Committee, *Report and Recommendations: Conference on Civil Society and the Organization of Civil Authority* (April 30 – May 4 1996), Himan-New Cush

p.   Speeches from the 1996 "Conference on Civil Society and the Organization of Civil Authority" mentioned in the text:

   1. James Wani, Secretary for Public Administration and Local Government, 'Keynote Address'.

   2. Daniel Awet Akot, 'Experiences and Problems Encountered in the Organization of Civil Authorities at [the] National Level'.

   3. John Okwaki, Deputy Governor Equatoria Region, 'Position Paper of Equatoria Region: Civil Authority Structure Its Establishment and Problems'.

   4. El Tahir Bior Abdallah Ajak, Secretary of Commerce and Supply, 'Speech'.

   5. Timothy Tot Chol, 'Civil Authority in the New Sudan: Organization, Func-tions and Problems'.

   6. Lawrence Lual Lual, 'Statement on the State of Education Services in the Liber-ated Areas of the Sudan Today'.

   7. Regional Governor Kuol Manyang Juuk of Upper Nile Region, 'Speech pre-sented to the Conference on Civil Society and the Organization of Civil Author-ity in the New Sudan, Sudan People's Liberation Movement (SPLM).

q.   'Report and Resolutions of The National Liberation Council (NLC) meeting held 25–27 December, 1998, Himan-New Cush, New Sudan.

r.   *Vision, Programme and Constitution of the Sudan People's Liberation Movement (SPLM)*, Yei and New Cush, New Sudan: SPLM Political Secretariat, March 1998.

s.   *Peace Through Development: Perspectives and Prospects in the Sudan*, the Sudan People's Liberation Movement, February 2000.

t.   Suzanne Samson Jambo, *SPLM Women's Conference 1998 held in New Cush, New Sudan on 21–25 August 1998, Full Report*.

u.   Professor George Tombe Lako, *Workshop on Economic Good Governance, Yambio – New Sudan, October 28 to November 3, 1999* [dated 4 December 1999].

UNPUBLISHED SOURCES: ARCHIVES

a.   Norwegian Archives
   1. Norwegian People's Aid archive, Oslo
   2. Norwegian Church Aid archive, Oslo

b. Nairobi archives

    1. Norwegian People's Aid archive

    2. Norwegian Church Aid archive

c. Southern Sudan archives

The archives consulted in the Southern Sudan reflected the status of the civil administration and were all in poor shape. Pre-war archives were all lost. The documents in the archives were all recent from after SPLM/A reoccupied the towns during 1997. Most documents were handwritten, some were typed. Archives visited were:

    1. Yei River County archive

    2. Rumbek County archive

    3. Yirol County archive

UNPUBLISHED SOURCES: OTHER DOCUMENTS

a. 'Testimony of Roger Winter, Director U.S. Committee for Refugees, on Terrorism and Sudan before the African Affairs Subcommittee, Senate Foreign Relations Committee', 15 May 1997.

b. 'Testimony of Jemera Rone, Human Rights Watch, on Crises in Sudan and Northern Uganda', before the House Subcommittee on International Operations, and Human Rights and the Subcommittee on Africa, 29 July, 1998. http://www.house.gov/international_relations/105th/hr/wshr729982.htm

UNPUBLISHED SOURCES: ORAL INTERVIEWS (ordered by date)

Most of the interviews were taped and are, for the time being, only available from the author. Below, a list of the most important informants consulted in Oslo and during the fieldwork in the period 02.02.02 - 26.03.03:

Place and Date	Informant
Oslo 03.01.02	Stein Erik Horjen, Progamme Officer NCA
Oslo 14.01.02	Helge Rohn, former NPA Resident Rep. Nairobi (1992–96)
Oslo 16.01.02	Halle Jørn Hanssen, former General Secretary NPA
Nairobi, 07.02.02	Anne Itto, Development Assistance Technical Office (DATO)
Rumbek, 11.02.02	Daniel Nok, BYDA Area Manager Rumbek
Yei, 14.02.02	Mary Apai, member of NLC
Yei, 16.02.02	Fabein Lasuba, Administrator Hqrs and E.O., Yei County
Yei, 18.02.02	Justin Mudi Samuel, Head of Adm., Otogo payam
Yei, 21.02.02	Agnes Asha Chairlady of the Christian Women's Empowerment Project (CWEP) and Azanda Umi, CWEP Secretary
Yei, 22.02.02	Samuel Abur John, SPLM/A Regional Secretary Equatoria Region
Yei, 22.02.02	Daniel Yumi
Yirol, 26.02.02	Daniel Wel, BYDA Area Manager/Project Manager Yirol
Agany, 25.02.02	Sisto Mapel Makeiny, Police captain Agany payam
Agany, 25.02.02	Joseph Mamot Mabor, Payam Administrator

Rumbek, 28.02.02	Adiel Maher, NSWA Chairlady, Rumbek County
Rumbek, 28.02.02	Ayan Magwat, manager of Panda Hotel, Rumbek
Rumbek, 28.02.02	Paul Macuei Malok, County Secretary Rumbek
Rumbek, 01.03.02	Mario Mayek Manum, NSCC BEG Ecumenical field officer Rumbek
Rumbek, 01.03.02	Elija Malok, Secretary General SRRA
Rumbek, 01.03.02	Daniel Deng Manydit, Deputy Regional Secretary BEG
Agany, 04.03.02	Daniel Kon, Executive Chief
Agany, 05.03.02	Chief Dut, Paramount Chief
Agany, 05.03.02	Dr. Michael, retired field surgeon for the SPLM/A
Rumbek, 06.03.02	Cdr. Majak d'Agoot, Regional Head of SPLA, Bahr el-Ghazal
Yirol, 07.03.02	Isaac Kon Anok, newly appointed County Secretary of Aweril, former Commissioner of Yirol (1994-96), Yirol
Yirol 07.03.02	Chief Bone and Chief Makeny Kamic Apetbiu
Yirol, 07.03.02	Cdr Rin, County Secretary Yirol
Mapur Dit, 08.03.02	John Maja, Payam Administrator
Nairobi, 12.03.02	Daniel Deng, SPLM/A
Nairobi, 15.03.02	Edward Lino, head of external security SPLM/A
Nairobi, 16.03.02	Cirino Hiteng, Assistant Professor of International Relations and Politics, School of Arts and Sciences, United States International University, Nairobi.
Nairobi, 19.03.02	Sitouna A. Osman, NSWF Managing Director
Nairobi, 20.03.02	Professor George Tombe Lako, Economic Society of New Sudan
Nairobi, 21.03.02	Suzanne Samson Jambo, New Sudan Indigenous NGOs Network (NESI)
Nairobi, 22.03.02	Sam Gudner, South Sudan officer OXFAM, Nairobi
Nairobi, 22.03.02	John Luk, Editor *South Sudan Post*
Nairobi, 22.03.02	Jerome Surur, Head of Southern Sudan programme, NCA
Nairobi, 22.03.02	Stein Villumstad, Regional Representative for Norwegian Church Aid in the Horn of Africa and Great Lakes Region
Nairobi, 26.03.02	Martin Okerruk, General Secretary NEC/Programme Director HACDAD
Nairobi, 26.03.02	Kosti Manibe, Commissioner for Education, SPLM/A
Nairobi, 26.03.02	Gillian Wilcox, Coordinator OLS Consortium (Southern Sector)

WEBPUBLISHED SOURCES

a. Sudan Catholic Information Office's web site provides a detailed chronology of events in the Sudan with emphasis on the South for the period August 1996–February 2001. Each monthly newsletter usually contains more than 50 separate news items, http://www.peacelink.it/africa/scio/previous.html.

b. *Commander Yousif Kuwa Makkie - The Man* http://www.mathaba.net/africa2020//sudan/kuwa.htm.

c. IGAD information site, http://www.igad.org/

d. t'Ende, Nanne op, *Interview with Yousif Kuwa Mekki*, London February 12 and 13, http://leden.tref.nl/~ende0098/articles/interviewNotE.htm, pp. 1–30.

e.   Zedong, Mao, *On Guerrilla Warfare*,
     http://www.marxists.org/reference/archive/mao/works/1937/guerrilla-
     warfare/index.htm.

PUBLISHED SOURCES: A. PERIODICALS, NEWSPAPERS, NEWSLETTERS

Africa Confidential

Horn of Africa Vision

Sudan Democratic Gazette

Sudan Up-date

South Sudan Post

PUBLISHED SOURCES: B. SECONDARY

Adedeji, Adebayo (ed.), *Comprehending and Mastering African Conflicts: The Search for Sustainable Peace and Good Governance*. London: Zed Books, 1999.

African Rights, 'Great Expectations: The Civil Roles of the Churches in Southern Sudan', Discussion Paper No. 6. London: African Rights, April 1995.

—, 'Imposing Development: Aid and Civil Institutions in Southern Sudan', Discussion Paper No. 7. London: African Rights, December 1995.

—, *Facing Genocide: The Nuba of Sudan*. London: African Rights, 1995.

—, *Food and Power: A Critique of Humanitarianism*. London: African Rights, 1997.

Africa Watch, 'Denying the Honour of Living: Sudan – A Human Rights Disaster'. London: Africa Watch Committee, 1990.

Ahmed, Abdel Ghaffar M. (et al.), *Anthropology in the Sudan: Reflections by a Sudanese Anthropologist*. Utrecht: International Books in association with OSSREA, 2003.

Ahmed, Ismail, 'Understanding Conflict in Somalia and Somaliland', in Adebayo Adedeji (ed.), *Comprehending and Mastering African Conflicts: The Search for Sustainable Peace and Good Governance*. London: Zed Books, 1999.

Akol, Lam, *Inside an African Revolution*, Khartoum: Khartoum University Press, 2001.

—, *SPLM/SPLA: The Nasir Declaration*. New York: iUniverse Inc., 2003.

Alier, Abel, *Southern Sudan: Too Many Agreements Dishonoured*. Reading: Ithaca Press, 1992 (2nd ed.).

Allen, Tim (ed.), *In Search of Cool Ground: War, Flight and Homecoming in Northeast Africa*. London: James Currey, 1996.

Behrend, Heike, 'War in Northern Uganda: The Holy Spirit Movements of Alice Lakwena, Severino Lukoya and Joseph Kony (1986–1997)', in Christopher Clapham (ed.), *African Guerrillas*. Oxford: James Currey, 1998.

Beshir, Mohamed Omer, *The Southern Sudan: Background to a Conflict*. Khartoum: Khartoum University Press, 1979 (3rd Impr.).

Bradbury, M., N. Leader and K. Mackintosh, 'The "Agreement on Ground Rules" in South Sudan'. HPG Report (4). London: Overseas Development Institute, March 2000.

Burr, Millard, 'A Working Document II: Quantifying Genocide in the Southern Sudan and the Nuba Mountains, 1983–1998', Issue brief / U.S. Committee for Refugees. Washington DC: US Committee for Refugees, 1998.

Burr, J.M. and R.O. Collins, *Requiem for Sudan: War, Drought, and Disaster Relief on the Nile*. Boulder, San Francisco and Oxford: Westview Press, 1995.

BYDA, 'BYDA's Basic Documents: Vision, Mission, Constitution, Leadership Code of Conduct, Internal Regulations'. Mapel: BYDA, May 2000.

Clapham, Christopher, *Africa and the International System: The Politics of State Survival*. Cambridge: Cambridge University Press, 1996.

— (ed.), *African Guerrillas*. Oxford: James Currey, 1998.

Cole, D.C. and R. Huntington, *Between a Swamp and a Hard Place: Developmental Challenges in Remote Rural Africa*. Cambridge: Harvard University Press, 1997.

Collier, P. and A. Hoeffler, 'Greed and Grievance in Civil War'. Policy research working paper (2355). Washington, DC: World Bank, 2000.

Collins, Robert O., *Shadows in the grass: Britain in the Southern Sudan, 1918–1956*, New Haven: Yale University Press, 1983.

Comaroff, J.L. and J. Comaroff (eds), *Civil Society and the Political Imagination in Africa: Critical Perspectives*. Chicago: University of Chicago Press, 1999.

Daly, M.W. and A.A. Sikainga (eds), *Civil War in the Sudan*, London: British Academic Press, 1993.

Deng, Francis M., *War of Visions*. Washington DC: Brookings Institute, 1995.

Deng, Luka Biong, 'Famine in the Sudan: Causes, Preparedness and Response: A Political, Social and Economic Analysis of the 1998 Bahr el Ghazal Famine'. Discussion paper 369. Brighton: Institute for Development Studies, 1999.

de Waal, Alex, 'Some Comments on Militias in the Contemporary Sudan', in M.W. Daly and A.A. Sikainga (eds), *Civil War in the Sudan*, London: British Academic Press, 1993.

—, *Famine Crimes: Politics and the Disaster Relief Industry in Africa*, Oxford: African Rights and The International African Institute in association with James Currey, 1997.

Duffield, Mark et al., *Sudan Emergency Operations Consortium (SEOC): A Review*. Birmingham: University of Birmingham, 1995.

—, 'Humanitarian Conditionality: Origins, Consequences and Implications of the Pursuit of Development in Conflict', in G. Loane and T. Schümer (eds), *The Wider Impact of Humanitarian Assistance: The Case of Sudan and the Implications for European Union Policy*. Baden-Baden: Nomos Verlagsgesellschaft, 2000.

Ellis, Stephen, 'Africa's Wars of Liberation: Some Historiographical Reflections', in P. Konings et al. (eds), *Trajectories de libération en Afrique contemporaine*. Paris: Karthala, 2000, pp. 69–91.

—, 'Writing Histories of Contemporary Africa', *Journal of African History*, 43 (2002), pp. 1–26.

Fukui, K. and J. Markakis (eds), *Ethnicity and Conflict in the Horn of Africa*. London: James Currey, 1994.

Groth, Anne Marie, 'Frivillige organisasjoner som aktører i norsk utenrikspolitikk: En studie av Kirkens Nødhjelp og Norsk Folkehjelps nødhjelpsarbeide i Sudan', Hovedoppgave (Dissertation) i statsvitenskap, University of Oslo University, 1995.

Harbeson, J.W., D. Rothchild and N. Chazan (eds), *Civil Society and the State in Africa.* Boulder: Lynne Rienner, 1998 (3rd ed.).

Harir, S. and T. Tvedt (eds), *Short-Cut to Decay: The Case of the Sudan,* Uppsala: Nordiska Afrikainstitutet, 1994.

Heinrich, Wolfgang, 'Memorandum of Misunderstanding: Relief Agencies in South Sudan Face Dilemma', *Development and Cooperation,* No. 5, 2000, pp. 21–23.

Henriksen, Torben, 'Gjennombrudd i Sikte? Kirkens Nødhjelps distriktsutviklings-program i Sør-Sudan 1975–1986 – Alternativ bistandskanal og kilde til organisa-torisk vekst'. Hovedoppgave (Dissertation) i Historie, University of Oslo, Spring 2000.

Herzog, Herbert, 'Report: Mission on Governance to Western Equatoria, Southern Sudan 27/07-22/08 1998'. Liebefelt: Herzog Consult, September 1998.

Holt, P.M. and M.W. Daly, *A History of the Sudan: From the Coming of Islam to the Present Day.* Harlow: Pearson Education, 2000 (5th ed.).

Human Rights Watch, 'Civilian Devastation: Abuses by All Parties in the War in Southern Sudan', New York, 1993.

—, *Sudan, Oil and Human Rights.* Washington DC, 2003.

—, 'Darfur Destroyed: Ethnic Cleansing by Government and Militia Forces in Western Sudan'. Washington DC, 7 May 2004.

Hutchinson, Sharon E., *Nuer Dilemmas: Coping with Money, War and the State.* Berkeley, Los Angeles and London: University of California Press, 1996.

—, 'A Curse from God? Religious and Political Dimensions of the post-1991 Rise of Ethnic Violence in South Sudan', *The Journal of Modern African Studies,* Vol. 39 (2) 2001.

Huntington Technical Services Ltd., 'Agricultural Extension Processing and Marketing Study East Bank Equatoria', Borehamwood: Huntington Technical Services Ltd, April 1984.

International Nuba Coordination Centre, *The Right to be Nuba: The Story of a Sudanese People's Struggle for Survival.* Lawrenceville: Red Sea Press, 2001.

Ireton, F., E. Denis and G. Prunier (eds), *Contemporary Sudan.* Oxford: James Currey, forthcoming.

Jackson, Robert H., *Quasi-States: Sovereignty, International Relations, and the Third World.* Cambridge: Cambridge University Press, 1990.

James, Wendy, '"People-Friendly" Projects and Practical Realities: Some Contradictions on the Sudan-Ethiopian Border'. Paper presented at *Sudan Workshop,* Copenhagen, 9 February 2001.

Johnson, Douglas, 'Destruction and Reconstruction in the Economy of the Southern Sudan', in S. Harir and T. Tvedt (eds), *Short-Cut to Decay: The Case of the Sudan,* Uppsala: Nordiska Afrikainstitutet, 1994.

—, 'Increasing the Trauma of Return: An Assessment of the UN's Emergency Response to the Evacuation of the Sudanese Refugee Camps in Ethiopia 1991', in Tim Allen (ed.), *In Search of Cool Ground: War, Flight and Homecoming in Northeast Africa.* London: James Currey, 1996.

—, 'The Sudan People's Liberation Army and the Problem of Factionalism', in Christoper Clapham (ed.), *African Guerrillas.* Oxford: James Currey, 1998.

—, 'The Sudan Conflict: Historical and Political Background', in G. Loane and T. Schümer (eds), *The Wider Impact of Humanitarian Assistance: The Case of Sudan and the Implications for European Union Policy.* Baden-Baden: Nomos Verlagesgesellschaft, 2000.

—, *The Root Causes of Sudan's Civil Wars.* Oxford: James Currey, 2003.

Joseph, Richard A. (ed.), *State, Conflict, and Democracy in Africa.* Boulder: Lynne Rienner, 1999.

Karim, Ataul et al., *Operation Lifeline Sudan: A Review.* Geneva: Operation Lifeline Sudan, 1996.

Keen, David, *The Benefits of Famine: A Political Economy of Famine and Relief in Southwestern Sudan, 1983–89.* Princeton: Princeton University Press, 1994.

Kevane, M. and E. Stiansen (eds), *Kordofan Invaded: Peripheral Incorporation and Social Transformation in Islamic Africa.* Leiden: Brill, 1998.

Kok, Peter N., *Governance and Conflict in the Sudan, 1985–1995: Analysis, Evaluation and Documentation.* Hamburg: Deutches Orient-Institut, 1996.

—, 'Sudan: Between Radical Restructuring and Deconstruction of State Systems', *Review of African Politics and Economy*, No. 70, 1996, p. 560.

Konings P. et al. (eds), *Trajectories de libération en Afrique contemporaine.* Paris: Karthala, 2000.

Kriger, Norma J., *Zimbabwe's Guerrilla War: Peasant Voices,* Cambridge: Cambridge University Press, 1992.

Kuol, M.L., 'Administration of Justice in (SPLA/M) Liberated Areas: Court Cases in War-Torn Southern Sudan'. Oxford: Oxford Refugee Studies Programme, February 1997.

—, 'The Anthropology of Law and Issues of Justice in the Southern Sudan Today'. University of Oxford: Trinity, 2000.

Lan, David, *Guns and Rain: Guerrillas and Spirit Mediums in Zimbabwe.* London: James Currey, 1985.

Lesch, Ann Mosley, *The Sudan: Contested National Identities.* Bloomington, Indiana: Indiana University Press, 1998.

Levine, Iain, 'Promoting Humanitarian Principles: The Southern Sudan Experience'. London: RRN Network Paper Overseas Development Institute, May 1997.

Loane, G., 'Literature Assessment of the Wider Impact of Humanitarian Assistance', in G. Loane and T. Schümer (eds), *The Wider Impact of Humanitarian Assistance: The Case of Sudan and the Implications for European Union Policy.* Baden-Baden: Nomos Verlagesgesellschaft, 2000.

Loane, G. and T. Schümer (eds), *The Wider Impact of Humanitarian Assistance: The Case of Sudan and the Implications for European Union Policy*. Baden-Baden: Nomos Verlagesgesellschaft, 2000.

Mamdani, Mahmood, *Citizen and Subject: Contemporary Africa and the Legacy of Late Colonialism*. Princeton: Princeton University Press, 1996.

Mansour, Khalid (ed.), *The Call for Democracy in Sudan*. New York: Kegan Paul International, 1992.

Medley, Michael, 'Humanitarian Assistance in Sudan: A Chronological Analysis of Shifting Mandates', in G. Loane and T. Schümer (eds), *The Wider Impact of Humanitarian Assistance: The Case of Sudan and the Implications for European Union Policy*. Baden-Baden: Nomos Verlagesgesellschaft, 2000.

Minear, Larry et al., *Humanitariansim under Siege: A Critical Review of Operation Lifeline Sudan*. Trenton: Red Sea Press, 1991.

Ministry of Foreign Affairs (conducted by COWI), 'Evaluation of Norwegian Humanitarian Assistance to the Sudan', 11.97. Oslo: The Royal Ministry of Foreign Affairs, 1997.

Murphy, Paul et al., 'Planning for Peace in Sudan: A Record of the Perspectives and Recommendations Made by People Living in Opposition Controlled Areas of Sudan on Building and Achieving Peace'. Final Report. Nairobi: IGAD Partners' Forum, August 2001.

Negash, T. and K. Tronvoll, *Brothers at War: Making Sense of the Eritrean-Ethiopian War*. Oxford: James Currey, 2000.

Nikkel, Marc R., *Dinka Christianity: The Origins and Development of Christianity among the Dinka of Sudan with Special Reference to the Songs of Dinka Christians*. Nairobi: Pauline Publications Africa, 2001.

Nordrum, Edvard, 2002, *Biskop Paride Taban – Fredskjempe i krig*. Oslo: Andersen and Butenschøn forlag.

Nyaba, Peter A., *The Politics of Liberation in South Sudan: An Insider's View*. Kampala: Fountain Publishers, 2000 (2nd ed.).

O'Ballance, Edgar, *The Secret War in the Sudan: 1955–197*. London: Faber, 1977.

—, *Sudan, Civil War and Terrorism, 1956–99*. Basingstoke: Macmillan, 2000.

Petterson, Donald D., *Inside Sudan: Political Islam, Conflict and Catastrophe*. Boulder: Westview Press, 1999.

Pierli, F. et al. (eds), *Gateway to the Heart of Africa*. Nairobi: Paulines Publications Africa, 1999.

Pool, David, *From Guerrilas to Government: The Eritrean People's Liberation Front*. Oxford: James Currey, 2001.

Prunier, Gérard, *From Peace to War: The Southern Sudan 1972–1984*. Occasional paper, Department of Sociology and Social Anthropology (3). Hull: University of Hull, 1986.

—, 'The SPLA Crisis', manuscript to be published as a chapter in F. Ireton, E. Denis and G. Prunier (eds), *Contemporary Sudan*, forthcoming.

Reno, William, *Warlord Politics and African States*. Boulder: Lynner Rienner Publishers, 1998.

Riehl, Volker, *Who is Ruling in South Sudan? The Role of NGOs in Rebuilding Socio-Political Order*. Studies on Emergencies and Disaster Relief (9). Uppsala: The Nordic Africa Institute, 2001.

Rohn, Adwok Nyaba and Maker Benjamin, 'Report on the Study of Local Structures in Maridi, Mundri and Yei Counties, West Bank Equatoria, South Sudan'. Aktion-Africa Hilfe e.V., 1997.

Rolandsen, Øystein H., 'Development Interventions. Illusions and Narratives: The Case of Norwegian Church Aid in Eastern Equatoria 1974–86'. MA Dissertation. London: School of Oriental and African Studies (SOAS), 2000.

Rone, Jemera, *Famine in Sudan, 1998: The Human Rights Causes*. New York: Human Rights Watch, 1999.

Ryle, John, 'SRRA Northern Sobat Basin: Agriculture & Fisheries Rehabilitation Project'. Save the Children (UK), 1989.

Salinas, A.T. and B.C. D'Silva, 'Evolution of a Transitional Strategy and Lessons Learned: USAID Funded Activities in the West Bank of Southern Sudan, 1993 to 1999', funded by the USAID Office of Foreign Disaster Assistance (OFDA), September 1999.

Stiansen, Endre, 'Democracy in the Sudan? An Evaluation of the Historical Legacy'. Paper presented at the conference *Democratization in Developing Countries: Social, Economic and Political Consequences*. Bergen: Chr. Michelsen Institute, 3–5 February 1994.

—, 'Expectations of Development'. Oslo: Norwegian Support Group for Peace in the Sudan, 2002.

—, 'GOS Revenue, Oil and the Cost of the Civil War'. Paper presented at the conference *Money Makes the War Go Round? The EU and Transforming the Economy of War in Sudan*, held by the Bonn International Centre for Conversion (BICC), Brussels, 12–13 June 2002.

Sudan: Staff Report for the 2000 Article IV Consultation and Fourth Review of the First Annual Programme under the Medium-Term Staff-Monitored Program, Washington DC: IMF, May 2000.

Tvedt, Terje, 'The Collapse of the State in Southern Sudan After the Addis Ababa Agreement. A Study of Internal Causes and the Role of the NGOs', in S. Harir and T. Tvedt (eds), *Short-Cut to Decay: The Case of the Sudan*, Uppsala: Nordiska Afrikainstitutet, 1994.

—, *Angels of Mercy or Development Diplomats? NGOs and Foreign Aid*, Oxford: Africa World Press, 1998.

—, et al., 'Chronology', in Terje Tvedt et al., *An Annotated Bibliography on the Southern Sudan, 1850–2000*. Bergen: University of Bergen, 2000.

—, et al., *An Annotated Bibliography on the Southern Sudan, 1850–2000*. Bergen: University of Bergen, 2000.

United Nations Lifeline Sudan, 'An Investigation into Production Capabilities in the Rural Southern Sudan: A Report on Food Sources and Needs'. Nairobi, June 1990.

Uribe, Solveig Ullaland, 'Norsk bistandshistorie 1972–1992. En studie an Kirkens Nødhjelp i Sør-Sudan'. Hovedoppgave (Dissertation) i Historie, University of Bergen, Spring 1996.

Wheeler, Andrew , 'Gateway to the Heart of Africa: Sudan's Missionary Story', in F. Pierli et al. (eds), *Gateway to the Heart of Africa*. Nairobi: Paulines Publications Africa, 1999.

— (ed.), *Land and Promise: Church Growth in a Sudan at War*. Limuru: Paulines Publications Africa, 1997.

Wöndu, S. and A. Lesch, *Battle for Peace in Sudan: An Analysis of the Abuja Conferences 1992–1993*. New York and Oxford: Uni Press of Africa Inc, Lanham, 2000.

Young, John, *Peasant Revolution in Ethiopia: The Tigray People's Liberation Front, 1975–1991*. Cambridge: Cambridge University Press, 1997.

—, 'Sudan's South Blue Nile Territory and the Struggle Against Marginalization', in P. Kingston and I.S. Spears, *States Within States: Incipient Political Entities in the Post-Cold War Era*. New York: Palgrave MacMillan, 2004.

Index